I0168757

ENGLISH
KYRGYZ

THEME-BASED
DICTIONARY

Contains over 9000 commonly
used words

T&P BOOKS PUBLISHING

Theme-based dictionary British English-Kyrgyz - 9000 words

By Andrey Taranov

T&P Books vocabularies are intended for helping you learn, memorize and review foreign words. The dictionary is divided into themes, covering all major spheres of everyday activities, business, science, culture, etc.

The process of learning words using T&P Books' theme-based dictionaries gives you the following advantages:

- Correctly grouped source information predetermines success at subsequent stages of word memorization
- Availability of words derived from the same root allowing memorization of word units (rather than separate words)
- Small units of words facilitate the process of establishing associative links needed for consolidation of vocabulary
- Level of language knowledge can be estimated by the number of learned words

T&P Books Publishing
www.tpbooks.com

ISBN: 978-1-78767-002-0

This book is also available in E-book formats.
Please visit www.tpbooks.com or the major online bookstores.

KYRGYZ THEME-BASED DICTIONARY
British English collection

T&P Books vocabularies are intended to help you learn, memorize, and review foreign words. The vocabulary contains over 9000 commonly used words arranged thematically.

- Vocabulary contains the most commonly used words
- Recommended as an addition to any language course
- Meets the needs of beginners and advanced learners of foreign languages
- Convenient for daily use, revision sessions, and self-testing activities
- Allows you to assess your vocabulary

Special features of the vocabulary

- Words are organized according to their meaning, not alphabetically
- Words are presented in three columns to facilitate the reviewing and self-testing processes
- Words in groups are divided into small blocks to facilitate the learning process
- The vocabulary offers a convenient and simple transcription of each foreign word

The vocabulary has 256 topics including:

Basic Concepts, Numbers, Colors, Months, Seasons, Units of Measurement, Clothing & Accessories, Food & Nutrition, Restaurant, Family Members, Relatives, Character, Feelings, Emotions, Diseases, City, Town, Sightseeing, Shopping, Money, House, Home, Office, Working in the Office, Import & Export, Marketing, Job Search, Sports, Education, Computer, Internet, Tools, Nature, Countries, Nationalities and more …

TABLE OF CONTENTS

PRONUNCIATION GUIDE

T&P phonetic alphabet	Kyrgyz example	English example
[a]	манжа [mandʒa]	shorter than in ask
[e]	келечек [keletʃek]	elm, medal
[i]	жигит [dʒigit]	shorter than in feet
[ɪ]	кубаныч [kubanɪtʃ]	big, America
[o]	мактоо [maktoo]	pod, John
[u]	узундук [uzunduk]	book
[ʉ]	алюминий [alʉminij]	youth, usually
[y]	түнкү [tynky]	fuel, tuna
[b]	ашкабак [aʃkabak]	baby, book
[d]	адам [adam]	day, doctor
[dʒ]	жыгач [dʒɪgatʃ]	joke, general
[f]	флейта [flejta]	face, food
[g]	тегерек [tegerek]	game, gold
[j]	бөйрөк [bøjrøk]	yes, New York
[k]	карапа [karapa]	clock, kiss
[l]	алтын [altɪn]	lace, people
[m]	бешмант [beʃmant]	magic, milk
[n]	найза [najza]	name, normal
[ŋ]	булуң [buluŋ]	ring
[p]	пайдубал [pajdubal]	pencil, private
[r]	рахмат [raχmat]	rice, radio
[s]	сагызган [sagɪzgan]	city, boss
[ʃ]	бурулуш [buruluʃ]	machine, shark
[t]	түтүн [tytyn]	tourist, trip
[χ]	пахтадан [paχtadan]	hot, hobby
[ts]	шприц [ʃprits]	cats, tsetse fly
[tʃ]	биринчи [birintʃi]	church, French
[v]	квартал [kvartal]	very, river
[z]	казуу [kazuu]	zebra, please
[ʲ]	руль, актёр [rulʲ, aktʲor]	palatalization sign
[ʰ]	объектив [obʰjektiv]	hard sign

ABBREVIATIONS
used in the dictionary

English abbreviations

ab.	-	about
adj	-	adjective
adv	-	adverb
anim.	-	animate
as adj	-	attributive noun used as adjective
e.g.	-	for example
etc.	-	et cetera
fam.	-	familiar
fem.	-	feminine
form.	-	formal
inanim.	-	inanimate
masc.	-	masculine
math	-	mathematics
mil.	-	military
n	-	noun
pl	-	plural
pron.	-	pronoun
sb	-	somebody
sing.	-	singular
sth	-	something
v aux	-	auxiliary verb
vi	-	intransitive verb
vi, vt	-	intransitive, transitive verb
vt	-	transitive verb

BASIC CONCEPTS

Basic concepts. Part 1

1. Pronouns

I, me	мен, мага	men, maga
you	сен	sen
he, she, it	ал	al
they	алар	alar

2. Greetings. Salutations. Farewells

Hello! (fam.)	Салам!	salam!
Hello! (form.)	Саламатсызбы!	salamatsızbı!
Good morning!	Кутман таңыңыз менен!	kutman taŋıŋız menen!
Good afternoon!	Кутман күнүңүз менен!	kutman kynyŋyz menen!
Good evening!	Кутман кечиңиз менен!	kutman ketʃiŋiz menen!

to say hello	учурашуу	utʃuraʃuu
Hi! (hello)	Кандай!	kandaj!
greeting (n)	салам	salam
to greet (vt)	саламдашуу	salamdaʃuu
How are you?	Иштериң кандай?	iʃteriŋ kandaj?
How are you? (form.)	Иштериңиз кандай?	iʃteriŋiz kandaj?
How are you? (fam.)	Иштер кандай?	iʃter kandaj?
What's new?	Эмне жаңылык?	emne dʒaŋılık?

Bye-Bye! Goodbye!	Көрүшкөнчө!	køryʃkøntʃø!
See you soon!	Эмки жолукканга чейин!	emki dʒolukkanga tʃejin!
Farewell! (to a friend)	Кош бол!	koʃ bol!
Farewell! (form.)	Кош болуңуз!	koʃ boluŋuz!
to say goodbye	коштошуу	koʃtoʃuu
Cheers!	Жакшы кал!	dʒakʃı kal!

Thank you! Cheers!	Рахмат!	raxmat!
Thank you very much!	Чоң рахмат!	tʃoŋ raxmat!
My pleasure!	Эч нерсе эмес	etʃ nerse emes
Don't mention it!	Алкышка арзыбайт	alkıʃka arzıbajt
It was nothing	Эчтеке эмес.	etʃteke emes

Excuse me! (fam.)	Кечир!	ketʃir!
Excuse me! (form.)	Кечирип коюңузчу!	ketʃirip kojuŋuztʃu!
to excuse (forgive)	кечирүү	ketʃiryy

to apologize (vi)	кечирим суроо	ketʃirim suroo
My apologies	Кечирим сурайм.	ketʃirim surajm

13

I'm sorry!	Кечиресиз!	ketʃiresiz!
to forgive (vt)	кечирүү	ketʃiryy
It's okay! (that's all right)	Эч капачылык жок.	etʃ kapatʃılık dʒok
please (adv)	суранам	suranam

Don't forget!	Унутуп калбаңыз!	unutup kalbaŋız!
Certainly!	Албетте!	albette!
Of course not!	Албетте жок!	albette dʒok!
Okay! (I agree)	Макул!	makul!
That's enough!	Жетишет!	dʒetiʃet!

3. How to address

Excuse me, ...	Кечиресиз!	ketʃiresiz!
mister, sir	мырза	mırza
madam	айым	ajım
miss	чоң кыз	tʃoŋ kız
young man	чоң жигит	tʃoŋ dʒigit
young man (little boy)	жаш бала	dʒaʃ bala
miss (little girl)	кызым	kızım

4. Cardinal numbers. Part 1

0 zero	нөл	nøl
1 one	бир	bir
2 two	эки	eki
3 three	үч	ytʃ
4 four	төрт	tørt

5 five	беш	beʃ
6 six	алты	altı
7 seven	жети	dʒeti
8 eight	сегиз	segiz
9 nine	тогуз	toguz

10 ten	он	on
11 eleven	он бир	on bir
12 twelve	он эки	on eki
13 thirteen	он үч	on ytʃ
14 fourteen	он төрт	on tørt

15 fifteen	он беш	on beʃ
16 sixteen	он алты	on altı
17 seventeen	он жети	on dʒeti
18 eighteen	он сегиз	on segiz
19 nineteen	он тогуз	on toguz

20 twenty	жыйырма	dʒıjırma
21 twenty-one	жыйырма бир	dʒıjırma bir
22 twenty-two	жыйырма эки	dʒıjırma eki
23 twenty-three	жыйырма үч	dʒıjırma ytʃ
30 thirty	отуз	otuz

31 thirty-one	отуз бир	otuz bir
32 thirty-two	отуз эки	otuz eki
33 thirty-three	отуз үч	otuz ytʃ

40 forty	кырк	kɩrk
42 forty-two	кырк эки	kɩrk eki
43 forty-three	кырк үч	kɩrk ytʃ

50 fifty	элүү	elyy
51 fifty-one	элүү бир	elyy bir
52 fifty-two	элүү эки	elyy eki
53 fifty-three	элүү үч	elyy ytʃ

60 sixty	алтымыш	altɩmɩʃ
61 sixty-one	алтымыш бир	altɩmɩʃ bir
62 sixty-two	алтымыш эки	altɩmɩʃ eki
63 sixty-three	алтымыш үч	altɩmɩʃ ytʃ

70 seventy	жетимиш	dʒetimiʃ
71 seventy-one	жетимиш бир	dʒetimiʃ bir
72 seventy-two	жетимиш эки	dʒetimiʃ eki
73 seventy-three	жетимиш үч	dʒetimiʃ ytʃ

80 eighty	сексен	seksen
81 eighty-one	сексен бир	seksen bir
82 eighty-two	сексен эки	seksen eki
83 eighty-three	сексен үч	seksen ytʃ

90 ninety	токсон	tokson
91 ninety-one	токсон бир	tokson bir
92 ninety-two	токсон эки	tokson eki
93 ninety-three	токсон үч	tokson ytʃ

5. Cardinal numbers. Part 2

100 one hundred	бир жүз	bir dʒyz
200 two hundred	эки жүз	eki dʒyz
300 three hundred	үч жүз	ytʃ dʒyz
400 four hundred	төрт жүз	tørt dʒyz
500 five hundred	беш жүз	beʃ dʒyz

600 six hundred	алты жүз	altɩ dʒyz
700 seven hundred	жети жүз	dʒeti dʒyz
800 eight hundred	сегиз жүз	segiz dʒyz
900 nine hundred	тогуз жүз	toguz dʒyz

1000 one thousand	бир миң	bir miŋ
2000 two thousand	эки миң	eki miŋ
3000 three thousand	үч миң	ytʃ miŋ
10000 ten thousand	он миң	on miŋ
one hundred thousand	жүз миң	dʒyz miŋ

| million | миллион | million |
| billion | миллиард | milliard |

6. Ordinal numbers

first (adj)	биринчи	birinʧi
second (adj)	экинчи	ekinʧi
third (adj)	үчүнчү	yʧynʧy
fourth (adj)	төртүнчү	tørtynʧy
fifth (adj)	бешинчи	beʃinʧi
sixth (adj)	алтынчы	altınʧı
seventh (adj)	жетинчи	dʒetinʧi
eighth (adj)	сегизинчи	segizinʧi
ninth (adj)	тогузунчу	toguzunʧu
tenth (adj)	онунчу	onunʧu

7. Numbers. Fractions

fraction	бөлчөк	bølʧøk
one half	экиден бир	ekiden bir
one third	үчтөн бир	yʧtøn bir
one quarter	төрттөн бир	tørttøn bir
one eighth	сегизден бир	segizden bir
one tenth	тогуздан бир	toguzdan bir
two thirds	үчтөн эки	yʧtøn eki
three quarters	төрттөн үч	tørttøn yʧ

8. Numbers. Basic operations

subtraction	кемитүү	kemityy
to subtract (vi, vt)	кемитүү	kemityy
division	бөлүү	bølyy
to divide (vt)	бөлүү	bølyy
addition	кошуу	koʃuu
to add up (vt)	кошуу	koʃuu
to add (vi)	кошуу	koʃuu
multiplication	көбөйтүү	købøjtyy
to multiply (vt)	көбөйтүү	købøjtyy

9. Numbers. Miscellaneous

digit, figure	санарип	sanarip
number	сан	san
numeral	сан атооч	san atooʧ
minus sign	кемитүү	kemityy
plus sign	плюс	plus
formula	формула	formula
calculation	эсептөө	eseptøø
to count (vi, vt)	саноо	sanoo

| to count up | эсептөө | eseptøø |
| to compare (vt) | салыштыруу | salıʃtıruu |

How much?	Канча?	kantʃa?
sum, total	жыйынтык	dʒıjıntık
result	натыйжа	natıjdʒa
remainder	калдык	kaldık

a few (e.g., ~ years ago)	бир нече	bir netʃe
little (I had ~ time)	биртике	bir az
few (I have ~ friends)	бир аз	bir az
a little (~ water)	кичине	kitʃine
the rest	калганы	kalganı
one and a half	бир жарым	bir dʒarım
dozen	он эки даана	on eki daana

in half (adv)	тең экиге	teŋ ekige
equally (evenly)	тең	teŋ
half	жарым	dʒarım
time (three ~s)	бир жолу	bir dʒolu

10. The most important verbs. Part 1

to advise (vt)	кеңеш берүү	keŋeʃ beryy
to agree (say yes)	макул болуу	makul boluu
to answer (vi, vt)	жооп берүү	dʒoop beryy
to apologize (vi)	кечирим суроо	ketʃirim suroo
to arrive (vi)	келүү	kelyy

to ask (~ oneself)	суроо	suroo
to ask (~ sb to do sth)	суроо	suroo
to be (vi)	болуу	boluu

to be afraid	жазкануу	dʒazkanuu
to be hungry	ачка болуу	atʃka boluu
to be interested in ...	... кызыгуу	... kızıguu
to be needed	керек болуу	kerek boluu
to be surprised	таң калуу	taŋ kaluu

to be thirsty	суусап калуу	suusap kaluu
to begin (vt)	баштоо	baʃtoo
to belong to ...	таандык болуу	taandık boluu
to boast (vi)	мактануу	maktanuu
to break (split into pieces)	сындыруу	sındıruu
to call (~ for help)	чакыруу	tʃakıruu

can (v aux)	жасай алуу	dʒasaj aluu
to catch (vt)	кармоо	karmoo
to change (vt)	өзгөртүү	øzgørtyy
to choose (select)	тандоо	tandoo
to come down (the stairs)	ылдый түшүү	ıldıj tyʃyy

| to compare (vt) | салыштыруу | salıʃtıruu |
| to complain (vi, vt) | арыздануу | arızdanuu |

to confuse (mix up)	адаштыруу	adaʃtıruu
to continue (vt)	улантуу	ulantuu
to control (vt)	башкаруу	baʃkaruu
to cook (dinner)	тамак бышыруу	tamak bıʃıruu

to cost (vt)	туруу	turuu
to count (add up)	саноо	sanoo
to count on ...	... ишенүү	... iʃenyy
to create (vt)	жаратуу	dʒaratuu
to cry (weep)	ыйлоо	ıjloo

11. The most important verbs. Part 2

to deceive (vi, vt)	алдоо	aldoo
to decorate (tree, street)	кооздоо	koozdoo
to defend (a country, etc.)	коргоо	korgoo
to demand (request firmly)	талап кылуу	talap kıluu
to dig (vt)	казуу	kazuu

to discuss (vt)	талкуулоо	talkuuloo
to do (vt)	кылуу	kıluu
to doubt (have doubts)	күмөн саноо	kymøn sanoo
to drop (let fall)	түшүрүп алуу	tyʃyryp aluu
to enter (room, house, etc.)	кирүү	kiryy

to excuse (forgive)	кечирүү	ketʃiryy
to exist (vi)	чыгуу	tʃıguu
to expect (foresee)	күтүү	kytyy
to explain (vt)	түшүндүрүү	tyʃyndyryy
to fall (vi)	жыгылуу	dʒıgıluu

to fancy (vt)	жактыруу	dʒaktıruu
to find (vt)	таап алуу	taap aluu
to finish (vt)	бүтүрүү	bytyryy
to fly (vi)	учуу	utʃuu
to follow ... (come after)	... ээрчүү	... eertʃyy

to forget (vi, vt)	унутуу	unutuu
to forgive (vt)	кечирүү	ketʃiryy
to give (vt)	берүү	beryy
to give a hint	четин чыгаруу	tʃetin tʃıgaruu
to go (on foot)	жөө басуу	dʒøø basuu

to go for a swim	суига түшүү	suuga tyʃyy
to go out (for dinner, etc.)	чыгуу	tʃıguu
to guess (the answer)	жандырмагын табуу	dʒandırmagın tabuu

to have (vt)	бар болуу	bar boluu
to have breakfast	эртең менен тамактануу	erteŋ menen tamaktanuu
to have dinner	кечки тамакты ичүү	ketʃki tamaktı itʃyy
to have lunch	түштөнүү	tyʃtønyy
to hear (vt)	угуу	uguu
to help (vt)	жардам берүү	dʒardam beryy
to hide (vt)	жашыруу	dʒaʃıruu

to hope (vi, vt)	үмүттөнүү	ymyttønyy
to hunt (vi, vt)	аңчылык кылуу	aŋʧılık kıluu
to hurry (vi)	шашуу	ʃaʃuu

12. The most important verbs. Part 3

to inform (vt)	маалымат берүү	maalımat beryy
to insist (vi, vt)	көшөрүү	køʃøryy
to insult (vt)	кемсинтүү	kemsintyy
to invite (vt)	чакыруу	ʧakıruu
to joke (vi)	тамашалоо	tamaʃaloo

to keep (vt)	сактоо	saktoo
to keep silent, to hush	унчукпоо	unʧukpoo
to kill (vt)	өлтүрүү	øltyryy
to know (sb)	таануу	taanuu
to know (sth)	билүү	bilyy
to laugh (vi)	күлүү	kylyy

to liberate (city, etc.)	бошотуу	boʃotuu
to look for ... (search)	... издөө	... izdøø
to love (sb)	сүйүү	syjyy
to make a mistake	ката кетирүү	kata ketiryy
to manage, to run	башкаруу	baʃkaruu
to mean (signify)	билдирүү	bildiryy
to mention (talk about)	айтып өтүү	ajtıp øtyy
to miss (school, etc.)	калтыруу	kaltıruu
to notice (see)	байкоо	bajkoo
to object (vi, vt)	каршы болуу	karʃı boluu

to observe (see)	байкоо салуу	bajkoo
to open (vt)	ачуу	aʧuu
to order (meal, etc.)	буйрутма кылуу	bujrutma kıluu
to order (mil.)	буйрук кылуу	bujruk kıluu
to own (possess)	ээ болуу	ee boluu
to participate (vi)	катышуу	katıʃuu
to pay (vi, vt)	төлөө	tøløø
to permit (vt)	уруксат берүү	uruksat beryy
to plan (vt)	пландаштыруу	plandaʃtıruu
to play (children)	ойноо	ojnoo

to pray (vi, vt)	дуба кылуу	duba kıluu
to prefer (vt)	артык көрүү	artık køryy
to promise (vt)	убада берүү	ubada beryy
to pronounce (vt)	айтуу	ajtuu
to propose (vt)	сунуштоо	sunuʃtoo
to punish (vt)	жазалоо	dʒazaloo

13. The most important verbs. Part 4

| to read (vi, vt) | окуу | okuu |
| to recommend (vt) | сунуштоо | sunuʃtoo |

to refuse (vi, vt)	баш тартуу	baʃ tartuu
to regret (be sorry)	өкүнүү	økynyy
to rent (sth from sb)	батирге алуу	batirge aluu
to repeat (say again)	кайталоо	kajtaloo
to reserve, to book	камдык буйрутмалоо	kamdık bujrutmaloo
to run (vi)	чуркоо	tʃurkoo
to save (rescue)	куткаруу	kutkaruu
to say (~ thank you)	айтуу	ajtuu
to scold (vt)	урушуу	uruʃuu
to see (vt)	көрүү	køryy
to sell (vt)	сатуу	satuu
to send (vt)	жөнөтүү	dʒønøtyy
to shoot (vi)	атуу	atuu
to shout (vi)	кыйкыруу	kıjkıruu
to show (vt)	көрсөтүү	kørsøtyy
to sign (document)	кол коюу	kol kojʉu
to sit down (vi)	отуруу	oturuu
to smile (vi)	жылмаюу	dʒılmadʒʉu
to speak (vi, vt)	сүйлөө	syjløø
to steal (money, etc.)	уурдоо	uurdoo
to stop (for pause, etc.)	токтоо	toktoo
to stop (please ~ calling me)	токтотуу	toktotuu
to study (vt)	окуу	okuu
to swim (vi)	сүзүү	syzyy
to take (vt)	алуу	aluu
to think (vi, vt)	ойлоо	ojloo
to threaten (vt)	коркутуу	korkutuu
to touch (with hands)	тийүү	tijyy
to translate (vt)	которуу	kotoruu
to trust (vt)	ишенүү	iʃenyy
to try (attempt)	аракет кылуу	araket kıluu
to turn (e.g., ~ left)	бурулуу	buruluu
to underestimate (vt)	баалабоо	baalaboo
to understand (vt)	түшүнүү	tyʃynyy
to unite (vt)	бириктирүү	biriktiryy
to wait (vt)	күтүү	kytyy
to want (wish, desire)	каалоо	kaaloo
to warn (vt)	эскертүү	eskertyy
to work (vi)	иштөө	iʃtøø
to write (vt)	жазуу	dʒazuu
to write down	кагазга түшүрүү	kagazga tyʃyryy

14. Colours

colour	түс	tys
shade (tint)	кошумча түс	koʃumtʃa tys

| hue | кубулуу | kubuluu |
| rainbow | күндүн кулагы | kyndyn kulagı |

white (adj)	ак	ak
black (adj)	кара	kara
grey (adj)	боз	boz

green (adj)	жашыл	dʒaʃıl
yellow (adj)	сары	sarı
red (adj)	кызыл	kızıl

blue (adj)	көк	køk
light blue (adj)	көгүлтүр	køgyltyr
pink (adj)	мала	mala
orange (adj)	кызгылт сары	kızgılt sarı
violet (adj)	сыя көк	sıja køk
brown (adj)	күрөң	kyrøŋ

| golden (adj) | алтын түстүү | altın tystyy |
| silvery (adj) | күмүш өңдүү | kymyʃ øŋdyy |

beige (adj)	сары боз	sarı boz
cream (adj)	саргылт	sargılt
turquoise (adj)	бирюза	birʉza
cherry red (adj)	кочкул кызыл	kotʃkul kızıl
lilac (adj)	кызгылт көгүш	kızgılt køgyʃ
crimson (adj)	ачык кызыл	atʃık kızıl

light (adj)	ачык	atʃık
dark (adj)	күңүрт	kyŋyrt
bright, vivid (adj)	ачык	atʃık

coloured (pencils)	түстүү	tystyy
colour (e.g. ~ film)	түстүү	tystyy
black-and-white (adj)	ак-кара	ak-kara
plain (one-coloured)	бир өңчөй түстө	bir øŋtʃøj tystø
multicoloured (adj)	ар түрдүү түстө	ar tyrdyy tystø

15. Questions

Who?	Ким?	kim?
What?	Эмне?	emne?
Where? (at, in)	Каерде?	kaerde?
Where (to)?	Каяка?	kajaka?
From where?	Каяктан?	kajaktan?
When?	Качан?	katʃan?
Why? (What for?)	Эмне үчүн?	emne ytʃyn?
Why? (~ are you crying?)	Эмнеге?	emnege?

What for?	Кайсы керекке?	kajsı kerekke?
How? (in what way)	Кандай?	kandaj?
What? (What kind of ...?)	Кайсы?	kajsı?
Which?	Кайсынысы?	kajsınısı?
To whom?	Кимге?	kimge?

About whom?	Ким жөнүндө?	kim dʒønyndø?
About what?	Эмне жөнүндө?	emne dʒønyndø?
With whom?	Ким менен?	kim menen?

How many? How much?	Канча?	kantʃa?
Whose?	Кимдики?	kimdiki?
Whose? (fem.)	Кимдики?	kimdiki?
Whose? (pl)	Кимдердики?	kimderdiki?

16. Prepositions

with (accompanied by)	менен	menen
without	-сыз, -сиз	-sɪz, -siz
to (indicating direction)	... көздөй	.,. køzdøj
about (talking ~ ...)	... жөнүндө	... dʒønyndø
before (in time)	... астында	... astɪnda
in front of ...	... алдында	... aldɪnda

under (beneath, below)	... астында	... astɪnda
above (over)	... өйдө	... øjdø
on (atop)	... үстүндө	... ystyndø
from (off, out of)	-дан	-dan
of (made from)	-дан	-dan

| in (e.g. ~ ten minutes) | ... ичинде | ... itʃinde |
| over (across the top of) | ... үстүнөн | ... ystynøn |

17. Function words. Adverbs. Part 1

Where? (at, in)	Каерде?	kaerde?
here (adv)	бул жерде	bul dʒerde
there (adv)	тээтигил жакта	teetigil dʒakta

| somewhere (to be) | бир жерде | bir dʒerde |
| nowhere (not in any place) | эч жакта | etʃ dʒakta |

| by (near, beside) | ... жанында | ... dʒanɪnda |
| by the window | терезенин жанында | terezenin dʒanɪnda |

Where (to)?	Каяка?	kajaka?
here (e.g. come ~!)	бери	beri
there (e.g. to go ~)	нары	narɪ
from here (adv)	бул жерден	bul dʒerden
from there (adv)	тигил жерден	tigil dʒerden

| close (adv) | жакын | dʒakɪn |
| far (adv) | алыс | alɪs |

near (e.g. ~ Paris)	... тегерегинде	... tegereginde
nearby (adv)	жакын арада	dʒakɪn arada
not far (adv)	алыс эмес	alɪs emes
left (adj)	сол	sol

| on the left | сол жакта | sol dʒakta |
| to the left | солго | solgo |

right (adj)	оӊ	oŋ
on the right	оӊ жакта	oŋ dʒakta
to the right	оӊго	oŋgo

in front (adv)	астыда	astıda
front (as adj)	алдыӊкы	aldıŋkı
ahead (the kids ran ~)	алдыга	aldıga

behind (adv)	артында	artında
from behind	артынан	artınan
back (towards the rear)	артка	artka

| middle | ортосу | ortosu |
| in the middle | ортосунда | ortosunda |

at the side	капталында	kaptalında
everywhere (adv)	бүт жерде	byt dʒerde
around (in all directions)	айланасында	ajlanasında

from inside	ичинде	itʃinde
somewhere (to go)	бир жерде	bir dʒerde
straight (directly)	түз	tyz
back (e.g. come ~)	кайра	kajra

| from anywhere | бир жерден | bir dʒerden |
| from somewhere | бир жактан | bir dʒaktan |

firstly (adv)	биринчиден	birintʃiden
secondly (adv)	экинчиден	ekintʃiden
thirdly (adv)	үчүнчүдөн	ytʃyntʃydøn

suddenly (adv)	күтпөгөн жерден	kytpøgøn dʒerden
at first (in the beginning)	башында	baʃında
for the first time	биринчи жолу	birintʃi dʒolu
long before ...	... алдында	... aldında
anew (over again)	башынан	baʃınan
for good (adv)	түбөлүккө	tybølykkø

never (adv)	эч качан	etʃ katʃan
again (adv)	кайра	kajra
now (at present)	эми	emi
often (adv)	көпчүлүк учурда	køptʃylyk utʃurda
then (adv)	анда	anda
urgently (quickly)	тезинен	tezinen
usually (adv)	көбүнчө	købyntʃø

by the way, ...	баса, ...	basa, ...
possibly	мүмкүн	mymkyn
probably (adv)	балким	balkim
maybe (adv)	ыктымал	ıktımal
besides ...	андан тышкары, ...	andan tıʃkarı, ...
that's why ...	ошондуктан ...	oʃonduktan ...
in spite of ...	... карабастан	... karabastan

thanks to ...	... кучу менен	... kytʃy menen
what (pron.)	эмне	emne
that (conj.)	эмне	emne
something	бир нерсе	bir nerse
anything (something)	бир нерсе	bir nerse
nothing	эч нерсе	etʃ nerse

who (pron.)	ким	kim
someone	кимдир бирөө	kimdir birøø
somebody	бирөө жарым	birøø dʒarım

nobody	эч ким	etʃ kim
nowhere (a voyage to ~)	эч жака	etʃ dʒaka
nobody's	эч кимдики	etʃ kimdiki
somebody's	бирөөнүкү	birøønyky

so (I'm ~ glad)	эми	emi
also (as well)	ошондой эле	oʃondoj ele
too (as well)	дагы	dagı

18. Function words. Adverbs. Part 2

Why?	Эмнеге?	emnege?
for some reason	эмнегедир	emnegedir
because ...	... себептен	... sebepten
for some purpose	эмне үчүндүр	emne ytʃyndyr

and	жана	dʒana
or	же	dʒe
but	бирок	birok
for (e.g. ~ me)	үчүн	ytʃyn

too (excessively)	өтө эле	øtø ele
only (exclusively)	азыр эле	azır ele
exactly (adv)	так	tak
about (more or less)	болжол менен	boldʒol menen

approximately (adv)	болжол менен	boldʒol menen
approximate (adj)	болжолдуу	boldʒolduu
almost (adv)	дээрлик	deerlik
the rest	калганы	kalganı

the other (second)	башка	baʃka
other (different)	башка бөлөк	baʃka bøløk
each (adj)	ар бири	ar biri
any (no matter which)	баардык	baardık
many, much (a lot of)	көп	køp
many people	көбү	køby
all (everyone)	баары	baarı

in return for ...	... алмашуу	... almaʃuu
in exchange (adv)	ордуна	orduna
by hand (made)	колго	kolgo
hardly (negative opinion)	ишенүүгө болбойт	iʃenyygø bolbojt

probably (adv)	балким	balkim
on purpose (intentionally)	атайын	atajın
by accident (adv)	кокустан	kokustan

very (adv)	аябай	ajabaj
for example (adv)	мисалы	misalı
between	ортосунда	ortosunda
among	арасында	arasında
so much (such a lot)	ошончо	oʃontʃo
especially (adv)	өзгөчө	øzgøtʃø

Basic concepts. Part 2

19. Weekdays

Monday	дүйшөмбү	dyjʃømby
Tuesday	шейшемби	ʃejʃembi
Wednesday	шаршемби	ʃarʃembi
Thursday	бейшемби	bejʃembi
Friday	жума	dʒuma
Saturday	ишенби	iʃenbi
Sunday	жекшемби	dʒekʃembi

today (adv)	бүгүн	bygyn
tomorrow (adv)	эртең	erteŋ
the day after tomorrow	бирсүгүнү	birsygyny
yesterday (adv)	кечээ	ketʃee
the day before yesterday	мурда күнү	murda kyny

day	күн	kyn
working day	иш күнү	iʃ kyny
public holiday	майрам күнү	majram kyny
day off	дем алыш күн	dem alɪʃ kyn
weekend	дем алыш күндөр	dem alɪʃ kyndør

all day long	күнү бою	kyny bojʉ
the next day (adv)	кийинки күнү	kijinki kyny
two days ago	эки күн мурун	eki kyn murun
the day before	жакында	dʒakɪnda
daily (adj)	күндө	kyndø
every day (adv)	күн сайын	kyn sajɪn

week	жума	dʒuma
last week (adv)	өткөн жумада	øtkøn dʒumada
next week (adv)	келаткан жумада	kelatkan dʒumada
weekly (adj)	жума сайын	dʒuma sajɪn
every week (adv)	жума сайын	dʒuma sajɪn
twice a week	жумасына эки жолу	dʒumasɪna eki dʒolu
every Tuesday	ар шейшемби	ar ʃejʃembi

20. Hours. Day and night

morning	таң	taŋ
in the morning	эртең менен	erteŋ menen
noon, midday	жарым күн	dʒarɪm kyn
in the afternoon	түштөн кийин	tyʃtøn kijin

evening	кеч	ketʃ
in the evening	кечинде	ketʃinde

night	түн	tyn
at night	түндө	tyndø
midnight	жарым түн	dʒarım tyn
second	секунда	sekunda
minute	мүнөт	mynøt
hour	саат	saat
half an hour	жарым саат	dʒarım saat
a quarter-hour	чейрек саат	tʃejrek saat
fifteen minutes	он беш мүнөт	on beʃ mynøt
24 hours	сутка	sutka
sunrise	күндүн чыгышы	kyndyn tʃıgıʃı
dawn	таң агаруу	taŋ agaruu
early morning	таң эрте	taŋ erte
sunset	күн батуу	kyn batuu
early in the morning	таң эрте	taŋ erte
this morning	бүгүн эртең менен	bygyn erteŋ menen
tomorrow morning	эртең эртең менен	erteŋ erteŋ menen
this afternoon	күндүзү	kyndyzy
in the afternoon	түштөн кийин	tyʃtøn kijin
tomorrow afternoon	эртең түштөн кийин	erteŋ tyʃtøn kijin
tonight (this evening)	бүгүн кечинде	bygyn ketʃinde
tomorrow night	эртең кечинде	erteŋ ketʃinde
at 3 o'clock sharp	туура саат үчтө	tuura saat ytʃtø
about 4 o'clock	болжол менен төрт саат	boldʒol menen tørt saat
by 12 o'clock	саат он экиде	saat on ekide
in 20 minutes	жыйырма мүнөттөн кийин	dʒıjırma mynøttøn kijin
in an hour	бир сааттан кийин	bir saattan kijin
on time (adv)	өз убагында	øz ubagında
a quarter to …	… он беш мүнөт калды	… on beʃ mynøt kaldı
within an hour	бир сааттын ичинде	bir saattın itʃinde
every 15 minutes	он беш мүнөт сайын	on beʃ mynøt sajın
round the clock	бир сутка бою	bir sutka boju

21. Months. Seasons

January	январь	janvarʲ
February	февраль	fevralʲ
March	март	mart
April	апрель	aprelʲ
May	май	maj
June	июнь	ijʉnʲ
July	июль	ijʉlʲ
August	август	avgust
September	сентябрь	sentʲabrʲ
October	октябрь	oktʲabrʲ
November	ноябрь	nojabrʲ
December	декабрь	dekabrʲ

spring	жаз	dʒaz
in spring	жазында	dʒazında
spring (as adj)	жазгы	dʒazgı

summer	жай	dʒaj
in summer	жайында	dʒajında
summer (as adj)	жайкы	dʒajkı

autumn	күз	kyz
in autumn	күзүндө	kyzyndø
autumn (as adj)	күздүк	kyzdyk

winter	кыш	kıʃ
in winter	кышында	kıʃında
winter (as adj)	кышкы	kıʃkı

month	ай	aj
this month	ушул айда	uʃul ajda
next month	кийинки айда	kijinki ajda
last month	өткөн айда	øtkøn ajda

a month ago	бир ай мурун	bir aj murun
in a month (a month later)	бир айдан кийин	bir ajdan kijin
in 2 months (2 months later)	эки айдан кийин	eki ajdan kijin
the whole month	ай бою	aj bojʉ
all month long	толук бир ай	toluk bir aj

monthly (~ magazine)	ай сайын	aj sajın
monthly (adv)	ай сайын	aj sajın
every month	ар бир айда	ar bir ajda
twice a month	айына эки жолу	ajına eki dʒolu

year	жыл	dʒıl
this year	бул жылы	bul dʒılı
next year	келаткан жылы	kelatkan dʒılı
last year	өткөн жылы	øtkøn dʒılı

a year ago	бир жыл мурун	bir dʒıl murun
in a year	бир жылдан кийин	bir dʒıldan kijin
in two years	эки жылдан кийин	eki dʒıldan kijin
the whole year	жыл бою	dʒıl bodʒʉ
all year long	толук бир жыл	toluk bir dʒıl

every year	ар жыл сайын	ar dʒıl sajın
annual (adj)	жыл сайын	dʒıl sajın
annually (adv)	жыл сайын	dʒıl sajın
4 times a year	жылына төрт жолу	dʒılına tørt dʒolu

date (e.g. today's ~)	число	tʃislo
date (e.g. ~ of birth)	күн	kyn
calendar	календарь	kalendarʲ

half a year	жарым жыл	dʒarım dʒıl
six months	жарым чейрек	dʒarım tʃejrek
season (summer, etc.)	мезгил	mezgil
century	кылым	kılım

22. Time. Miscellaneous

time	убакыт	ubakıt
moment	учур	utʃur
instant (n)	көз ирмемде	køz irmemde
instant (adj)	көз ирмемде	køz irmemde
lapse (of time)	убакыттын бир бөлүгү	ubakıttın bir bølygy
life	жашоо	dʒaʃoo
eternity	түбөлүк	tybølyk
epoch	доор	door
era	заман	zaman
cycle	мерчим	mertʃim
period	мезгил	mezgil
term (short-~)	мөөнөт	møønøt
the future	келечек	keletʃek
future (as adj)	келечек	keletʃek
next time	кийинки жолу	kijinki dʒolu
the past	өткөн	øtkøn
past (recent)	өткөн	øtkøn
last time	өткөндө	øtkøndø
later (adv)	кийнчерээк	kijntʃereek
after (prep.)	кийин	kijin
nowadays (adv)	азыр, учурда	azır, utʃurda
now (at this moment)	азыр	azır
immediately (adv)	тез арада	tez arada
soon (adv)	жакында	dʒakında
in advance (beforehand)	алдын ала	aldın ala
a long time ago	көп убакыт мурун	køp ubakıt murun
recently (adv)	жакындан бери	dʒakından beri
destiny	тагдыр	tagdır
memories (childhood ~)	эсте калганы	este kalganı
archives	архив	arχiv
during ...	... убагында	... ubagında
long, a long time (adv)	узак	uzak
not long (adv)	узак эмес	uzak emes
early (in the morning)	эрте	erte
late (not early)	кеч	ketʃ
forever (for good)	түбөлүк	tybølyk
to start (begin)	баштоо	baʃtoo
to postpone (vt)	жылдыруу	dʒıldıruu
at the same time	бир учурда	bir utʃurda
permanently (adv)	үзгүлтүксүз	yzgyltyksyz
constant (noise, pain)	үзгүлтүксүз	yzgyltyksyz
temporary (adj)	убактылуу	ubaktıluu
sometimes (adv)	кээдээ	kedee
rarely (adv)	чанда	tʃanda
often (adv)	көпчүлүк учурда	køptʃylyk utʃurda

23. Opposites

| rich (adj) | бай | baj |
| poor (adj) | кедей | kedej |

| ill, sick (adj) | оорулуу | ooruluu |
| well (not sick) | дени сак | deni sak |

| big (adj) | чоң | ʧoŋ |
| small (adj) | кичине | kiʧine |

| quickly (adv) | тез | tez |
| slowly (adv) | жай | ʤaj |

| fast (adj) | тез | tez |
| slow (adj) | жай | ʤaj |

| glad (adj) | шайыр | ʃajır |
| sad (adj) | муңдуу | muŋduu |

| together (adv) | бирге | birge |
| separately (adv) | өзүнчө | øzynʧø |

| aloud (to read) | үн чыгарып | yn ʧıgarıp |
| silently (to oneself) | үн чыгарбай | yn ʧıgarbaj |

| tall (adj) | бийик | bijik |
| low (adj) | жапыз | ʤapız |

| deep (adj) | терең | tereŋ |
| shallow (adj) | тайыз | tajız |

| yes | ооба | ooba |
| no | жок | ʤok |

| distant (in space) | алыс | alıs |
| nearby (adj) | жакын | ʤakın |

| far (adv) | алыс | alıs |
| nearby (adv) | жакын арада | ʤakın arada |

| long (adj) | узун | uzun |
| short (adj) | кыска | kıska |

| good (kindhearted) | кайрымдуу | kajrımduu |
| evil (adj) | каардуу | kaarduu |

| married (adj) | аялы бар | ajalı bar |
| single (adj) | бойдок | bojdok |

| to forbid (vt) | тыюу салуу | tıjuu saluu |
| to permit (vt) | уруксат берүү | uruksat beryy |

| end | аягы | ajagı |
| beginning | башталыш | baʃtalıʃ |

left (adj)	сол	sol
right (adj)	оң	oŋ
first (adj)	биринчи	birintʃi
last (adj)	акыркы	akırkı
crime	кылмыш	kılmıʃ
punishment	жаза	dʒaza
to order (vt)	буйрук кылуу	bujruk kıluu
to obey (vi, vt)	баш ийүү	baʃ ijyy
straight (adj)	түз	tyz
curved (adj)	кыйшак	kıʃak
paradise	бейиш	bejiʃ
hell	тозок	tozok
to be born	төрөлүү	tørølyy
to die (vi)	өлүү	ølyy
strong (adj)	күчтүү	kytʃtyy
weak (adj)	алсыз	alsız
old (adj)	эски	eski
young (adj)	жаш	dʒaʃ
old (adj)	эски	eski
new (adj)	жаңы	dʒaŋı
hard (adj)	катуу	katuu
soft (adj)	жумшак	dʒumʃak
warm (tepid)	жылуу	dʒıluu
cold (adj)	муздак	muzdak
fat (adj)	семиз	semiz
thin (adj)	арык	arık
narrow (adj)	тар	tar
wide (adj)	кең	keŋ
good (adj)	жакшы	dʒakʃı
bad (adj)	жаман	dʒaman
brave (adj)	кайраттуу	kajrattuu
cowardly (adj)	суу жүрөк	suu dʒyrøk

24. Lines and shapes

square	чарчы	tʃartʃı
square (as adj)	чарчы	tʃartʃı
circle	тегерек	tegerek
round (adj)	тегерек	tegerek

triangle	үч бурчтук	ytʃ burtʃtuk
triangular (adj)	үч бурчтуу	ytʃ burtʃtuu
oval	жумуру	ʤumuru
oval (as adj)	жумуру	ʤumuru
rectangle	тик бурчтук	tik burtʃtuk
rectangular (adj)	тик бурчтуу	tik burtʃtuu
pyramid	пирамида	piramida
rhombus	ромб	romb
trapezium	трапеция	trapetsija
cube	куб	kub
prism	призма	prizma
circumference	айлана	ajlana
sphere	сфера	sfera
ball (solid sphere)	шар	ʃar
diameter	диаметр	diametr
radius	радиус	radius
perimeter (circle's ~)	периметр	perimetr
centre	борбор	borbor
horizontal (adj)	туурасынан	tuurasınan
vertical (adj)	тикесинен	tikesinen
parallel (n)	параллель	parallelʲ
parallel (as adj)	параллель	parallelʲ
line	сызык	sızık
stroke	сызык	sızık
straight line	түз сызык	tyz sızık
curve (curved line)	кыйшык сызык	kıjʃık sızık
thin (line, etc.)	ичке	itʃke
contour (outline)	караан	karaan
intersection	кесилиш	kesiliʃ
right angle	тик бурч	tik burtʃ
segment	сегмент	segment
sector (circular ~)	сектор	sektor
side (of triangle)	каптал	kaptal
angle	бурч	burtʃ

25. Units of measurement

weight	салмак	salmak
length	узундук	uzunduk
width	жазылык	ʤazılık
height	бийиктик	bijiktik
depth	терендик	terendik
volume	көлөм	køløm
area	аянт	ajant
gram	грамм	gramm
milligram	миллиграмм	milligramm

kilogram	килограмм	kilogramm
ton	тонна	tonna
pound	фунт	funt
ounce	унция	untsija

metre	метр	metr
millimetre	миллиметр	millimetr
centimetre	сантиметр	santimetr
kilometre	километр	kilometr
mile	миля	milʲa

inch	дюйм	dʉjm
foot	фут	fut
yard	ярд	jard

| square metre | квадраттык метр | kvadrattık metr |
| hectare | гектар | gektar |

litre	литр	litr
degree	градус	gradus
volt	вольт	volʲt
ampere	ампер	amper
horsepower	ат күчү	at kytʃy

quantity	саны	sanı
a little bit of ...	... бир аз	... bir az
half	жарым	dʒarım
dozen	он эки даана	on eki daana
piece (item)	даана	daana

| size | чоңдук | tʃoŋduk |
| scale (map ~) | өлчөмчен | øltʃømtʃen |

minimal (adj)	минималдуу	minimalduu
the smallest (adj)	эң кичинекей	eŋ kitʃinekej
medium (adj)	орточо	ortotʃo
maximal (adj)	максималдуу	maksimalduu
the largest (adj)	эң чоң	eŋ tʃoŋ

26. Containers

canning jar (glass ~)	банка	banka
tin, can	банка	banka
bucket	чака	tʃaka
barrel	бочка	botʃka

wash basin (e.g., plastic ~)	дагара	dagara
tank (100L water ~)	бак	bak
hip flask	фляжка	flʲadʒka
jerrycan	канистра	kanistra
tank (e.g., tank car)	цистерна	tsısterna

| mug | кружка | krudʒka |
| cup (of coffee, etc.) | чөйчөк | tʃøjtʃøk |

saucer	табак	tabak
glass (tumbler)	ыстакан	ıstakan
wine glass	бокал	bokal
stock pot (soup pot)	мискей	miskej

| bottle (~ of wine) | бөтөлкө | bøtølkø |
| neck (of the bottle, etc.) | оозу | oozu |

carafe (decanter)	графин	grafin
pitcher	кумура	kumura
vessel (container)	идиш	idiʃ
pot (crock, stoneware ~)	карапа	karapa
vase	ваза	vaza

flacon, bottle (perfume ~)	флакон	flakon
vial, small bottle	кичине бөтөлкө	kitʃine bøtølkø
tube (of toothpaste)	тюбик	tubik

sack (bag)	кап	kap
bag (paper ~, plastic ~)	пакет	paket
packet (of cigarettes, etc.)	пачке	patʃke

box (e.g. shoebox)	куту	kutu
crate	үкөк	ykøk
basket	себет	sebet

27. Materials

material	материал	material
wood (n)	жыгач	dʒıgatʃ
wood-, wooden (adj)	жыгач	dʒıgatʃ

| glass (n) | айнек | ajnek |
| glass (as adj) | айнек | ajnek |

| stone (n) | таш | taʃ |
| stone (as adj) | таш | taʃ |

| plastic (n) | пластик | plastik |
| plastic (as adj) | пластик | plastik |

| rubber (n) | резина | rezina |
| rubber (as adj) | резина | rezina |

| cloth, fabric (n) | кездеме | kezdeme |
| fabric (as adj) | кездеме | kezdeme |

| paper (n) | кагаз | kagaz |
| paper (as adj) | кагаз | kagaz |

cardboard (n)	картон	karton
cardboard (as adj)	картон	karton
polyethylene	полиэтилен	polietilen
cellophane	целлофан	tsellofan

| linoleum | линолеум | linoleum |
| plywood | фанера | fanera |

porcelain (n)	фарфор	farfor
porcelain (as adj)	фарфор	farfor
clay (n)	чопо	ʧopo
clay (as adj)	чопо	ʧopo
ceramic (n)	карапа	karapa
ceramic (as adj)	карапа	karapa

28. Metals

metal (n)	металл	metall
metal (as adj)	металл	metall
alloy (n)	эритме	eritme

gold (n)	алтын	altın
gold, golden (adj)	алтын	altın
silver (n)	күмүш	kymyʃ
silver (as adj)	күмүш	kymyʃ

iron (n)	темир	temir
iron-, made of iron (adj)	темир	temir
steel (n)	болот	bolot
steel (as adj)	болот	bolot
copper (n)	жез	ʤez
copper (as adj)	жез	ʤez

aluminium (n)	алюминий	alɯminij
aluminium (as adj)	алюминий	alɯminij
bronze (n)	коло	kolo
bronze (as adj)	коло	kolo

brass	латунь	latunʲ
nickel	никель	nikelʲ
platinum	платина	platina
mercury	сымап	sımap
tin	калай	kalaj
lead	коргошун	korgoʃun
zinc	цинк	ʦınk

HUMAN BEING

Human being. The body

29. Humans. Basic concepts

human being	адам	adam
man (adult male)	эркек	erkek
woman	аял	ajal
child	бала	bala
girl	кыз бала	kız bala
boy	бала	bala
teenager	өспүрүм	øspyrym
old man	абышка	abıʃka
old woman	кемпир	kempir

30. Human anatomy

organism (body)	организм	organizm
heart	жүрөк	dʒyrøk
blood	кан	kan
artery	артерия	arterija
vein	вена	vena
brain	мээ	mee
nerve	нерв	nerv
nerves	нервдер	nervder
vertebra	омуртка	omurtka
spine (backbone)	кыр арка	kır arka
stomach (organ)	ашказан	aʃkazan
intestines, bowels	ичеги-карын	itʃegi-karın
intestine (e.g. large ~)	ичеги	itʃegi
liver	боор	boor
kidney	бөйрөк	bøjrøk
bone	сөөк	søøk
skeleton	скелет	skelet
rib	кабырга	kabırga
skull	баш сөөгү	baʃ søøgy
muscle	булчуң	bultʃuŋ
biceps	бицепс	bitseps
triceps	трицепс	tritseps
tendon	тарамыш	taramıʃ
joint	муундар	muundar

lungs	өпкө	øpkø
genitals	жан жер	dʒan dʒer
skin	тери	teri

31. Head

head	баш	baʃ
face	бет	bet
nose	мурун	murun
mouth	ооз	ooz

eye	көз	køz
eyes	көздөр	køzdør
pupil	карек	karek
eyebrow	каш	kaʃ
eyelash	кирпик	kirpik
eyelid	кабак	kabak

tongue	тил	til
tooth	тиш	tiʃ
lips	эриндер	erinder
cheekbones	бет сөөгү	bet søøgy
gum	тиш эти	tiʃ eti
palate	таңдай	taŋdaj

nostrils	мурун тешиги	murun teʃigi
chin	ээк	eek
jaw	жаак	dʒaak
cheek	бет	bet

forehead	чеке	tʃeke
temple	чыкый	tʃɪkɪj
ear	кулак	kulak
back of the head	желке	dʒelke
neck	моюн	mojʉn
throat	тамак	tamak

hair	чач	tʃatʃ
hairstyle	чач жасоо	tʃatʃ dʒasoo
haircut	чач кыркуу	tʃatʃ kɪrkuu
wig	парик	parik

moustache	мурут	murut
beard	сакал	sakal
to have (a beard, etc.)	мурут коюу	murut kojʉu
plait	өрүм чач	ørym tʃatʃ
sideboards	бакенбарда	bakenbarda

red-haired (adj)	сары	sarɪ
grey (hair)	ак чачтуу	ak tʃatʃtuu
bald (adj)	таз	taz
bald patch	кашка	kaʃka
ponytail	куйрук	kujruk
fringe	көкүл	køkyl

32. Human body

| hand | беш манжа | beʃ mandʒa |
| arm | кол | kol |

finger	манжа	mandʒa
toe	манжа	mandʒa
thumb	бармак	barmak
little finger	чыпалак	ʧɪpalak
nail	тырмак	tɪrmak

fist	муштум	muʃtum
palm	алакан	alakan
wrist	билек	bilek
forearm	каруу	karuu
elbow	чыканак	ʧɪkanak
shoulder	ийин	ijin

leg	бут	but
foot	таман	taman
knee	тизе	tize
calf (part of leg)	балтыр	baltɪr
hip	сан	san
heel	согончок	sogonʧok

body	дене	dene
stomach	курсак	kursak
chest	төш	tøʃ
breast	эмчек	emʧek
flank	каптал	kaptal
back	арка жон	arka dʒon
lower back	бел	bel
waist	бел	bel

navel (belly button)	киндик	kindik
buttocks	жамбаш	dʒambaʃ
bottom	көчүк	køʧyk

beauty spot	мең	meŋ
birthmark (café au lait spot)	кал	kal
tattoo	татуировка	tatuirovka
scar	тырык	tɪrɪk

Clothing & Accessories

33. Outerwear. Coats

clothes	кийим	kijim
outerwear	үстүнкү кийим	ystyŋky kijim
winter clothing	кышкы кийим	kıʃkı kijim
coat (overcoat)	пальто	palʲto
fur coat	тон	ton
fur jacket	чолок тон	tʃolok ton
down coat	мамык олпок	mamık olpok
jacket (e.g. leather ~)	күрмө	kyrmø
raincoat (trenchcoat, etc.)	плащ	plaʃtʃ
waterproof (adj)	суу өткүс	suu øtkys

34. Men's & women's clothing

shirt (button shirt)	көйнөк	køjnøk
trousers	шым	ʃım
jeans	джинсы	dʒinsı
suit jacket	бешмант	beʃmant
suit	костюм	kostɥm
dress (frock)	көйнөк	køjnøk
skirt	юбка	jɥbka
blouse	блузка	bluzka
knitted jacket (cardigan, etc.)	кофта	kofta
jacket (of woman's suit)	кыска бешмант	kıska beʃmant
T-shirt	футболка	futbolka
shorts (short trousers)	чолок шым	tʃolok ʃım
tracksuit	спорт кийими	sport kijimi
bathrobe	халат	χalat
pyjamas	пижама	pidʒama
jumper (sweater)	свитер	sviter
pullover	пуловер	pulover
waistcoat	жилет	dʒilet
tailcoat	фрак	frak
dinner suit	смокинг	smoking
uniform	форма	forma
workwear	жумуш кийим	dʒumuʃ kijim
boiler suit	комбинезон	kombinezon
coat (e.g. doctor's smock)	халат	χalat

35. Clothing. Underwear

underwear	ич кийим	iʧ kijim
pants	эркектер чолок дамбалы	erkekter ʧolok dambalı
panties	аялдар трусиги	ajaldar trusigi
vest (singlet)	майка	majka
socks	байпак	bajpak

nightdress	жатаарда кийүүчү көйнөк	ʤataarda kijyyʧy køjnøk
bra	бюстгальтер	bʉstgalʲter
knee highs (knee-high socks)	гольфы	golʲfı
tights	колготки	kolgotki
stockings (hold ups)	байпак	bajpak
swimsuit, bikini	купальник	kupalʲnik

36. Headwear

hat	топу	topu
trilby hat	шляпа	ʃlʲapa
baseball cap	бейсболка	bejsbolka
flatcap	кепка	kepka

beret	берет	beret
hood	капюшон	kapʉʃon
panama hat	панамка	panamka
knit cap (knitted hat)	токулган шапка	tokulgan ʃapka

headscarf	жоолук	ʤooluk
women's hat	шляпа	ʃlʲapa

hard hat	каска	kaska
forage cap	пилотка	pilotka
helmet	шлем	ʃlem

bowler	котелок	kotelok
top hat	цилиндр	tsılindr

37. Footwear

footwear	бут кийим	but kijim
shoes (men's shoes)	ботинка	botinka
shoes (women's shoes)	туфли	tufli
boots (e.g., cowboy ~)	өтүк	øtyk
carpet slippers	тапочка	tapotʃka

trainers	кроссовка	krossovka
trainers	кеды	kedı
sandals	сандалии	sandalii

cobbler (shoe repairer)	өтүкчү	øtykʧy
heel	така	taka

pair (of shoes)	түгөй	tygøj
lace (shoelace)	боо	boo
to lace up (vt)	боолоо	booloo
shoehorn	кашык	kaʃık
shoe polish	өтүк май	øtyk maj

38. Textile. Fabrics

cotton (n)	пахта	paχta
cotton (as adj)	пахтадан	paχtadan
flax (n)	зыгыр	zıgır
flax (as adj)	зыгырдан	zıgırdan

silk (n)	жибек	dʒibek
silk (as adj)	жибек	dʒibek
wool (n)	жүн	dʒyn
wool (as adj)	жүндөн	dʒyndøn

velvet	баркыт	barkıt
suede	күдөрү	kydøry
corduroy	чий баркыт	ʧij barkıt

nylon (n)	нейлон	nejlon
nylon (as adj)	нейлон	nejlon
polyester (n)	полиэстер	poliester
polyester (as adj)	полиэстер	poliester

leather (n)	булгаары	bulgaarı
leather (as adj)	булгаары	bulgaarı
fur (n)	тери	teri
fur (e.g. ~ coat)	тери	teri

39. Personal accessories

gloves	колкап	kolkap
mittens	мээлей	meelej
scarf (muffler)	моюн орогуч	mojʉn oroguʧ

glasses	көз айнек	køz ajnek
frame (eyeglass ~)	алкак	alkak
umbrella	чатырча	ʧatırʧa
walking stick	аса таяк	asa tajak
hairbrush	тарак	tarak
fan	желпингич	dʒelpingiʧ

tie (necktie)	галстук	galstuk
bow tie	галстук-бабочка	galstuk-babotʃka
braces	шым тарткыч	ʃım tartkıʧ
handkerchief	бетаарчы	betaarʧı

| comb | тарак | tarak |
| hair slide | чачсайгы | ʧaʧsajgı |

| hairpin | шпилька | ʃpilʲka |
| buckle | таралга | taralga |

| belt | кайыш кур | kajıʃ kur |
| shoulder strap | илгич | ilgitʃ |

bag (handbag)	колбаштык	kolbaʃtık
handbag	кичине колбаштык	kitʃine kolbaʃtık
rucksack	жонбаштык	dʒonbaʃtık

40. Clothing. Miscellaneous

fashion	мода	moda
in vogue (adj)	саркеч	sarketʃ
fashion designer	модельер	modeljer

collar	жака	dʒaka
pocket	чөнтөк	tʃøntøk
pocket (as adj)	чөнтөк	tʃøntøk
sleeve	жең	dʒeŋ
hanging loop	илгич	ilgitʃ
flies (on trousers)	ширинка	ʃirinka

zip (fastener)	молния	molnija
fastener	топчулук	toptʃuluk
button	топчу	toptʃu
buttonhole	илмек	ilmek
to come off (ab. button)	үзүлүү	yzylyy

to sew (vi, vt)	тигүү	tigyy
to embroider (vi, vt)	сайма саюу	sajma sajʉu
embroidery	сайма	sajma
sewing needle	ийне	ijne
thread	жип	dʒip
seam	тигиш	tigiʃ

to get dirty (vi)	булгап алуу	bulgap aluu
stain (mark, spot)	так	tak
to crease, crumple (vi)	бырышып калуу	bırıʃıp kaluu
to tear, to rip (vt)	айрылуу	ajrıluu
clothes moth	күбө	kybø

41. Personal care. Cosmetics

toothpaste	тиш пастасы	tiʃ pastası
toothbrush	тиш щёткасы	tiʃ ʃtʃotkası
to clean one's teeth	тиш жуу	tiʃ dʒuu

razor	устара	ustara
shaving cream	кырынуу үчүн көбүк	kırınuu ytʃyn købyk
to shave (vi)	кырынуу	kırınuu
soap	самын	samın

shampoo	шампунь	ʃampunʲ
scissors	кайчы	kajtʃı
nail file	тырмак өгөө	tırmak øgøø
nail clippers	тырмак кычкачы	tırmak kıtʃkatʃı
tweezers	искек	iskek

cosmetics	упа-эндик	upa-endik
face mask	маска	maska
manicure	маникюр	manikʉr
to have a manicure	маникюр жасоо	manikdʒʉr dʒasoo
pedicure	педикюр	pedikʉr

make-up bag	косметичка	kosmetitʃka
face powder	упа	upa
powder compact	упа кутусу	upa kutusu
blusher	эндик	endik

perfume (bottled)	атыр	atır
toilet water (lotion)	туалет атыр суусу	tualet atır suusu
lotion	лосьон	losʲon
cologne	одеколон	odekolon

eyeshadow	көз боёгу	køz bojogu
eyeliner	көз карандашы	køz karandaʃı
mascara	кирпик үчүн боек	kirpik ytʃyn boek

lipstick	эрин помадасы	erin pomadası
nail polish	тырмак үчүн лак	tırmak ytʃyn lak
hair spray	чач үчүн лак	tʃatʃ ytʃyn lak
deodorant	дезодорант	dezodorant

cream	крем	krem
face cream	бетмай	betmaj
hand cream	кол үчүн май	kol ytʃyn maj
anti-wrinkle cream	бырыштарга каршы бет май	bırıʃtarga karʃı bet maj

day cream	күндүзгү бет май	kyndyzgy bet maj
night cream	түнкү бет май	tynky bet maj
day (as adj)	күндүзгү	kyndyzgy
night (as adj)	түнкү	tynky

tampon	тампон	tampon
toilet paper (toilet roll)	даарат кагазы	daarat kagazı
hair dryer	фен	fen

42. Jewellery

jewellery, jewels	зер буюмдар	zer bujumdar
precious (e.g. ~ stone)	баалуу	baaluu
hallmark stamp	проба	proba

ring	шакек	ʃakek
wedding ring	нике шакеги	nike ʃakegi
bracelet	билерик	bilerik

earrings	сөйкө	søjkø
necklace (~ of pearls)	шуру	ʃuru
crown	таажы	taadʒı
bead necklace	мончок	montʃok

diamond	бриллиант	brilliant
emerald	зымырыт	zımırıt
ruby	лаал	laal
sapphire	сапфир	sapfir
pearl	бермет	bermet
amber	янтарь	jantarʲ

43. Watches. Clocks

watch (wristwatch)	кол саат	kol saat
dial	циферблат	tsıferblat
hand (of clock, watch)	жебе	dʒebe
metal bracelet	браслет	braslet
watch strap	кайыш кур	kajıʃ kur

battery	батарейка	batarejka
to be flat (battery)	зарядканын түгөнүүсү	zarʲadkanın tygønyysy
to change a battery	батарейка алмаштыруу	batarejka almaʃtıruu
to run fast	алдыга кетүү	aldıga ketyy
to run slow	калуу	kaluu

wall clock	дубалга тагуучу саат	dubalga taguutʃu saat
hourglass	кум саат	kum saat
sundial	күн саат	kyn saat
alarm clock	ойготкуч саат	ojgotkutʃ saat
watchmaker	саат устасы	saat ustası
to repair (vt)	оңдоо	oŋdoo

Food. Nutricion

44. Food

meat	эт	et
chicken	тоок	took
poussin	балапан	balapan
duck	өрдөк	ørdøk
goose	каз	kaz
game	илбээсин	ilbeesin
turkey	күрп	kyrp
pork	чочко эти	ʧoʧko eti
veal	торпок эти	torpok eti
lamb	кой эти	koj eti
beef	уй эти	uj eti
rabbit	коен	koen
sausage (bologna, etc.)	колбаса	kolbasa
vienna sausage (frankfurter)	сосиска	sosiska
bacon	бекон	bekon
ham	ветчина	vetʧina
gammon	сан эт	san et
pâté	паштет	paʃtet
liver	боор	boor
mince (minced meat)	фарш	farʃ
tongue	тил	til
egg	жумуртка	ʤumurtka
eggs	жумурткалар	ʤumurtkalar
egg white	жумурттканын агы	ʤumurtkanın agı
egg yolk	жумурттканын сарысы	ʤumurtkanın sarısı
fish	балык	balık
seafood	деңиз азыктары	deŋiz azıktarı
crustaceans	рак сыяктуулар	rak sıjaktuular
caviar	урук	uruk
crab	краб	krab
prawn	креветка	krevetka
oyster	устрица	ustriʦa
spiny lobster	лангуст	langust
octopus	сегиз бут	segiz but
squid	кальмар	kalʲmar
sturgeon	осетрина	osetrina
salmon	лосось	lososʲ
halibut	палтус	paltus
cod	треска	treska

mackerel	скумбрия	skumbrija
tuna	тунец	tunels
eel	угорь	ugorⁱ

trout	форель	forelʲ
sardine	сардина	sardina
pike	чортон	ʧorton
herring	сельдь	selʲdʲ

bread	нан	nan
cheese	сыр	sır
sugar	кум шекер	kum-ʃeker
salt	туз	tuz

rice	күрүч	kyryʧ
pasta (macaroni)	макарон	makaron
noodles	кесме	kesme

butter	ак май	ak maj
vegetable oil	өсүмдүк майы	øsymdyk majı
sunflower oil	күн карама майы	kyn karama majı
margarine	маргарин	margarin

olives	зайтун	zajtun
olive oil	зайтун майы	zajtun majı

milk	сүт	syt
condensed milk	коютулган сүт	kojutulgan syt
yogurt	йогурт	jogurt
soured cream	сметана	smetana
cream (of milk)	каймак	kajmak

mayonnaise	майонез	majonez
buttercream	крем	krem

groats (barley ~, etc.)	акшак	akʃak
flour	ун	un
tinned food	консерва	konserva

cornflakes	жарылган жүгөрү	ʤarılgan ʤygøry
honey	бал	bal
jam	джем, конфитюр	ʤem, konfitur
chewing gum	сагыз	sagız

45. Drinks

water	суу	suu
drinking water	ичүүчү суу	iʧyyʧy suu
mineral water	минерал суусу	mineral suusu

still (adj)	газсыз	gazsız
carbonated (adj)	газдалган	gazdalgan
sparkling (adj)	газы менен	gazı menen
ice	муз	muz

with ice	музу менен	muzu menen
non-alcoholic (adj)	алкоголсуз	alkogolsuz
soft drink	алкоголсуз ичимдик	alkogolsuz itʃimdik
refreshing drink	суусундук	suusunduk
lemonade	лимонад	limonad

spirits	спирт ичимдиктери	spirt itʃimdikteri
wine	шарап	ʃarap
white wine	ак шарап	ak ʃarap
red wine	кызыл шарап	kızıl ʃarap

liqueur	ликёр	likʲor
champagne	шампан	ʃampan
vermouth	вермут	vermut

whisky	виски	viski
vodka	арак	arak
gin	джин	dʒin
cognac	коньяк	konjak
rum	ром	rom

coffee	кофе	kofe
black coffee	кара кофе	kara kofe
white coffee	сүттөлгөн кофе	syttølgøn kofe
cappuccino	капучино	kaputʃino
instant coffee	эрүүчү кофе	eryytʃy kofe

milk	сүт	syt
cocktail	коктейль	koktejlʲ
milkshake	сүт коктейли	syt koktejli

juice	шире	ʃire
tomato juice	томат ширеси	tomat ʃiresi
orange juice	апельсин ширеси	apelʲsin ʃiresi
freshly squeezed juice	түз сыгылып алынган шире	tyz sıgılıp alıngan ʃire

beer	сыра	sıra
lager	ачык сыра	atʃık sıra
bitter	коңур сыра	koŋur sıra

tea	чай	tʃaj
black tea	кара чай	kara tʃaj
green tea	жашыл чай	dʒaʃıl tʃaj

46. Vegetables

| vegetables | жашылча | dʒaʃıltʃa |
| greens | көк чөп | køk tʃøp |

tomato	помидор	pomidor
cucumber	бадыраң	badıraŋ
carrot	сабиз	sabiz
potato	картошка	kartoʃka

| onion | пияз | pijaz |
| garlic | сарымсак | sarımsak |

cabbage	капуста	kapusta
cauliflower	гүлдүү капуста	gyldyy kapusta
Brussels sprouts	брюссель капустасы	brusseli kapustası
broccoli	брокколи капустасы	brokkoli kapustası

beetroot	кызылча	kızıltʃa
aubergine	баклажан	bakladʒan
courgette	кабачок	kabatʃok
pumpkin	ашкабак	aʃkabak
turnip	шалгам	ʃalgam

parsley	петрушка	petruʃka
dill	укроп	ukrop
lettuce	салат	salat
celery	сельдерей	seliderej
asparagus	спаржа	spardʒa
spinach	шпинат	ʃpinat

pea	нокот	nokot
beans	буурчак	buurtʃak
maize	жүгөрү	dʒygøry
kidney bean	төө буурчак	tøø buurtʃak

sweet paper	таттуу перец	tattuu perets
radish	шалгам	ʃalgam
artichoke	артишок	artiʃok

47. Fruits. Nuts

fruit	мөмө	mømø
apple	алма	alma
pear	алмурут	almurut
lemon	лимон	limon
orange	апельсин	apelisin
strawberry (garden ~)	кулпунай	kulpunaj

tangerine	мандарин	mandarin
plum	кара өрүк	kara øryk
peach	шабдаалы	ʃabdaalı
apricot	өрүк	øryk
raspberry	дан куурай	dan kuuraj
pineapple	ананас	ananas

banana	банан	banan
watermelon	арбуз	arbuz
grape	жүзүм	dʒyzym
sour cherry	алча	altʃa
sweet cherry	гилас	gilas
melon	коон	koon
grapefruit	грейпфрут	grejpfrut
avocado	авокадо	avokado

papaya	папайя	papaja
mango	манго	mango
pomegranate	анар	anar

redcurrant	кызыл карагат	kızıl karagat
blackcurrant	кара карагат	kara karagat
gooseberry	крыжовник	krıʤovnik
bilberry	кара моюл	kara mojʉl
blackberry	кара бүлдүркөн	kara byldyrkøn

raisin	мейиз	mejiz
fig	анжир	anʤir
date	курма	kurma

peanut	арахис	araχis
almond	бадам	badam
walnut	жаңгак	ʤaŋgak
hazelnut	токой жаңгагы	tokoj ʤaŋgagı
coconut	кокос жаңгагы	kokos ʤaŋgagı
pistachios	мисте	miste

48. Bread. Sweets

bakers' confectionery (pastry)	кондитер азыктары	konditer azıktarı
bread	нан	nan
biscuits	печенье	petʃenje

chocolate (n)	шоколад	ʃokolad
chocolate (as adj)	шоколаддан	ʃokoladdan
candy (wrapped)	конфета	konfeta
cake (e.g. cupcake)	пирожное	piroʤnoe
cake (e.g. birthday ~)	торт	tort

| pie (e.g. apple ~) | пирог | pirog |
| filling (for cake, pie) | начинка | natʃinka |

jam (whole fruit jam)	кыям	kıjam
marmalade	мармелад	marmelad
wafers	вафли	vafli
ice-cream	бал муздак	bal muzdak
pudding (Christmas ~)	пудинг	puding

49. Cooked dishes

course, dish	тамак	tamak
cuisine	даам	daam
recipe	тамак жасоо ыкмасы	tamak ʤasoo ıkması
portion	порция	portsija

salad	салат	salat
soup	сорпо	sorpo
clear soup (broth)	ынак сорпо	ınak sorpo

sandwich (bread)	бутерброд	buterbrod
fried eggs	куурулган жумуртка	kuurulgan ʤumurtka
hamburger (beefburger)	гамбургер	gamburger
beefsteak	бифштекс	bifʃteks
side dish	гарнир	garnir
spaghetti	спагетти	spagetti
mash	эзилген картошка	ezilgen kartoʃka
pizza	пицца	pitsa
porridge (oatmeal, etc.)	ботко	botko
omelette	омлет	omlet
boiled (e.g. ~ beef)	сууга бышырылган	suuga bɪʃɪrɪlgan
smoked (adj)	ышталган	ɪʃtalgan
fried (adj)	куурулган	kuurulgan
dried (adj)	кургатылган	kurgatɪlgan
frozen (adj)	тоңдурулган	toŋdurulgan
pickled (adj)	маринаддагы	marinaddagɪ
sweet (sugary)	таттуу	tattuu
salty (adj)	туздуу	tuzduu
cold (adj)	муздак	muzdak
hot (adj)	ысык	ɪsɪk
bitter (adj)	ачуу	atʃuu
tasty (adj)	даамдуу	daamduu
to cook in boiling water	кайнатуу	kajnatuu
to cook (dinner)	тамак бышыруу	tamak bɪʃɪruu
to fry (vt)	куур уу	kuuruu
to heat up (food)	жылытуу	ʤɪlɪtuu
to salt (vt)	туздоо	tuzdoo
to pepper (vt)	калемпир кошуу	kalempir koʃuu
to grate (vt)	сүргүлөө	syrgyløø
peel (n)	сырты	sɪrtɪ
to peel (vt)	тазалоо	tazaloo

50. Spices

salt	туз	tuz
salty (adj)	туздуу	tuzduu
to salt (vt)	туздоо	tuzdoo
black pepper	кара мурч	kara murtʃ
red pepper (milled ~)	кызыл калемпир	kɪzɪl kalempir
mustard	горчица	gortʃitsa
horseradish	хрен	χren
condiment	татымал	tatɪmal
spice	татымал	tatɪmal
sauce	соус	sous
vinegar	уксус	uksus
anise	анис	anis

basil	райхон	rajχon
cloves	гвоздика	gvozdika
ginger	имбирь	imbirʲ
coriander	кориандр	koriandr
cinnamon	корица	koritsa

sesame	кунжут	kundʒut
bay leaf	лавр жалбырагы	lavr dʒalbıragı
paprika	паприка	paprika
caraway	зира	zira
saffron	заапаран	zaaparan

51. Meals

food	тамак	tamak
to eat (vi, vt)	тамактануу	tamaktanuu

breakfast	таңкы тамак	taŋkı tamak
to have breakfast	эртең менен тамактануу	erteŋ menen tamaktanuu
lunch	түшкү тамак	tyʃky tamak
to have lunch	түштөнүү	tyʃtønyy
dinner	кечки тамак	ketʃki tamak
to have dinner	кечки тамакты ичүү	ketʃki tamaktı itʃyy

appetite	табит	tabit
Enjoy your meal!	Тамагыңыз таттуу болсун!	tamagıŋız tattuu bolsun!

to open (~ a bottle)	ачуу	atʃuu
to spill (liquid)	төгүп алуу	tøgyp aluu
to spill out (vi)	төгүлүү	tøgylyy
to boil (vi)	кайноо	kajnoo
to boil (vt)	кайнатуу	kajnatuu
boiled (~ water)	кайнатылган	kajnatılgan
to chill, cool down (vt)	суутуу	suutuu
to chill (vi)	сууп туруу	suup turuu

taste, flavour	даам	daam
aftertaste	даамдануу	daamdanuu

to slim down (lose weight)	арыктоо	arıktoo
diet	мүнөз тамак	mynøz tamak
vitamin	витамин	vitamin
calorie	калория	kalorija
vegetarian (n)	эттен чанган	etten tʃangan
vegetarian (adj)	этсиз даярдалган	etsiz dajardalgan

fats (nutrient)	майлар	majlar
proteins	белоктор	beloktor
carbohydrates	көмүрсуулар	kømyrsuular

slice (of lemon, ham)	кесим	kesim
piece (of cake, pie)	бөлүк	bølyk
crumb (of bread, cake, etc.)	күкүм	kykym

52. Table setting

spoon	кашык	kaʃık
knife	бычак	bıʧak
fork	вилка	vilka

cup (e.g., coffee ~)	чөйчөк	ʧøjʧøk
plate (dinner ~)	табак	tabak
saucer	табак	tabak
serviette	майлык	majlık
toothpick	тиш чукугуч	tiʃ ʧukuguʧ

53. Restaurant

restaurant	ресторан	restoran
coffee bar	кофекана	kofekana
pub, bar	бар	bar
tearoom	чай салону	ʧaj salonu

waiter	официант	ofitsiant
waitress	официант кыз	ofitsiant kız
barman	бармен	barmen

menu	меню	menü
wine list	шарап картасы	ʃarap kartası
to book a table	столду камдык буйрутмалоо	stoldu kamdık bujrutmaloo

course, dish	тамак	tamak
to order (meal)	буйрутма кылуу	bujrutma kıluu
to make an order	буйрутма берүү	bujrutma beryy

aperitif	аперитив	aperitiv
starter	ысылык	ısılık
dessert, pudding	десерт	desert

bill	эсеп	esep
to pay the bill	эсеп төлөө	esep tøløø
to give change	майда акчаны кайтаруу	majda akʧanı kajtaruu
tip	чайпул	ʧajpul

Family, relatives and friends

54. Personal information. Forms

name (first name)	аты	atı
surname (last name)	фамилиясы	familijası
date of birth	төрөлгөн күнү	tørølgøn kyny
place of birth	туулган жери	tuulgan ʤeri
nationality	улуту	ulutu
place of residence	жашаган жери	ʤaʃagan ʤeri
country	өлкө	ølkø
profession (occupation)	кесиби	kesibi
gender, sex	жынысы	ʤınısı
height	бою	boju
weight	салмак	salmak

55. Family members. Relatives

mother	эне	ene
father	ата	ata
son	уул	uul
daughter	кыз	kız
younger daughter	кичүү кыз	kitʃyy kız
younger son	кичүү уул	kitʃyy uul
eldest daughter	улуу кыз	uluu kız
eldest son	улуу уул	uluu uul
brother	бир тууган	bir tuugan
elder brother	байке	bajke
younger brother	ини	ini
sister	бир тууган	bir tuugan
elder sister	эже	eʤe
younger sister	синди	siŋdi
cousin (masc.)	атасы же энеси бир тууган	atası ʤe enesi bir tuugan
cousin (fem.)	атасы же энеси бир тууган	atası ʤe enesi bir tuugan
mummy	апа	apa
dad, daddy	ата	ata
parents	ата-эне	ata-ene
child	бала	bala
children	балдар	baldar
grandmother	чоң апа	tʃoŋ apa

grandfather	чоӊ ата	tʃoŋ ata
grandson	небере бала	nebere bala
granddaughter	небере кыз	nebere kız
grandchildren	неберелер	nebereler

uncle	таяке	tajake
aunt	таяже	tajadʒe
nephew	ини	ini
niece	жээн	dʒeen

mother-in-law (wife's mother)	кайын эне	kajın ene
father-in-law (husband's father)	кайын ата	kajın ata
son-in-law (daughter's husband)	күйөө бала	kyjøø bala
stepmother	өгөй эне	øgøj ene
stepfather	өгөй ата	øgøj ata

infant	эмчектеги бала	emtʃektegi bala
baby (infant)	ымыркай	ımırkaj
little boy, kid	бөбөк	bøbøk

wife	аял	ajal
husband	эр	er
spouse (husband)	күйөө	kyjøø
spouse (wife)	зайып	zajıp

married (masc.)	аялы бар	ajalı bar
married (fem.)	күйөөдө	kyjøødø
single (unmarried)	бойдок	bojdok
bachelor	бойдок	bojdok
divorced (masc.)	ажырашкан	adʒıraʃkan
widow	жесир	dʒesir
widower	жесир	dʒesir

relative	тууган	tuugan
close relative	жакын тууган	dʒakın tuugan
distant relative	алыс тууган	alıs tuugan
relatives	бир тууган	bir tuugan

orphan (boy or girl)	жетим	dʒetim
guardian (of a minor)	камкорчу	kamkortʃu
to adopt (a boy)	уул кылып асырап алуу	uul kılıp asırap aluu
to adopt (a girl)	кыз кылып асырап алуу	kız kılıp asırap aluu

56. Friends. Colleagues

friend (masc.)	дос	dos
friend (fem.)	курбу	kurbu
friendship	достук	dostuk
to be friends	достошуу	dostoʃuu
pal (masc.)	шерик	ʃerik
pal (fem.)	шерик кыз	ʃerik kız

partner	өнөктөш	ønøktøʃ
chief (boss)	башчы	baʃʧı
superior (n)	башчы	baʃʧı
owner, proprietor	кожоюн	koʤoʤʉn
subordinate (n)	кол астындагы	kol astındagı
colleague	кесиптеш	kesipteʃ

acquaintance (person)	тааныш	taanıʃ
fellow traveller	жолдош	ʤoldoʃ
classmate	классташ	klasstaʃ

neighbour (masc.)	кошуна	koʃuna
neighbour (fem.)	кошуна	koʃuna
neighbours	кошуналар	koʃunalar

57. Man. Woman

woman	аял	ajal
girl (young woman)	кыз	kız
bride	колукту	koluktu

beautiful (adj)	сулуу	suluu
tall (adj)	бою узун	bojʉ uzun
slender (adj)	сымбаттуу	sımbattuu
short (adj)	орто бойлуу	orto bojluu

blonde (n)	ак саргыл чачтуу	ak sargıl ʧatʃtuu
brunette (n)	кара чачтуу	kara ʧatʃtuu
ladies' (adj)	аялдардын	ajaldardın
virgin (girl)	эркек көрө элек кыз	erkek kørø elek kız
pregnant (adj)	кош бойлуу	koʃ bojluu

man (adult male)	эркек	erkek
blonde haired man	ак саргыл чачтуу	ak sargıl ʧatʃtuu
dark haired man	кара чачтуу	kara ʧatʃtuu
tall (adj)	бийик бойлуу	bijik bojluu
short (adj)	орто бойлуу	orto bojluu
rude (rough)	орой	oroj
stocky (adj)	жапалдаш бой	ʤapaldaʃ boj
robust (adj)	чымыр	ʧımır
strong (adj)	күчтүү	kytʃtyy
strength	күч	kytʃ

stout, fat (adj)	толук	toluk
swarthy (adj)	кара тору	kara toru
slender (well-built)	сымбаттуу	sımbattuu
elegant (adj)	жарашып кийинген	ʤaraʃıp kijingen

58. Age

age	жаш	ʤaʃ
youth (young age)	жаштык	ʤaʃtık

young (adj)	жаш	dʒaʃ
younger (adj)	кичүү	kitʃyy
older (adj)	улуу	uluu

young man	улан	ulan
teenager	өспүрүм	øspyrym
guy, fellow	жигит	dʒigit

| old man | абышка | abıʃka |
| old woman | кемпир | kempir |

adult (adj)	чоң киши	tʃoŋ kiʃi
middle-aged (adj)	орто жаш	orto dʒaʃ
elderly (adj)	жашап калган	dʒaʃap kalgan
old (adj)	картаң	kartaŋ

retirement	бааракы	baarakı
to retire (from job)	ардактуу эс алууга чыгуу	ardaktuu es aluuga tʃıguu
pensioner	бааргер	baarger

59. Children

child	бала	bala
children	балдар	baldar
twins	эгиздер	egizder

cradle	бешик	beʃik
rattle	шырылдак	ʃırıldak
nappy	жалаяк	dʒalajak

dummy, comforter	упчу	uptʃu
pram	бешик араба	beʃik araba
nursery	бала бакча	bala baktʃa
babysitter	бала баккыч	bala bakkıtʃ

childhood	балалык	balalık
doll	куурчак	kuurtʃak
toy	оюнчук	ojuntʃuk
construction set (toy)	конструктор	konstruktor
well-bred (adj)	тарбия көргөн	tarbija kørgøn
ill-bred (adj)	жетесиз	dʒetesiz
spoilt (adj)	эрке	erke

to be naughty	тентектик кылуу	tentektik kıluu
mischievous (adj)	тентек	tentek
mischievousness	шоктук, тентектик	ʃoktuk, tentektik
mischievous child	тентек	tentek

| obedient (adj) | элпек | elpek |
| disobedient (adj) | тил албас | til albas |

docile (adj)	зээндүү	zeendyy
clever (intelligent)	акылдуу	akılduu
child prodigy	вундеркинд	vunderkind

60. Married couples. Family life

to kiss (vt)	өбүү	øbyy
to kiss (vi)	өбүшүү	øbyʃyy
family (n)	үй-бүлө	yj-bylø
family (as adj)	үй-бүлөлүү	yj-bylølyy
couple	эрди-катын	erdi-katın
marriage (state)	нике	nike
hearth (home)	үй очогу	yj otʃogu
dynasty	династия	dinastija
date	жолугушуу	dʒoluguʃuu
kiss	өбүү	øbyy
love (for sb)	сүйүү	syjyy
to love (sb)	сүйүү	syjyy
beloved	жакшы көргөн	dʒakʃı kørgøn
tenderness	назиктик	naziktik
tender (affectionate)	назик	nazik
faithfulness	берилгендик	berilgendik
faithful (adj)	ишенимдүү	iʃenimdyy
care (attention)	кам көрүү	kam køryy
caring (~ father)	камкор	kamkor
newlyweds	жаңы үйлөнүшкөндөр	dʒaŋı yjlønyʃkøndør
honeymoon	таттуулашуу	tattuulaʃuu
to get married (ab. woman)	күйөөгө чыгуу	kyjøøgø tʃıguu
to get married (ab. man)	аял алуу	ajal aluu
wedding	үйлөнүү той	yjlønyy toy
golden wedding	алтын үлпөт той	altın ylpøt toj
anniversary	жылдык	dʒıldık
lover (masc.)	ойнош	ojnoʃ
mistress (lover)	ойнош	ojnoʃ
adultery	көзгө чөп салуу	køzgø tʃøp saluu
to cheat on ... (commit adultery)	көзгө чөп салуу	køzgø tʃøp saluu
jealous (adj)	кызгануу	kızganuu
to be jealous	кызгануу	kızganuu
divorce	ажырашуу	adʒıraʃuu
to divorce (vi)	ажырашуу	adʒıraʃuu
to quarrel (vi)	урушуу	uruʃuu
to be reconciled (after an argument)	жарашуу	dʒaraʃuu
together (adv)	бирге	birge
sex	жыныстык катнаш	dʒınıstık katnaʃ
happiness	бакыт	bakıt
happy (adj)	бактылуу	baktıluu
misfortune (accident)	кырсык	kırsık
unhappy (adj)	бактысыз	baktısız

Character. Feelings. Emotions

61. Feelings. Emotions

feeling (emotion)	сезим	sezim
feelings	сезим	sezim
to feel (vt)	сезүү	sezyy
hunger	ачка болуу	atʃka boluu
to be hungry	ачка болуу	atʃka boluu
thirst	чаңкоо	tʃaŋkoo
to be thirsty	суусап калуу	suusap kaluu
sleepiness	уйкусу келүү	ujkusu kelyy
to feel sleepy	уйкусу келүү	ujkusu kelyy
tiredness	чарчоо	tʃartʃoo
tired (adj)	чарчаңкы	tʃartʃaŋkɪ
to get tired	чарчоо	tʃartʃoo
mood (humour)	көңүл	køŋyl
boredom	зеригүү	zerigyy
to be bored	зеригүү	zerigyy
seclusion	элден качуу	elden katʃuu
to seclude oneself	элден качуу	elden katʃuu
to worry (make anxious)	көңүлүн бөлүү	køŋylyn bølyy
to be worried	сарсанаа болуу	sarsanaa boluu
worrying (n)	кабатырлануу	kabatırlanuu
anxiety	чочулоо	tʃotʃuloo
preoccupied (adj)	бушайман	buʃajman
to be nervous	тынчы кетүү	tıntʃı ketyy
to panic (vi)	дүрбөлөңгө түшүү	dyrbøløŋgø tyʃyy
hope	үмүт	ymyt
to hope (vi, vt)	үмүттөнүү	ymyttønyy
certainty	ишенимдүүлүк	iʃenimdyylyk
certain, sure (adj)	ишеничтүү	iʃenitʃtyy
uncertainty	ишенбегендик	iʃenbegendik
uncertain (adj)	ишенбеген	iʃenbegen
drunk (adj)	мас	mas
sober (adj)	соо	soo
weak (adj)	бошоң	boʃoŋ
happy (adj)	бактылуу	baktıluu
to scare (vt)	жүрөгүн түшүрүү	dʒyrøgyn tyʃyryy
fury (madness)	жинденүү	dʒindenyy
rage (fury)	жаалдануу	dʒaaldanuu
depression	көңүлү чөгүү	køŋyly tʃøgyy
discomfort (unease)	ыңгайсыз	ıŋgajsız

comfort	ыңгайлуу	ıŋgajluu
to regret (be sorry)	өкүнүү	økynyy
regret	өкүнүп калуу	økynyp kaluu
bad luck	жолу болбоо	dʒolu bolboo
sadness	капалануу	kapalanuu

shame (remorse)	уят	ujat
gladness	кубаныч	kubanıtʃ
enthusiasm, zeal	ынта менен	ınta menen
enthusiast	ынтызар	ıntızar
to show enthusiasm	ынтасын көрсөтүү	ıntasın kørsøtyy

62. Character. Personality

character	мүнөз	mynøz
character flaw	кемчилик	kemtʃilik
mind	эс-акыл	es-akıl
reason	акыл	akıl

conscience	абийир	abijir
habit (custom)	адат	adat
ability (talent)	жөндөм	dʒøndøm
can (e.g. ~ swim)	билүү	bilyy

patient (adj)	көтөрүмдүү	køtørymdyy
impatient (adj)	чыдамы жок	tʃıdamı dʒok
curious (inquisitive)	ынтызар	ıntızar
curiosity	кызыгуучулук	kızıguutʃuluk

modesty	жөнөкөйлүк	dʒønøkøjlyk
modest (adj)	жөнөкөй	dʒønøkøj
immodest (adj)	чекилик	tʃekilik

laziness	жалкоолук	dʒalkooluk
lazy (adj)	жалкоо	dʒalkoo
lazy person (masc.)	эринчээк	erintʃeek

cunning (n)	куулук	kuuluk
cunning (as adj)	куу	kuu
distrust	ишенбөөчүлүк	iʃenbøøtʃylyk
distrustful (adj)	ишенбеген	iʃenbegen

generosity	берешендик	bereʃendik
generous (adj)	берешен	bereʃen
talented (adj)	зээндүү	zeendyy
talent	талант	talant

courageous (adj)	кайраттуу	kajrattuu
courage	кайрат	kajrat
honest (adj)	чынчыл	tʃıntʃıl
honesty	чынчылдык	tʃıntʃıldık

| careful (cautious) | сак | sak |
| brave (courageous) | тайманбас | tajmanbas |

| serious (adj) | оор басырыктуу | oor basırıktuu |
| strict (severe, stern) | сүрдүү | syrdyy |

decisive (adj)	чечкиндүү	tʃetʃkindyy
indecisive (adj)	чечкинсиз	tʃetʃkinsiz
shy, timid (adj)	тартынчаак	tartıntʃaak
shyness, timidity	жүрөкзаада	dʒyrøkzaada

confidence (trust)	ишеним артуу	iʃenim artuu
to believe (trust)	ишенүү	iʃenyy
trusting (credulous)	ишенчээк	iʃentʃeek

sincerely (adv)	чын жүрөктөн	tʃın dʒyrøktøn
sincere (adj)	ак ниеттен	ak nietten
sincerity	ак ниеттүүлүк	ak niettyylyk
open (person)	ачык	atʃık

calm (adj)	жоош	dʒooʃ
frank (sincere)	ачык	atʃık
naïve (adj)	ишенчээк	iʃentʃeek
absent-minded (adj)	унутчаак	unuttʃaak
funny (odd)	кызык	kızık

greed, stinginess	ач көздүк	atʃ køzdyk
greedy, stingy (adj)	сараң	saraŋ
stingy (adj)	сараң	saraŋ
evil (adj)	каардуу	kaarduu
stubborn (adj)	көк	køk
unpleasant (adj)	жагымсыз	dʒagımsız

selfish person (masc.)	өзүмчүл	øzymtʃyl
selfish (adj)	өзүмчүл	øzymtʃyl
coward	суу жүрөк	suu dʒyrøk
cowardly (adj)	суу жүрөк	suu dʒyrøk

63. Sleep. Dreams

to sleep (vi)	уктоо	uktoo
sleep, sleeping	уйку	ujku
dream	түш	tyʃ
to dream (in sleep)	түш көрүү	tyʃ køryy
sleepy (adj)	уйкусураган	ujkusuragan

bed	керебет	kerebet
mattress	матрас	matras
blanket (eiderdown)	жууркан	dʒuurkan
pillow	жаздык	dʒazdık
sheet	шейшеп	ʃejʃep

insomnia	уйкусуздук	ujkusuzduk
sleepless (adj)	уйкусуз	ujkusuz
sleeping pill	уйку дарысы	ujku darısı
to take a sleeping pill	уйку дарысын ичүү	ujku darısın itʃyy
to feel sleepy	уйкусу келүү	ujkusu kelyy

to yawn (vi)	эстөө	estøø
to go to bed	уктоого кетүү	uktoogo ketyy
to make up the bed	төшөк салуу	tøʃøk saluu
to fall asleep	уктап калуу	uktap kaluu
nightmare	коркунучтуу түш	korkunuʧtuu tyʃ
snore, snoring	коңурук	koŋuruk
to snore (vi)	коңурук тартуу	koŋuruk tartuu
alarm clock	ойготкуч саат	ojgotkuʧ saat
to wake (vt)	ойготуу	ojgotuu
to wake up	ойгонуу	ojgonuu
to get up (vi)	төшөктөн туруу	tøʃøktøn turuu
to have a wash	бети-колду жуу	beti-koldu dʒuu

64. Humour. Laughter. Gladness

humour (wit, fun)	күлкү салуу	kylky saluu
sense of humour	тамашага чалуу	tamaʃaga ʧaluu
to enjoy oneself	көңүл ачуу	køŋyl aʧuu
cheerful (merry)	көңүлдүү	køŋyldyy
merriment (gaiety)	көңүлдүүлүк	køŋyldyylyk
smile	жылмайыш	dʒılmajıʃ
to smile (vi)	жылмаюу	dʒılmadʒuu
to start laughing	күлүп жиберүү	kylyp dʒiberyy
to laugh (vi)	күлүү	kylyy
laugh, laughter	күлкү	kylky
anecdote	күлкүлүү окуя	kylkylyy okuja
funny (anecdote, etc.)	күлкүлүү	kylkylyy
funny (odd)	кызык	kızık
to joke (vi)	тамашалоо	tamaʃaloo
joke (verbal)	тамаша	tamaʃa
joy (emotion)	кубаныч	kubanıʧ
to rejoice (vi)	кубануу	kubanuu
joyful (adj)	кубанычтуу	kubanıʧtuu

65. Discussion, conversation. Part 1

communication	баарлашуу	baarlaʃuu
to communicate	баарлашуу	baarlaʃuu
conversation	сүйлөшүү	syjløʃyy
dialogue	маек	maek
discussion (discourse)	талкуу	talkuu
dispute (debate)	талаш	talaʃ
to dispute	талашуу	talaʃuu
interlocutor	аңгемелешкен	aŋgemeleʃken
topic (theme)	тема	tema

point of view	көз караш	køz karaʃ
opinion (point of view)	ой-пикир	oj-pikir
speech (talk)	сөз	søz

discussion (of report, etc.)	талкуу	talkuu
to discuss (vt)	талкуулоо	talkuuloo
talk (conversation)	маек	maek
to talk (to chat)	маектешүү	maekteʃyy
meeting (encounter)	жолугушуу	dʒoluguʃuu
to meet (vi, vt)	жолугушуу	dʒoluguʃuu

proverb	макал-лакап	makal-lakap
saying	лакап	lakap
riddle (poser)	табышмак	tabıʃmak
to pose a riddle	табышмак айтуу	tabıʃmak ajtuu
password	сырсөз	sırsøz
secret	сыр	sır

oath (vow)	ант	ant
to swear (an oath)	ант берүү	ant beryy
promise	убада	ubada
to promise (vt)	убада берүү	ubada beryy

advice (counsel)	кеңеш	keŋeʃ
to advise (vt)	кеңеш берүү	keŋeʃ beryy
to follow one's advice	кеңешин жолдоо	keŋeʃin dʒoldoo
to listen to ... (obey)	угуу	uguu

news	жаңылык	dʒaŋılık
sensation (news)	дүң салуу	dyŋ saluu
information (report)	маалымат	maalımat
conclusion (decision)	корутунду	korutundu
voice	үн	yn
compliment	мактоо	maktoo
kind (nice)	сылык	sılık

word	сөз	søz
phrase	сүйлөм	syjløm
answer	жооп	dʒoop

| truth | чындык | tʃındık |
| lie | жалган | dʒalgan |

thought	ой	oj
idea (inspiration)	ой	oj
fantasy	ойдон чыгаруу	ojdon tʃıgaruu

66. Discussion, conversation. Part 2

respected (adj)	урматтуу	urmattuu
to respect (vt)	сыйлоо	sıjloo
respect	урмат	urmat
Dear ... (letter)	Урматтуу ...	urmattuu ...
to introduce (sb to sb)	тааныштыруу	taanıʃtıruu

to make acquaintance	таанышуу	taanıʃuu
intention	ниет	niet
to intend (have in mind)	ниеттенүү	niettenyy
wish	каалоо	kaaloo
to wish (~ good luck)	каалоо айтуу	kaaloo ajtuu

surprise (astonishment)	таңгалыч	taŋgalıtʃ
to surprise (amaze)	таң калтыруу	taŋ kaltıruu
to be surprised	таң калуу	taŋ kaluu

to give (vt)	берүү	beryy
to take (get hold of)	алуу	aluu
to give back	кайтарып берүү	kajtarıp beryy
to return (give back)	кайра берүү	kajra beryy

to apologize (vi)	кечирим суроо	ketʃirim suroo
apology	кечирим	ketʃirim
to forgive (vt)	кечирүү	ketʃiryy

to talk (speak)	сүйлөшүү	syjløʃyy
to listen (vi)	угуу	uguu
to hear out	кулак салуу	kulak saluu
to understand (vt)	түшүнүү	tyʃynyy

to show (to display)	көрсөтүү	kørsøtyy
to look at ...	... кароо	... karoo
to call (yell for sb)	чакыруу	tʃakıruu
to distract (disturb)	тынчын алуу	tıntʃın aluu
to disturb (vt)	тынчын алуу	tıntʃın aluu
to pass (to hand sth)	узатып коюу	uzatıp kojʉu

demand (request)	сураныч	suranıtʃ
to request (ask)	суроо	suroo
demand (firm request)	талап	talap
to demand (request firmly)	талап кылуу	talap kıluu

to tease (call names)	кыжырына тийүү	kıdʒırına tijyy
to mock (make fun of)	шылдыңдоо	ʃıldıŋdoo
mockery, derision	шылдың	ʃıldıŋ
nickname	лакап ат	lakap at

insinuation	кыйытма	kıjıtma
to insinuate (imply)	кыйытып айтуу	kıjıtıp aytuu
to mean (vt)	билдирүү	bildiryy

description	сүрөттөө	syrøttøø
to describe (vt)	сүрөттөп берүү	syrøttøp beryy
praise (compliments)	алкыш	alkıʃ
to praise (vt)	мактоо	maktoo

disappointment	көңүлү калуу	køŋyly kaluu
to disappoint (vt)	көңүлүн калтыруу	køŋylyn kaltıruu
to be disappointed	көңүл калуу	køŋyl kaluu

supposition	божомол	bodʒomol
to suppose (assume)	божомолдоо	bodʒomoldoo

warning (caution)	эскертүү	eskertyy
to warn (vt)	эскертүү	eskertyy

67. Discussion, conversation. Part 3

to talk into (convince)	көндүрүү	køndyryy
to calm down (vt)	тынчтандыруу	tıntʃtandıruu

silence (~ is golden)	жымжырт	dʒımdʒırt
to be silent (not speaking)	унчукпоо	untʃukpoo
to whisper (vi, vt)	шыбыроо	ʃıbıroo
whisper	шыбыр	ʃıbır

frankly, sincerely (adv)	ачык айтканда	atʃık ajtkanda
in my opinion ...	менин оюмча ...	menin ojumtʃa ...

detail (of the story)	ийне-жиби	ijne-dʒibi
detailed (adj)	тетиктелген	tetiktelgen
in detail (adv)	тетикке чейин	tetikke tʃejin

hint, clue	четин чыгаруу	tʃetin tʃıgaruu
to give a hint	четин чыгаруу	tʃetin tʃıgaruu

look (glance)	көз	køz
to have a look	карап коюу	karap kojuu
fixed (look)	тиктеген	tiktegen
to blink (vi)	көз ирмөө	køz irmøø
to wink (vi)	көз кысуу	køz kısuu
to nod (in assent)	баш ийкөө	baʃ ijkøø

sigh	дем чыгаруу	dem tʃıgaruu
to sigh (vi)	дем алуу	dem aluu
to shudder (vi)	селт этүү	selt etyy
gesture	жаңсоо	dʒaŋsoo
to touch (one's arm, etc.)	тийип кетүү	tijip ketyy
to seize (e.g., ~ by the arm)	кармоо	karmoo
to tap (on the shoulder)	таптоо	taptoo

Look out!	Абайлагыла!	abajlagıla!
Really?	Чын элеби?!	tʃın elebi?!
Are you sure?	Жаңылган жоксуңбу?	dʒaŋılgan dʒoksuŋbu?
Good luck!	Ийгилик!	ijgilik!
I see!	Түшүнүктүү!	tyʃynyktyy!
What a pity!	Кап!	kap!

68. Agreement. Refusal

consent	макулдук	makulduk
to consent (vi)	макул болуу	makul boluu
approval	колдоо	koldoo
to approve (vt)	колдоо	koldoo
refusal	баш тартуу	baʃ tartuu

to refuse (vi, vt)	баш тартуу	baʃ tartuu
Great!	Эң жакшы!	eŋ ʤakʃı!
All right!	Жакшы!	ʤakʃı!
Okay! (I agree)	Макул!	makul!

forbidden (adj)	тыюу салынган	tıjʉu salıngan
it's forbidden	болбойт	bolbojt
it's impossible	мүмкүн эмес	mymkyn emes
incorrect (adj)	туура эмес	tuura emes

to reject (~ a demand)	четке кагуу	ʧetke kaguu
to support (cause, idea)	колдоо	koldoo
to accept (~ an apology)	кабыл алуу	kabıl aluu

to confirm (vt)	ырастоо	ırastoo
confirmation	ырастоо	ırastoo
permission	уруксат	uruksat
to permit (vt)	уруксат берүү	uruksat beryy
decision	чечим	ʧeʧim
to say nothing (hold one's tongue)	унчукпоо	unʧukpoo

condition (term)	шарт	ʃart
excuse (pretext)	шылтоо	ʃıltoo
praise (compliments)	алкыш	alkıʃ
to praise (vt)	мактоо	maktoo

69. Success. Good luck. Failure

success	ийгилик	ijgilik
successfully (adv)	ийгиликтүү	ijgiliktyy
successful (adj)	ийгиликтүү	ijgiliktyy

luck (good luck)	жол болуу	ʤol boluu
Good luck!	Ийгилик!	ijgilik!
lucky (e.g. ~ day)	ийгиликтүү	ijgiliktyy
lucky (fortunate)	жолу бар	ʤolu bar

failure	жолу болбостук	ʤolu bolbostuk
misfortune	жолу болбостук	ʤolu bolbostuk
bad luck	жолу болбоо	ʤolu bolboo
unsuccessful (adj)	жолу болбогон	ʤolu bolbogon
catastrophe	киши көрбөсүн	kiʃi kørbøsyn

pride	сыймык	sıjmık
proud (adj)	көтөрүнгөн	køtøryngøn
to be proud	сыймыктануу	sıjmıktanuu

winner	жеңүүчү	ʤeŋyyʧy
to win (vi)	жеңүү	ʤeŋyy
to lose (not win)	жеңилүү	ʤeŋilyy
try	аракет	araket
to try (vi)	аракет кылуу	araket kıluu
chance (opportunity)	мүмкүнчүлүк	mymkynʧylyk

70. Quarrels. Negative emotions

shout (scream)	кыйкырык	kıjkırık
to shout (vi)	кыйкыруу	kıjkıruu
to start to cry out	кыйкырып алуу	kıjkırıp aluu

quarrel	уруш	uruʃ
to quarrel (vi)	урушуу	uruʃuu
fight (squabble)	чатак	ʧatak
to make a scene	чатакташуу	ʧataktaʃuu
conflict	чыр-чатак	ʧır-ʧatak
misunderstanding	түшүнбөстүк	tyʃynbøstyk

insult	кордоо	kordoo
to insult (vt)	кемсинтүү	kemsintyy
insulted (adj)	катуу тийген	katuu tijgen
resentment	таарыныч	taarınıʧ
to offend (vt)	көңүлгө тийүү	køŋylgø tijyy
to take offence	таарынып калуу	taarınıp kaluu

indignation	нааразылык	naarazılık
to be indignant	нааразы болуу	naarazı boluu
complaint	арыз	arız
to complain (vi, vt)	арыздануу	arızdanuu

apology	кечирим	ketʃirim
to apologize (vi)	кечирим суроо	ketʃirim suroo
to beg pardon	кечирим суроо	ketʃirim suroo

criticism	сын-пикир	sın-pikir
to criticize (vt)	сындоо	sındoo
accusation (charge)	айыптоо	ajıptoo
to accuse (vt)	айыптоо	ajıptoo

revenge	өч алуу	øʧ aluu
to avenge (get revenge)	өч алуу	øʧ aluu

disdain	киши катары көрбөө	kiʃi katarı kørbøø
to despise (vt)	киши катарына албоо	kiʃi katarına alboo
hatred, hate	жек көрүү	dʒek køryy
to hate (vt)	жек көрүү	dʒek køryy

nervous (adj)	тынчы кеткен	tınʧı ketken
to be nervous	тынчы кетүү	tınʧı ketyy
angry (mad)	ачууланган	atʃuulangan
to make angry	ачуусун келтирүү	atʃuusun keltiryy

humiliation	кемсинтүү	kemsintyy
to humiliate (vt)	кемсинтүү	kemsintyy
to humiliate oneself	байкуш болуу	bajkuʃ boluu

shock	дендирөө	dendirøø
to shock (vt)	дендиретүү	dendiretyy
trouble (e.g. serious ~)	жагымсыз жагдай	dʒagımsız dʒagdaj
unpleasant (adj)	жагымсыз	dʒagımsız

fear (dread)	коркунуч	korkunuʧ
terrible (storm, heat)	каардуу	kaarduu
scary (e.g. ~ story)	коркунучтуу	korkunuʧtuu
horror	үрөй учуу	yrøj uʧuu
awful (crime, news)	үрөй учуруу	yrøj uʧuruu

to begin to tremble	калтырап баштоо	kaltırap baʃtoo
to cry (weep)	ыйлоо	ıjloo
to start crying	ыйлап жиберүү	ıjlap dʒiberyy
tear	көз жаш	køz dʒaʃ

fault	күнөө	kynøø
guilt (feeling)	күнөө сезими	kynøø sezimi
dishonor (disgrace)	уят	ujat
protest	нааразылык	naarazılık
stress	бушайман болуу	buʃajman boluu

to disturb (vt)	тынчын алуу	tınʧın aluu
to be furious	жини келүү	dʒini kelyy
angry (adj)	ачуулуу	aʧuuluu
to end (~ a relationship)	токтотуу	toktotuu
to swear (at sb)	урушуу	uruʃuu

to scare (become afraid)	чоочуу	ʧooʧuu
to hit (strike with hand)	уруу	uruu
to fight (street fight, etc.)	мушташуу	muʃtaʃuu

to settle (a conflict)	жөндөө	dʒøndøø
discontented (adj)	нааразы	naarazı
furious (adj)	жаалданган	dʒaaldangan

| It's not good! | Бул жакшы эмес! | bul dʒakʃı emes! |
| It's bad! | Бул жаман! | bul dʒaman! |

Medicine

71. Diseases

illness	оору	ooru
to be ill	ооруу	ooruu
health	ден-соолук	den-sooluk

runny nose (coryza)	мурдунан суу агуу	murdunan suu aguu
tonsillitis	ангина	angina
cold (illness)	суук тийүү	suuk tijyy
to catch a cold	суук тийгизип алуу	suuk tijgizip aluu

bronchitis	бронхит	bronχit
pneumonia	кабыргадан сезгенүү	kabırgadan sezgenyy
flu, influenza	сасык тумоо	sasık tumoo

shortsighted (adj)	алыстан көрө албоо	alıstan kørø alboo
longsighted (adj)	жакындан көрө албоо	dʒakından kørø alboo
strabismus (crossed eyes)	кылый көздүүлүк	kılıj køzdyylyk
squint-eyed (adj)	кылый көздүүлүк	kılıj køzdyylyk
cataract	челкөз	tʃelkøz
glaucoma	глаукома	glaukoma

stroke	мээге кан куюлуу	meege kan kujuluu
heart attack	инфаркт	infarkt
myocardial infarction	инфаркт миокарда	infarkt miokarda
paralysis	шал	ʃal
to paralyse (vt)	шал болуу	ʃal boluu

allergy	аллергия	allergija
asthma	астма	astma
diabetes	диабет	diabet

| toothache | тиш оорусу | tiʃ oorusu |
| caries | кариес | karies |

diarrhoea	ич өткү	itʃ øtky
constipation	ич катуу	itʃ katuu
stomach upset	ич бузулгандык	itʃ buzulgandık
food poisoning	уулануу	uulanuu
to get food poisoning	уулануу	uulanuu

arthritis	артрит	artrit
rickets	итий	itij
rheumatism	кызыл жүгүрүк	kızıl dʒygyryk
atherosclerosis	атеросклероз	ateroskleroz

| gastritis | карын сезгенүүсу | karın sezgenyysu |
| appendicitis | аппендицит | appenditsit |

| cholecystitis | холецистит | χoletsistit |
| ulcer | жара | dʒara |

measles	кызылча	kızıltʃa
rubella (German measles)	кызамык	kızamık
jaundice	сарык	sarık
hepatitis	гепатит	gepatit

schizophrenia	шизофрения	ʃizofrenija
rabies (hydrophobia)	кутурма	kuturma
neurosis	невроз	nevroz
concussion	мээнин чайкалышы	meenin tʃajkalıʃı

cancer	рак	rak
sclerosis	склероз	skleroz
multiple sclerosis	жайылган склероз	dʒajılgan skleroz

alcoholism	аракечтик	araketʃtik
alcoholic (n)	аракеч	araketʃ
syphilis	котон жара	koton dʒara
AIDS	СПИД	spid

tumour	шишик	ʃiʃik
malignant (adj)	залалдуу	zalalduu
benign (adj)	залалсыз	zalalsız

fever	безгек	bezgek
malaria	безгек	bezgek
gangrene	кабыз	kabız
seasickness	деңиз оорусу	deŋiz oorusu
epilepsy	талма	talma

epidemic	эпидемия	epidemija
typhus	келте	kelte
tuberculosis	кургак учук	kurgak utʃuk
cholera	холера	χolera
plague (bubonic ~)	кара тумоо	kara tumoo

72. Symptoms. Treatments. Part 1

symptom	белги	belgi
temperature	дене табынын көтөрүлүшү	dene tabının køtørylyʃy
high temperature (fever)	жогорку температура	dʒogorku temperatura
pulse (heartbeat)	тамыр кагышы	tamır kagıʃı

dizziness (vertigo)	баш айлануу	baʃ ajlanuu
hot (adj)	ысык	ısık
shivering	чыйрыгуу	tʃijrıguu
pale (e.g. ~ face)	купкуу	kupkuu

cough	жөтөл	dʒøtøl
to cough (vi)	жөтөлүү	dʒøtølyy
to sneeze (vi)	чүчкүрүү	tʃytʃkyryy

| faint | эси оо | esi oo |
| to faint (vi) | эси ооп жыгылуу | esi oop dʒɪgɪluu |

bruise (hématome)	көк-ала	køk-ala
bump (lump)	шишик	ʃiʃik
to bang (bump)	урунуп алуу	urunup aluu
contusion (bruise)	көгөртүп алуу	køgørtyp aluu
to get a bruise	көгөртүп алуу	køgørtyp aluu

to limp (vi)	аксоо	aksoo
dislocation	муундун чыгып кетүүсү	muundun ʧɪgɪp ketyysy
to dislocate (vt)	чыгарып алуу	ʧɪgarɪp aluu
fracture	сынуу	sɪnuu
to have a fracture	сындырып алуу	sɪndɪrɪp aluu

cut (e.g. paper ~)	кесилген жер	kesilgen dʒer
to cut oneself	кесип алуу	kesip aluu
bleeding	кан кетүү	kan ketyy

| burn (injury) | күйүк | kyjyk |
| to get burned | күйгүзүп алуу | kyjgyzyp aluu |

to prick (vt)	саюу	sajuu
to prick oneself	сайып алуу	sajɪp aluu
to injure (vt)	кокустатып алуу	kokustatɪp aluu
injury	кокустатып алуу	kokustatɪp aluu
wound	жара	dʒara
trauma	жаракат	dʒarakat

to be delirious	жөлүү	dʒølyy
to stutter (vi)	кекечтенүү	keketʧenyy
sunstroke	күн өтүү	kyn øtyy

73. Symptoms. Treatments. Part 2

| pain, ache | оору | ooru |
| splinter (in foot, etc.) | тикен | tiken |

sweat (perspiration)	тер	ter
to sweat (perspire)	тердөө	terdøø
vomiting	кусуу	kusuu
convulsions	тарамыш карышуусу	taramɪʃ karɪʃuusu

pregnant (adj)	кош бойлуу	koʃ bojluu
to be born	төрөлүү	tørølyy
delivery, labour	төрөт	tørøt
to deliver (~ a baby)	төрөө	tørøø
abortion	бойдон түшүрүү	bojdon tyʃyryy

breathing, respiration	дем алуу	dem aluu
in-breath (inhalation)	дем алуу	dem aluu
out-breath (exhalation)	дем чыгаруу	dem ʧɪgaruu
to exhale (breathe out)	дем чыгаруу	dem ʧɪgaruu
to inhale (vi)	дем алуу	dem aluu

disabled person	майып	majıp
cripple	мунжу	mundʒu
drug addict	баӊги	baŋgi

deaf (adj)	дүлөй	dyløj
mute (adj)	дудук	duduk
deaf mute (adj)	дудук	duduk

mad, insane (adj)	жин тийген	dʒin tijgen
madman (demented person)	жинди чалыш	dʒindi ʧalıʃ
madwoman	жинди чалыш	dʒindi ʧalıʃ
to go insane	мээси айныган	meesi ajnıgan

gene	ген	gen
immunity	иммунитет	immunitet
hereditary (adj)	тукум куучулук	tukum kuuʧuluk
congenital (adj)	тубаса	tubasa

virus	вирус	virus
microbe	микроб	mikrob
bacterium	бактерия	bakterija
infection	жугуштуу илдет	dʒuguʃtuu ildet

74. Symptoms. Treatments. Part 3

| hospital | оорукана | oorukana |
| patient | бейтап | bejtap |

diagnosis	дарт аныктоо	dart anıktoo
cure	дарылоо	darıloo
medical treatment	дарылоо	darıloo
to get treatment	дарылануу	darılanuu
to treat (~ a patient)	дарылоо	darıloo
to nurse (look after)	кароо	karoo
care (nursing ~)	кароо	karoo

operation, surgery	операция	operatsija
to bandage (head, limb)	жараны таӊуу	dʒaranı taŋuu
bandaging	таӊуу	taŋuu

vaccination	эмдөө	emdøø
to vaccinate (vt)	эмдөө	emdøø
injection	ийне салуу	ijne saluu
to give an injection	ийне сайдыруу	ijne sajdıruu

attack	оору кармап калуу	ooru karmap kaluu
amputation	кесүү	kesyy
to amputate (vt)	кесип таштоо	kesip taʃtoo
coma	кома	koma
to be in a coma	комада болуу	komada boluu
intensive care	реанимация	reanimatsija
to recover (~ from flu)	сакаюу	sakajuu
condition (patient's ~)	абал	abal

consciousness	эсинде	esinde
memory (faculty)	эс тутум	es tutum
to pull out (tooth)	тишти жулуу	tiʃti dʒuluu
filling	пломба	plomba
to fill (a tooth)	пломба салуу	plomba saluu
hypnosis	гипноз	gipnoz
to hypnotize (vt)	гипноз кылуу	gipnoz kıluu

75. Doctors

doctor	доктур	doktur
nurse	медсестра	medsestra
personal doctor	жекелик доктур	dʒekelik doktur
dentist	тиш доктур	tiʃ doktur
optician	көз доктур	køz doktur
general practitioner	терапевт	terapevt
surgeon	хирург	χirurg
psychiatrist	психиатр	psiχiatr
paediatrician	педиатр	pediatr
psychologist	психолог	psiχolog
gynaecologist	гинеколог	ginekolog
cardiologist	кардиолог	kardiolog

76. Medicine. Drugs. Accessories

medicine, drug	дары-дармек	darı-darmek
remedy	дары	darı
to prescribe (vt)	жазып берүү	dʒazıp beryy
prescription	рецепт	retsept
tablet, pill	таблетка	tabletka
ointment	май	maj
ampoule	ампула	ampula
mixture, solution	аралашма	aralaʃma
syrup	сироп	sirop
capsule	пилюля	pilulʲa
powder	күкүм	kykym
gauze bandage	бинт	bint
cotton wool	пахта	paχta
iodine	йод	jod
plaster	лейкопластырь	lejkoplastırⁱ
eyedropper	дары тамызгыч	darı tamızgıtʃ
thermometer	градусник	gradusnik
syringe	шприц	ʃprits
wheelchair	майып арабасы	majıp arabası
crutches	колтук таяк	koltuk tajak

painkiller	оору сездирбөөчү дары	ooru sezdirbøøtʃy darı
laxative	ич алдыруучу дары	itʃ aldıruutʃu darı
spirits (ethanol)	спирт	spirt
medicinal herbs	дары чөптөр	darı tʃøptør
herbal (~ tea)	чөп чайы	tʃøp tʃajı

77. Smoking. Tobacco products

tobacco	тамеки	tameki
cigarette	чылым	tʃılım
cigar	чылым	tʃılım
pipe	трубка	trubka
packet (of cigarettes)	пачке	patʃke

matches	ширеңке	ʃireŋke
matchbox	ширеңке кутусу	ʃireŋke kutusu
lighter	зажигалка	zadʒigalka
ashtray	күл салгыч	kyl salgıtʃ
cigarette case	портсигар	portsigar

cigarette holder	мундштук	mundʃtuk
filter (cigarette tip)	фильтр	filʲtr

to smoke (vi, vt)	тамеки тартуу	tameki tartuu
to light a cigarette	күйгүзүп алуу	kyjgyzyp aluu
smoking	чылым чегүү	tʃılım tʃegyy
smoker	тамекичи	tamekitʃi

cigarette end	чылым калдыгы	tʃılım kaldıgı
smoke, fumes	түтүн	tytyn
ash	күл	kyl

HUMAN HABITAT

City

78. City. Life in the city

city, town	шаар	ʃaar
capital city	борбор	borbor
village	кыштак	kɪʃtak
city map	шаардын планы	ʃaardın planı
city centre	шаардын борбору	ʃaardın borboru
suburb	шаардын чет жакасы	ʃaardın ʧet dʒakası
suburban (adj)	шаардын чет жакасындагы	ʃaardın ʧet dʒakasındagı
outskirts	чет-жака	ʧet-dʒaka
environs (suburbs)	чет-жака	ʧet-dʒaka
city block	квартал	kvartal
residential block (area)	турак-жай кварталы	turak-dʒaj kvartalı
traffic	көчө кыймылы	køʧø kıjmılı
traffic lights	светофор	svetofor
public transport	шаар транспорту	ʃaar transportu
crossroads	кесилиш	kesiliʃ
zebra crossing	жөө жүрүүчүлөр жолу	dʒøø dʒyryytʃylør dʒolu
pedestrian subway	жер астындагы жол	dʒer astındagı dʒol
to cross (~ the street)	жолду өтүү	dʒoldu øtyy
pedestrian	жөө жүрүүчү	dʒøø dʒyryytʃy
pavement	жанжол	dʒandʒol
bridge	көпүрө	køpyrø
embankment (river walk)	жээк жол	dʒeek dʒol
fountain	фонтан	fontan
allée (garden walkway)	аллея	alleja
park	сейил багы	sejil bagı
boulevard	бульвар	bulʲvar
square	аянт	ajant
avenue (wide street)	проспект	prospekt
street	көчө	køʧø
side street	чолок көчө	ʧolok køʧø
dead end	туюк көчө	tujʉk køʧø
house	үй	yj
building	имарат	imarat
skyscraper	көк тиреген көп кабаттуу үй	køk tiregen køp kabattuu yj

facade	үйдүн алды	yjdyn aldı
roof	чатыр	tʃatır
window	терезе	tereze
arch	түркүк	tyrkyk
column	мамы	mamı
corner	бурч	burtʃ

shop window	көрсөтмө айнек үкөк	kørsøtmø ajnek ykøk
signboard (store sign, etc.)	көрнөк	kørnøk
poster (e.g., playbill)	афиша	afiʃa
advertising poster	көрнөк-жарнак	kørnøk-dʒarnak
hoarding	жарнамалык такта	dʒarnamalık takta

rubbish	таштанды	taʃtandı
rubbish bin	таштанды челек	taʃtandı tʃelek
to litter (vi)	таштоо	taʃtoo
rubbish dump	таштанды үйүлгөн жер	taʃtandı yjylgøn dʒer

telephone box	телефон будкасы	telefon budkası
lamppost	чырак мамы	tʃırak mamı
bench (park ~)	отургуч	oturgutʃ

police officer	полиция кызматкери	politsija kızmatkeri
police	полиция	politsija
beggar	кайырчы	kajırtʃı
homeless (n)	селсаяк	selsajak

79. Urban institutions

shop	дүкөн	dykøn
chemist, pharmacy	дарыкана	darıkana
optician (spectacles shop)	оптика	optika
shopping centre	соода борбору	sooda borboru
supermarket	супермаркет	supermarket

bakery	нан дүкөнү	nan dykøny
baker	навайчы	navajtʃı
cake shop	кондитердик дүкөн	konditerdik dykøn
grocery shop	азык-түлүк	azık-tylyk
butcher shop	эт дүкөнү	et dykøny

| greengrocer | жашылча дүкөнү | dʒaʃiltʃa dykøny |
| market | базар | bazar |

coffee bar	кофекана	kofekana
restaurant	ресторан	restoran
pub, bar	сыракана	sırakana
pizzeria	пиццерия	pitserija

hairdresser	чач тарач	tʃatʃ taratʃ
post office	почта	potʃta
dry cleaners	химиялык тазалоо	χimijalık tazaloo
photo studio	фотоателье	fotoatelje
shoe shop	бут кийим дүкөнү	but kijim dykøny

| bookshop | китеп дүкөнү | kitep dykøny |
| sports shop | спорт буюмдар дүкөнү | sport bujumdar dykøny |

clothes repair shop	кийим ондоочу жай	kijim ondooʧu ʤaj
formal wear hire	кийимди ижарага берүү	kijimdi iʤaraga beryy
video rental shop	тасмаларды ижарага берүү	tasmalardı iʤaraga beryy

circus	цирк	tsırk
zoo	зоопарк	zoopark
cinema	кинотеатр	kinoteatr
museum	музей	muzej
library	китепкана	kitepkana

theatre	театр	teatr
opera (opera house)	опера	opera
nightclub	түнкү клуб	tynky klub
casino	казино	kazino

mosque	мечит	meʧit
synagogue	синагога	sinagoga
cathedral	чоң чиркөө	ʧoŋ ʧirkøø
temple	ибадаткана	ibadatkana
church	чиркөө	ʧirkøø

college	коллеж	kolleʤ
university	университет	universitet
school	мектеп	mektep

prefecture	префектура	prefektura
town hall	мэрия	merija
hotel	мейманкана	mejmankana
bank	банк	bank

embassy	элчилик	elʧilik
travel agency	турагенттиги	turagenttigi
information office	маалымат бюросу	maalımat burosu
currency exchange	алмаштыруу пунктy	almaʃtıruu punktu

| underground, tube | метро | metro |
| hospital | оорукана | oorukana |

| petrol station | май куюучу станция | maj kujuuʧu stantsija |
| car park | унаа токтоочу жай | unaa toktooʧu ʤaj |

80. Signs

signboard (store sign, etc.)	көрнөк	kørnøk
notice (door sign, etc.)	жазуу	ʤazuu
poster	көрнөк	kørnøk
direction sign	көрсөткүч	kørsøtkyʧ
arrow (sign)	жебе	ʤebe
caution	экертме	ekertme
warning sign	эскертүү белгиси	eskertyy belgisi

to warn (vt)	эскертүү	eskertyy
rest day (weekly ~)	дем алыш күн	dem alıʃ kyn
timetable (schedule)	ырааттама	ıraattama
opening hours	иш сааттары	iʃ saattarı

WELCOME!	КОШ КЕЛИҢИЗДЕР!	koʃ keliŋizder!
ENTRANCE	КИРҮҮ	kiryy
WAY OUT	ЧЫГУУ	ʧıguu

PUSH	ӨЗҮҢҮЗДӨН ТҮРТҮҢҮЗ	øzyŋyzdøn tyrtyŋyz
PULL	ӨЗҮҢҮЗГӨ ТАРТЫҢЫЗ	øzyŋyzgø tartıŋız
OPEN	АЧЫК	aʧık
CLOSED	ЖАБЫК	dʒabık

| WOMEN | АЙЫМДАР ҮЧҮН | ajımdar yʧyn |
| MEN | ЭРКЕКТЕР ҮЧҮН | erkekter yʧyn |

DISCOUNTS	АРЗАНДАТУУЛАР	arzandatuular
SALE	САТЫП ТҮГӨТҮҮ	satıp tygøtyy
NEW!	СААМАЛЫК!	saamalık!
FREE	БЕКЕР	beker

ATTENTION!	КӨҢҮЛ БУРУҢУЗ!	køŋyl buruŋuz!
NO VACANCIES	ОРУН ЖОК	orun dʒok
RESERVED	КАМДЫК БУЙРУТМАЛАГАН	kamdık bujrutmalagan

| ADMINISTRATION | АДМИНИСТРАЦИЯ | administratsija |
| STAFF ONLY | ЖААМАТ ҮЧҮН ГАНА | dʒaamat yʧyn gana |

BEWARE OF THE DOG!	КАБАНААК ИТ	kabanaak it
NO SMOKING	ТАМЕКИ ЧЕГҮҮГӨ БОЛБОЙТ!	tameki ʧegyygø bolbojt!
DO NOT TOUCH!	КОЛУҢАР МЕНЕН КАРМАБАГЫЛА!	koluŋar menen karmabagıla!

DANGEROUS	КООПТУУ	kooptuu
DANGER	КОРКУНУЧ	korkunuʧ
HIGH VOLTAGE	ЖОГОРКУ ЧЫҢАЛУУ	dʒogorku ʧıŋaluu
NO SWIMMING!	СУУГА ТҮШҮҮГӨ БОЛБОЙТ	suuga tyʃyygø bolbojt
OUT OF ORDER	ИШТЕБЕЙТ	iʃtebejt

FLAMMABLE	ӨРТ ЧЫГУУ КОРКУНУЧУ	ørt ʧıguu korkunuʧu
FORBIDDEN	ТЫЮУ САЛЫНГАН	tıjuu salıngan
NO TRESPASSING!	ӨТҮҮГӨ БОЛБОЙТ	øtyygø bolbojt
WET PAINT	СЫРДАЛГАН	sırdalgan

81. Urban transport

bus, coach	автобус	avtobus
tram	трамвай	tramvaj
trolleybus	троллейбус	trollejbus
route (of bus, etc.)	каттам	kattam

number (e.g. bus ~)	номер	nomer
to go by ...	... жүрүү	... dʒyryy
to get on (~ the bus)	... отуруу	... oturuu
to get off ...	... түшүп калуу	... tyʃyp kaluu

stop (e.g. bus ~)	аялдама	ajaldama
next stop	кийинки аялдама	kijinki ajaldama
terminus	акыркы аялдама	akırkı ajaldama
timetable	ырааттама	ıraattama
to wait (vt)	күтүү	kytyy

ticket	билет	bilet
fare	билеттин баасы	bilettin baası

cashier (ticket seller)	кассир	kassir
ticket inspection	текшерүү	tekʃeryy
ticket inspector	текшерүүчү	tekʃeryytʃy

to be late (for ...)	кечигүү	ketʃigyy
to miss (~ the train, etc.)	кечигип калуу	ketʃigip kaluu
to be in a hurry	шашуу	ʃaʃuu

taxi, cab	такси	taksi
taxi driver	такси айдоочу	taksi ajdootʃu
by taxi	таксиде	takside
taxi rank	такси токтоочу жай	taksi toktootʃu dʒaj
to call a taxi	такси чакыруу	taksi tʃakıruu
to take a taxi	такси кармоо	taksi karmoo

traffic	көчө кыймылы	køtʃø kıjmılı
traffic jam	тыгын	tıgın
rush hour	кызуу маал	kızuu maal
to park (vi)	токтотуу	toktotuu
to park (vt)	машинаны жайлаштыруу	maʃinanı dʒajlaʃtıruu
car park	унаа токтоочу жай	unaa toktootʃu dʒaj

underground, tube	метро	metro
station	бекет	beket
to take the tube	метродо жүрүү	metrodo dʒyryy
train	поезд	poezd
train station	вокзал	vokzal

82. Sightseeing

monument	эстелик	estelik
fortress	чеп	tʃep
palace	сарай	saraj
castle	сепил	sepil
tower	мунара	munara
mausoleum	күмбөз	kymbøz

architecture	архитектура	arχitektura
medieval (adj)	орто кылымдык	orto kılımdık
ancient (adj)	байыркы	bajırkı

| national (adj) | улуттук | uluttuk |
| famous (monument, etc.) | тааным ал | taanımal |

tourist	турист	turist
guide (person)	гид	gid
excursion, sightseeing tour	экскурсия	ekskursija
to show (vt)	көрсөтүү	kørsøtyy
to tell (vt)	айтып берүү	ajtıp beryy

to find (vt)	табуу	tabuu
to get lost (lose one's way)	адашып кетүү	adaʃıp ketyy
map (e.g. underground ~)	схема	sχema
map (e.g. city ~)	план	plan

souvenir, gift	асембелек	asembelek
gift shop	асембелек дүкөнү	asembelek dykøny
to take pictures	сүрөткө тартуу	syrøtkø tartuu
to have one's picture taken	сүрөткө түшүү	syrøtkø tyʃyy

83. Shopping

to buy (purchase)	сатып алуу	satıp aluu
shopping	сатып алуу	satıp aluu
to go shopping	сатып алууга чыгуу	satıp aluuga tʃıguu
shopping	базарчылоо	bazartʃıloo

| to be open (ab. shop) | иштөө | iʃtøø |
| to be closed | жабылуу | dʒabıluu |

footwear, shoes	бут кийим	but kijim
clothes, clothing	кийим-кече	kijim-ketʃe
cosmetics	упа-эндик	upa-endik
food products	азык-түлүк	azık-tylyk
gift, present	белек	belek

| shop assistant (masc.) | сатуучу | satuutʃu |
| shop assistant (fem.) | сатуучу кыз | satuutʃu kız |

cash desk	касса	kassa
mirror	күзгү	kyzgy
counter (shop ~)	прилавок	prilavok
fitting room	кийим ченөөчү бөлмө	kijim tʃenøøtʃy bølmø

to try on	кийим ченөө	kijim tʃenøø
to fit (ab. dress, etc.)	ылайык келүү	ılajık kelyy
to fancy (vt)	жактыруу	dʒaktıruu

price	баа	baa
price tag	баа	baa
to cost (vt)	туруу	turuu
How much?	Канча?	kantʃa?
discount	арзандатуу	arzandatuu
inexpensive (adj)	кымбат эмес	kımbat emes
cheap (adj)	арзан	arzan

| expensive (adj) | кымбат | kımbat |
| It's expensive | Бул кымбат | bul kımbat |

hire (n)	ижара	idʒara
to hire (~ a dinner jacket)	ижарага алуу	idʒaraga aluu
credit (trade credit)	насыя	nasıja
on credit (adv)	насыяга алуу	nasıjaga aluu

84. Money

money	акча	aktʃa
currency exchange	алмаштыруу	almaʃtıruu
exchange rate	курс	kurs
cashpoint	банкомат	bankomat
coin	тыйын	tıjın

| dollar | доллар | dollar |
| euro | евро | evro |

lira	италиялык лира	italijalık lira
Deutschmark	немис маркасы	nemis markası
franc	франк	frank
pound sterling	фунт стерлинг	funt sterling
yen	йена	jena

debt	карыз	karız
debtor	карыздар	karızdar
to lend (money)	карызга берүү	karızga beryy
to borrow (vi, vt)	карызга алуу	karızga aluu

bank	банк	bank
account	эсеп	esep
to deposit (vt)	салуу	saluu
to deposit into the account	эсепке акча салуу	esepke aktʃa saluu
to withdraw (vt)	эсептен акча чыгаруу	esepten aktʃa tʃıgaruu

credit card	насыя картасы	nasıja kartası
cash	накталай акча	naktalaj aktʃa
cheque	чек	tʃek
to write a cheque	чек жазып берүү	tʃek dʒazıp beryy
chequebook	чек китепчеси	tʃek kiteptʃesi

wallet	намыян	namıjan
purse	капчык	kaptʃık
safe	сейф	sejf

heir	мураскер	murasker
inheritance	мурас	muras
fortune (wealth)	мүлк	mylk

lease	ижара	idʒara
rent (money)	батир акысы	batir akısı
to rent (sth from sb)	батирге алуу	batirge aluu
price	баа	baa

cost	баа	baa
sum	сумма	summa

to spend (vt)	коротуу	korotuu
expenses	чыгым	ʧïgïm
to economize (vi, vt)	үнөмдөө	ynømdøø
economical	сарамжал	saramdʒal

to pay (vi, vt)	төлөө	tøløø
payment	акы төлөө	akï tøløø
change (give the ~)	кайтарылган майда акча	kajtarïlgan majda akʧa

tax	салык	salïk
fine	айып	ajïp
to fine (vt)	айып пул салуу	ajïp pul saluu

85. Post. Postal service

post office	почта	poʧta
post (letters, etc.)	почта	poʧta
postman	кат ташуучу	kat taʃuuʧu
opening hours	иш сааттары	iʃ saattarï

letter	кат	kat
registered letter	тапшырык кат	tapʃïrïk kat
postcard	открытка	otkrïtka
telegram	телеграмма	telegramma
parcel	посылка	posïlka
money transfer	акча которуу	akʧa kotoruu

to receive (vt)	алуу	aluu
to send (vt)	жөнөтүү	dʒønøtyy
sending	жөнөтүү	dʒønøtyy

address	дарек	darek
postcode	индекс	indeks
sender	жөнөтүүчү	dʒønøtyyʧy
receiver	алуучу	aluuʧu

name (first name)	аты	atï
surname (last name)	фамилиясы	familijasï

postage rate	тариф	tarif
standard (adj)	жөнөкөй	dʒønøkøj
economical (adj)	үнөмдүү	ynømdyy

weight	салмак	salmak
to weigh (~ letters)	таразалоо	tarazaloo
envelope	конверт	konvert
postage stamp	марка	marka
to stamp an envelope	марка жабыштыруу	marka dʒabïʃtïruu

Dwelling. House. Home

86. House. Dwelling

house	үй	yj
at home (adv)	үйүндө	yjyndø
yard	эшик	eʃik
fence (iron ~)	тосмо	tosmo
brick (n)	кыш	kıʃ
brick (as adj)	кыштан	kıʃtan
stone (n)	таш	taʃ
stone (as adj)	таш	taʃ
concrete (n)	бетон	beton
concrete (as adj)	бетон	beton
new (new-built)	жаңы	dʒaŋı
old (adj)	эски	eski
decrepit (house)	эскирген	eskirgen
modern (adj)	заманбап	zamanbap
multistorey (adj)	көп кабаттуу	køp kabattuu
tall (~ building)	бийик	bijik
floor, storey	кабат	kabat
single-storey (adj)	бир кабаттуу	bir kabat
ground floor	ылдыйкы этаж	ıldıjkı etadʒ
top floor	үстүнкү этаж	ystyŋky etadʒ
roof	чатыр	tʃatır
chimney	мор	mor
roof tiles	чатыр карапа	tʃatır karapa
tiled (adj)	карапалуу	karapaluu
loft (attic)	чердак	tʃerdak
window	терезе	tereze
glass	айнек	ajnek
window ledge	текче	tektʃe
shutters	терезе жапкычы	tereze dʒapkıtʃı
wall	дубал	dubal
balcony	балкон	balkon
downpipe	суу аккан түтүк	suu akkan tytyk
upstairs (to be ~)	өйдө	øjdø
to go upstairs	көтөрүлүү	køtørylyy
to come down (the stairs)	ылдый түшүү	ıldıj tyʃyy
to move (to new premises)	көчүү	køtʃyy

87. House. Entrance. Lift

entrance	подъезд	podʰjezd
stairs (stairway)	тепкич	tepkitʃ
steps	тепкичтер	tepkitʃter
banisters	тосмо	tosmo
lobby (hotel ~)	холл	χoll

postbox	почта ящиги	potʃta jaʃtʃigi
waste bin	таштанды челеги	taʃtandı tʃelegi
refuse chute	таштанды түтүгү	taʃtandı tytygy

lift	лифт	lift
goods lift	жүк ташуучу лифт	dʒyk taʃuutʃu lift
lift cage	кабина	kabina
to take the lift	лифтке түшүү	liftke tyʃyy

flat	батир	batir
residents (~ of a building)	жашоочулар	dʒaʃootʃular
neighbour (masc.)	кошуна	koʃuna
neighbour (fem.)	кошуна	koʃuna
neighbours	кошуналар	koʃunalar

88. House. Electricity

electricity	электр кубаты	elektr kubatı
light bulb	чырак	tʃırak
switch	өчүргүч	øtʃyrgytʃ
fuse (plug fuse)	эриме сактагыч	erime saktagıtʃ

cable, wire (electric ~)	зым	zım
wiring	электр зымы	elektr zımı
electricity meter	электр эсептегич	elektr eseptegitʃ
readings	көрсөтүү ченем	kørsøtyy tʃenem

89. House. Doors. Locks

door	эшик	eʃik
gate (vehicle ~)	дарбаза	darbaza
handle, doorknob	тутка	tutka
to unlock (unbolt)	кулпусун ачуу	kulpusun atʃuu
to open (vt)	ачуу	atʃuu
to close (vt)	жабуу	dʒabuu

key	ачкыч	atʃkıtʃ
bunch (of keys)	ачкычтар тизмеси	atʃkıtʃtar tizmesi
to creak (door, etc.)	кычыратуу	kıtʃıratuu
creak	чыйкылдоо	tʃıjkıldoo
hinge (door ~)	петля	petlʲa
doormat	килемче	kilemtʃe
door lock	кулпу	kulpu

keyhole	кулпу тешиги	kulpu teʃigi
crossbar (sliding bar)	бекитме	bekitme
door latch	тээк	teek
padlock	асма кулпу	asma kulpu

to ring (~ the door bell)	чалуу	ʧaluu
ringing (sound)	шыңгыраш	ʃıŋgıraʃ
doorbell	конгуроо	konguroo
doorbell button	конгуроо баскычы	konguroo baskıʧı
knock (at the door)	такылдатуу	takıldatuu
to knock (vi)	такылдатуу	takıldatuu

code	код	kod
combination lock	код кулпусу	kod kulpusu
intercom	домофон	domofon
number (on the door)	номер	nomer
doorplate	тактача	taktaʧa
peephole	көзчө	køzʧø

90. Country house

village	кыштак	kıʃtak
vegetable garden	чарбак	ʧarbak
fence	тосмо	tosmo
picket fence	кашаа	kaʃaa
wicket gate	каалга	kaalga

granary	кампа	kampa
cellar	ороо	oroo
shed (garden ~)	сарай	saraj
water well	кудук	kuduk

stove (wood-fired ~)	меш	meʃ
to stoke the stove	меш жагуу	meʃ dʒaguu
firewood	отун	otun
log (firewood)	бир кертим жыгач	bir kertim dʒıgaʧ

veranda	веранда	veranda
deck (terrace)	терасса	terassa
stoop (front steps)	босого	bosogo
swing (hanging seat)	селкинчек	selkinʧek

91. Villa. Mansion

country house	шаар четиндеги үй	ʃaar ʧetindegi yj
country-villa	вилла	villa
wing (~ of a building)	канат	kanat

garden	бакча	bakʧa
park	сейил багы	sejil bagı
conservatory (greenhouse)	күнөскана	kynøskana
to look after (garden, etc.)	кароо	karoo

swimming pool	бассейн	bassejn
gym (home gym)	машыгуу залы	maʃıguu zalı
tennis court	теннис корту	tennis kortu
home theater (room)	кинотеатр	kinoteatr
garage	гараж	garadʒ

| private property | жеке менчик | dʒeke mentʃik |
| private land | жеке ээликте | dʒeke eelikte |

| warning (caution) | эскертүү | eskertyy |
| warning sign | эскертүү белгиси | eskertyy belgisi |

security	күзөт	kyzøt
security guard	кароолчу	karooltʃu
burglar alarm	сигнализация	signalizatsija

92. Castle. Palace

castle	сепил	sepil
palace	сарай	saraj
fortress	чеп	tʃep
wall (round castle)	дубал	dubal
tower	мунара	munara
keep, donjon	баш мунара	baʃ munara

portcullis	көтөрүлүүчү дарбаза	køtørylyytʃy darbaza
subterranean passage	жер астындагы жол	dʒer astındagı dʒol
moat	сепил аңгеги	sepil aŋgegi
chain	чынжыр	tʃındʒır
arrow loop	атуучу тешик	atuutʃu teʃik

magnificent (adj)	сонун	sonun
majestic (adj)	даңазалуу	daŋazaluu
impregnable (adj)	бекем чеп	bekem tʃep
medieval (adj)	орто кылымдык	orto kılımdık

93. Flat

flat	батир	batir
room	бөлмө	bølmø
bedroom	уктоочу бөлмө	uktootʃu bølmø
dining room	ашкана	aʃkana
living room	конок үйү	konok yjy
study (home office)	иш бөлмөсү	iʃ bølmøsy

entry room	кире бериш	kire beriʃ
bathroom	ванная	vannaja
water closet	даараткана	daaratkana

ceiling	шып	ʃıp
floor	пол	pol
corner	бурч	burtʃ

94. Flat. Cleaning

| to clean (vi, vt) | жыйноо | dʒɪjnoo |
| to put away (to stow) | жыйноо | dʒɪjnoo |

dust	чаң	ʧaŋ
dusty (adj)	чаң баскан	ʧaŋ baskan
to dust (vt)	чаң сүртүү	ʧaŋ syrtyy
vacuum cleaner	чаң соргуч	ʧaŋ sorguʧ
to vacuum (vt)	чаң сордуруу	ʧaŋ sorduruu

to sweep (vi, vt)	шыпыруу	ʃɪpɪruu
sweepings	шыпырынды	ʃɪpɪrɪndɪ
order	иреттелген	irettelgen
disorder, mess	чачылган	ʧaʧɪlgan

mop	швабра	ʃvabra
duster	чүпүрөк	ʧypyrøk
short broom	шыпыргы	ʃɪpɪrgɪ
dustpan	калак	kalak

95. Furniture. Interior

furniture	эмерек	emerek
table	стол	stol
chair	стул	stul
bed	керебет	kerebet
sofa, settee	диван	divan
armchair	олпок отургуч	olpok oturguʧ

| bookcase | китеп шкафы | kitep ʃkafɪ |
| shelf | текче | tekʧe |

wardrobe	шкаф	ʃkaf
coat rack (wall-mounted ~)	кийим илгич	kijim ilgiʧ
coat stand	кийим илгич	kijim ilgiʧ

| chest of drawers | комод | komod |
| coffee table | журнал столу | dʒurnal stolu |

mirror	күзгү	kyzgy
carpet	килем	kilem
small carpet	килемче	kilemʧe

fireplace	очок	oʧok
candle	шам	ʃam
candlestick	шамдал	ʃamdal

drapes	парда	parda
wallpaper	туш кагаз	tuʃ kagaz
blinds (jalousie)	жалюзи	dʒaldʒɐzi
table lamp	стол чырагы	stol ʧɪragɪ
wall lamp (sconce)	чырак	ʧɪrak

| standard lamp | торшер | torʃer |
| chandelier | асма шам | asma ʃam |

leg (of chair, table)	бут	but
armrest	чыканак такооч	tʃıkanak takootʃ
back (backrest)	жөлөнгүч	dʒøløngytʃ
drawer	суурма	suurma

96. Bedding

bedclothes	шейшеп	ʃejʃep
pillow	жаздык	dʒazdık
pillowslip	жаздык кап	dʒazdık kap
duvet	жууркан	dʒuurkan
sheet	шейшеп	ʃejʃep
bedspread	жапкыч	dʒapkıtʃ

97. Kitchen

kitchen	ашкана	aʃkana
gas	газ	gaz
gas cooker	газ плитасы	gaz plitası
electric cooker	электр плитасы	elektr plitası
oven	духовка	duχovka
microwave oven	микротолкун меши	mikrotolkun meʃi

refrigerator	муздаткыч	muzdatkıtʃ
freezer	тоңдургуч	toŋdurgutʃ
dishwasher	идиш жуучу машина	idiʃ dʒuutʃu maʃina

mincer	эт туурагыч	et tuuragıtʃ
juicer	шире сыккыч	ʃire sıkkıtʃ
toaster	тостер	toster
mixer	миксер	mikser

coffee machine	кофе кайнаткыч	kofe kajnatkıtʃ
coffee pot	кофе кайнатуучу идиш	kofe kajnatuutʃu idiʃ
coffee grinder	кофе майдалагыч	kofe majdalagıtʃ

kettle	чайнек	tʃajnek
teapot	чайнек	tʃajnek
lid	капкак	kapkak
tea strainer	чыпка	tʃıpka

spoon	кашык	kaʃık
teaspoon	чай кашык	tʃaj kaʃık
soup spoon	аш кашык	aʃ kaʃık
fork	вилка	vilka
knife	бычак	bıtʃak

| tableware (dishes) | идиш-аяк | idiʃ-ajak |
| plate (dinner ~) | табак | tabak |

saucer	табак	tabak
shot glass	рюмка	rumka
glass (tumbler)	ыстакан	ıstakan
cup	чөйчөк	ʧøjʧøk

sugar bowl	кум шекер салгыч	kum ʃeker salgıʧ
salt cellar	туз салгыч	tuz salgıʧ
pepper pot	мурч салгыч	murʧ salgıʧ
butter dish	май салгыч	maj salgıʧ

stock pot (soup pot)	мискей	miskej
frying pan (skillet)	табак	tabak
ladle	чөмүч	ʧømyʧ
colander	депкир	depkir
tray (serving ~)	батыныс	batınıs

bottle	бөтөлкө	bøtølkø
jar (glass)	банка	banka
tin (can)	банка	banka

bottle opener	ачкыч	aʧkıʧ
tin opener	ачкыч	aʧkıʧ
corkscrew	штопор	ʃtopor
filter	чыпка	ʧıpka
to filter (vt)	чыпкалоо	ʧıpkaloo

| waste (food ~, etc.) | таштанды | taʃtandı |
| waste bin (kitchen ~) | таштанды чака | taʃtandı ʧaka |

98. Bathroom

bathroom	ванная	vannaja
water	суу	suu
tap	чорго	ʧorgo
hot water	ысык суу	ısık suu
cold water	муздак суу	muzdak suu

toothpaste	тиш пастасы	tiʃ pastası
to clean one's teeth	тиш жуу	tiʃ dʒuu
toothbrush	тиш щёткасы	tiʃ ʃʧotkası

to shave (vi)	кырынуу	kırınuu
shaving foam	кырынуу үчүн көбүк	kırınuu yʧyn købyk
razor	устара	ustara

to wash (one's hands, etc.)	жуу	dʒuu
to have a bath	жуунуу	dʒuunuu
shower	душ	duʃ
to have a shower	душка түшүү	duʃka tyʃyy

bath	ванна	vanna
toilet (toilet bowl)	унитаз	unitaz
sink (washbasin)	раковина	rakovina
soap	самын	samın

soap dish	самын салгыч	samın salgıʧ
sponge	губка	gubka
shampoo	шампунь	ʃampunʲ
towel	сүлгү	sylgy
bathrobe	халат	χalat

laundry (laundering)	кир жуу	kir ʤuu
washing machine	кир жуучу машина	kir ʤuuʧu maʃina
to do the laundry	кир жуу	kir ʤuu
washing powder	кир жуучу порошок	kir ʤuuʧu poroʃok

99. Household appliances

TV, telly	сыналгы	sınalgı
tape recorder	магнитофон	magnitofon
video	видеомагнитофон	videomagnitofon
radio	үналгы	ynalgı
player (CD, MP3, etc.)	плеер	pleer

video projector	видеопроектор	videoproektor
home cinema	үй кинотеатры	yj kinoteatrı
DVD player	DVD ойноткуч	dividi ojnotkuʧ
amplifier	күчөткүч	kyʧʃøtkyʧ
video game console	оюн приставкасы	ojᴈn pristavkası

video camera	видеокамера	videokamera
camera (photo)	фотоаппарат	fotoapparat
digital camera	санарип камерасы	sanarip kamerası

vacuum cleaner	чаң соргуч	ʧaŋ sorguʧ
iron (e.g. steam ~)	үтүк	ytyk
ironing board	үтүктөөчү тактай	ytyktøøʧy taktaj

telephone	телефон	telefon
mobile phone	мобилдик	mobildik
typewriter	машинка	maʃinka
sewing machine	кийим тигүүчү машинка	kijim tigyyʧy maʃinka

microphone	микрофон	mikrofon
headphones	кулакчын	kulakʧın
remote control (TV)	пульт	pulʲt

CD, compact disc	CD, компакт-диск	sidi, kompakt-disk
cassette, tape	кассета	kasseta
vinyl record	пластинка	plastinka

100. Repairs. Renovation

renovations	ремонт	remont
to renovate (vt)	ремонт жасоо	remont ʤasoo
to repair, to fix (vt)	оңдоо	oŋdoo
to put in order	иретке келтирүү	iretke keltiryy

to redo (do again)	кайра жасатуу	kajra dʒasatuu
paint	сыр	sɪr
to paint (~ a wall)	боео	boeo
house painter	боекчу	boektʃu
paintbrush	кисть	kistⁱ

| whitewash | акиташ | akitaʃ |
| to whitewash (vt) | актоо | aktoo |

wallpaper	туш кагаз	tuʃ kagaz
to wallpaper (vt)	туш кагаз менен чаптоо	tuʃ kagaz menen tʃaptoo
varnish	лак	lak
to varnish (vt)	лак менен жабуу	lak menen dʒabuu

101. Plumbing

water	суу	suu
hot water	ысык суу	ɪsɪk suu
cold water	муздак суу	muzdak suu
tap	чорго	tʃorgo

drop (of water)	тамчы	tamtʃɪ
to drip (vi)	тамчылоо	tamtʃɪloo
to leak (ab. pipe)	агуу	aguu
leak (pipe ~)	суу өтүү	suu øtyy
puddle	көлчүк	køltʃyk

pipe	түтүк	tytyk
valve (e.g., ball ~)	чорго	tʃorgo
to be clogged up	тыгылуу	tɪgɪluu

tools	аспаптар	aspaptar
adjustable spanner	бурама ачкыч	burama atʃkɪtʃ
to unscrew (lid, filter, etc.)	бурап чыгаруу	burap tʃɪgaruu
to screw (tighten)	бурап бекитүү	burap bekityy

to unclog (vt)	тазалоо	tazaloo
plumber	сантехник	santeχnik
basement	жер асты	dʒer astɪ
sewerage (system)	канализация	kanalizatsija

102. Fire. Conflagration

fire (accident)	өрт	ørt
flame	жалын	dʒalɪn
spark	учкун	utʃkun
smoke (from fire)	түтүн	tytyn
torch (flaming stick)	шамана	ʃamana
campfire	от	ot

| petrol | күйүүчү май | kyjyytʃy may |
| paraffin | керосин | kerosin |

flammable (adj)	күйүүчү	kyjyytʃy
explosive (adj)	жарылуу коркунучу	dʒarıluu korkunutʃu
NO SMOKING	ТАМЕКИ ЧЕГҮҮГӨ БОЛБОЙТ!	tameki tʃegyygø bolbojt!

safety	коопсуз	koopsuz
danger	коркунуч	korkunutʃ
dangerous (adj)	кооптуу	kooptuu

to catch fire	от алуу	ot aluu
explosion	жарылуу	dʒarıluu
to set fire	өрттөө	ørttøø
arsonist	өрттөөчү	ørttøøtʃy
arson	өрттөө	ørttøø

to blaze (vi)	жалындап күйүү	dʒalındap kyjyy
to burn (be on fire)	күйүү	kyjyy
to burn down	күйүп кетүү	kyjyp ketyy

to call the fire brigade	өрт өчүргүчтөрдү чакыруу	ørt øtʃyrgytʃtørdy tʃakıruu
firefighter, fireman	өрт өчүргүч	ørt øtʃyrgytʃ
fire engine	өрт өчүрүүчү машина	ørt øtʃyryytʃy maʃina
fire brigade	өрт өчүрүү командасы	ørt øtʃyryy komandası
fire engine ladder	өрт өчүрүүчү шаты	ørt øtʃyryytʃy ʃatı

fire hose	шланг	ʃlang
fire extinguisher	өрт өчүргүч	ørt øtʃyrgytʃ
helmet	каска	kaska
siren	сирена	sirena

to cry (for help)	айгай салуу	ajgaj saluu
to call for help	жардамга чакыруу	dʒardamga tʃakıruu
rescuer	куткаруучу	kutkaruutʃu
to rescue (vt)	куткаруу	kutkaruu

to arrive (vi)	келүү	kelyy
to extinguish (vt)	өчүрүү	øtʃyryy
water	суу	suu
sand	кум	kum

ruins (destruction)	уранды	urandı
to collapse (building, etc.)	уроо	uroo
to fall down (vi)	кулоо	kuloo
to cave in (ceiling, floor)	урап тушүү	urap tuʃyy

| piece of debris | сынык | sınık |
| ash | күл | kyl |

| to suffocate (die) | тумчугуу | tumtʃuguu |
| to be killed (perish) | өлүү | ølyy |

HUMAN ACTIVITIES

Job. Business. Part 1

103. Office. Working in the office

office (company ~)	офис	ofis
office (of director, etc.)	кабинет	kabinet
reception desk	кабыл алуу катчысы	kabıl aluu kattʃısı
secretary	катчы	kattʃı
secretary (fem.)	катчы аял	kattʃı ajal
director	директор	direktor
manager	башкаруучу	baʃkaruutʃu
accountant	бухгалтер	buχgalter
employee	кызматкер	kızmatker
furniture	эмерек	emerek
desk	стол	stol
desk chair	кресло	kreslo
drawer unit	үкөк	ykøk
coat stand	кийим илгич	kijim ilgitʃ
computer	компьютер	kompjuter
printer	принтер	printer
fax machine	факс	faks
photocopier	көчүрүүчү аппарат	køtʃyryytʃy apparat
paper	кагаз	kagaz
office supplies	кеңсе буюмдары	keŋse bujumdarı
mouse mat	килемче	kilemtʃe
sheet of paper	баракча	baraktʃa
binder	папка	papka
catalogue	каталог	katalog
phone directory	абоненттердин тизмеси	abonentterdin tizmesi
documentation	документтер	dokumentter
brochure (e.g. 12 pages ~)	китепче	kiteptʃe
leaflet (promotional ~)	баракча	baraktʃa
sample	үлгү	ylgy
training meeting	окутуу	okutuu
meeting (of managers)	кеңеш	keŋeʃ
lunch time	түшкү танапис	tyʃky tanapis
to make a copy	көчүрмө алуу	køtʃyrmø aluu
to make multiple copies	көбөйтүү	købøjtyy
to receive a fax	факс алуу	faks aluu
to send a fax	факс жөнөтүү	faks dʒønøtyy

to call (by phone)	чалуу	tʃaluu
to answer (vt)	жооп берүү	dʒoop beryy
to put through	байланыштыруу	bajlanɪʃtɪruu

to arrange, to set up	уюштуруу	ujʉʃturuu
to demonstrate (vt)	көрсөтүү	kørsøtyy
to be absent	келбей калуу	kelbej kaluu
absence	барбай калуу	barbaj kaluu

104. Business processes. Part 1

| business | иш | iʃ |
| occupation | жумуш | dʒumuʃ |

firm	фирма	firma
company	компания	kompanija
corporation	корпорация	korporatsija
enterprise	ишкана	iʃkana
agency	агенттик	agenttik

agreement (contract)	келишим	keliʃim
contract	контракт	kontrakt
deal	бүтүм	bytym
order (to place an ~)	буйрутма	bujrutma
terms (of the contract)	шарт	ʃart

wholesale (adv)	дүңү менен	dyŋy menen
wholesale (adj)	дүңүнөн	dyŋynøn
wholesale (n)	дүң соода	dyŋ sooda
retail (adj)	чекене	tʃekene
retail (n)	чекене соода	tʃekene sooda

competitor	атаандаш	ataandaʃ
competition	атаандаштык	ataandaʃtɪk
to compete (vi)	атаандашуу	ataandaʃuu

| partner (associate) | өнөктөш | ønøktøʃ |
| partnership | өнөктөштүк | ønøktøʃtyk |

crisis	каатчылык	kaattʃɪlɪk
bankruptcy	кудуретсиздик	kuduretsizdik
to go bankrupt	кудуретсиз калуу	kuduretsiz kaluu
difficulty	кыйынчылык	kɪjɪntʃɪlɪk
problem	кейгей	køjgøj
catastrophe	киши көрбөсүн	kiʃi kørbøsyn

economy	экономика	ekonomika
economic (~ growth)	экономикалык	ekonomikalɪk
economic recession	экономикалык төмөндөө	ekonomikalɪk tømøndøø

goal (aim)	максат	maksat
task	маселе	masele
to trade (vi)	соодалашуу	soodalaʃuu
network (distribution ~)	тармак	tarmak

| inventory (stock) | кампа | kampa |
| range (assortment) | ассортимент | assortiment |

leader (leading company)	алдыңкы катардагы	aldıŋkı katardagı
large (~ company)	ири	iri
monopoly	монополия	monopolija

theory	теория	teorija
practice	тажрыйба	tadʒrıjba
experience (in my ~)	тажрыйба	tadʒrıjba
trend (tendency)	умтулуу	umtuluu
development	өнүгүү	ønygyy

105. Business processes. Part 2

| profit (foregone ~) | пайда | pajda |
| profitable (~ deal) | майнаптуу | majnaptuu |

delegation (group)	делегация	delegatsija
salary	кызмат акы	kızmat akı
to correct (an error)	түзөтүү	tyzøtyy
business trip	иш сапар	iʃ sapar
commission	комиссия	komissija

to control (vt)	башкаруу	baʃkaruu
conference	иш жыйын	iʃ dʒıjın
licence	лицензия	litsenzija
reliable (~ partner)	ишеничтүү	iʃenitʃtyy

initiative (undertaking)	демилге	demilge
norm (standard)	стандарт	standart
circumstance	жагдай	dʒagdaj
duty (of employee)	милдет	mildet

organization (company)	уюм	ujʉm
organization (process)	уюштуруу	ujʉʃturuu
organized (adj)	уюштурулган	ujʉʃturulgan
cancellation	токтотуу	toktotuu
to cancel (call off)	жокко чыгаруу	dʒokko tʃıgaruu
report (official ~)	отчет	ottʃet

patent	патент	patent
to patent (obtain patent)	патентөө	patentøø
to plan (vt)	пландаштыруу	plandaʃtıruu

bonus (money)	сыйлык	sıjlık
professional (adj)	кесипкөй	kesipkøj
procedure	тартип	tartip

to examine (contract, etc.)	карап чыгуу	karap tʃıguu
calculation	эсеп-кысап	esep-kısap
reputation	аброй	abroj
risk	тобокел	tobokel
to manage, to run	башкаруу	baʃkaruu

information (report)	маалымат	maalımat
property	менчик	menҭik
union	бирикме	birikme

life insurance	жашоону камсыздандыруу	dʒaʃoonu kamsızdandıruu
to insure (vt)	камсыздандыруу	kamsızdandıruu
insurance	камсыздандыруу	kamsızdandıruu

auction (~ sale)	тоорук	tooruk
to notify (inform)	билдирүү	bildiryy
management (process)	башкаруу	baʃkaruu
service (~ industry)	кызмат	kızmat

forum	форум	forum
to function (vi)	иш-милдетти аткаруу	iʃ-mildetti atkaruu
stage (phase)	кадам	kadam
legal (~ services)	укуктуу	ukuktuu
lawyer (legal advisor)	юрист	jɵrist

106. Production. Works

plant	завод	zavod
factory	фабрика	fabrika
workshop	цех	tseҳ
works, production site	өндүрүш	øndyryʃ

industry (manufacturing)	өнөр-жай	ønør-dʒaj
industrial (adj)	өнөр-жай	ønør-dʒaj
heavy industry	оор өнөр-жай	oor ønør-dʒaj
light industry	жеңил өнөр-жай	dʒeɲil ønør-dʒaj

products	өндүрүм	øndyrym
to produce (vt)	өндүрүү	øndyryy
raw materials	чийки зат	tʃijki zat

foreman (construction ~)	бригадир	brigadir
workers team (crew)	бригада	brigada
worker	жумушчу	dʒumuʃtʃu

working day	иш күнү	iʃ kyny
pause (rest break)	тыныгуу	tınıguu
meeting	чогулуш	tʃoguluʃ
to discuss (vt)	талкуулоо	talkuuloo

plan	план	plan
to fulfil the plan	планды аткаруу	plandı atkaruu
rate of output	иштеп чыгаруу коюму	iʃtep tʃıgaruu kojɵmu
quality	сапат	sapat
control (checking)	текшерүү	tekʃeryy
quality control	сапат текшерүү	sapat tekʃeryy

| workplace safety | эмгек коопсуздугу | emgek koopsuzdugu |
| discipline | тартип | tartip |

| violation (of safety rules, etc.) | бузуу | buzuu |
| to violate (rules) | бузуу | buzuu |

strike	ишти калтыруу	iʃti kaltıruu
striker	иш калтыргыч	iʃ kaltırgıtʃ
to be on strike	ишти калтыруу	iʃti kaltıruu
trade union	профсоюз	profsojɥz

to invent (machine, etc.)	ойлоп табуу	ojlop tabuu
invention	ойлоп табылган нерсе	ojlop tabılgan nerse
research	изилдөө	izildøø
to improve (make better)	жакшыртуу	dʒakʃırtuu
technology	технология	teχnologija
technical drawing	чийме	tʃijme

load, cargo	жүк	dʒyk
loader (person)	жүк ташуучу	dʒyk taʃuutʃu
to load (vehicle, etc.)	жүктөө	dʒyktøø
loading (process)	жүктөө	dʒyktøø
to unload (vi, vt)	жүк түшүрүү	dʒyk tyʃuryy
unloading	жүк түшүрүү	dʒyk tyʃyryy

transport	транспорт	transport
transport company	транспорттук компания	transporttuk kompanija
to transport (vt)	транспорт менен ташуу	transport menen taʃuu

wagon	вагон	vagon
tank (e.g., oil ~)	цистерна	tsısterna
lorry	жүк ташуучу машина	dʒyk taʃuutʃu maʃina

| machine tool | станок | stanok |
| mechanism | механизм | meχanizm |

industrial waste	таштандылар	taʃtandılar
packing (process)	таңгактоо	taŋgaktoo
to pack (vt)	таңгактоо	taŋgaktoo

107. Contract. Agreement

contract	контракт	kontrakt
agreement	макулдашуу	makuldaʃuu
addendum	тиркеме	tirkeme

to sign a contract	контракт түзүү	kontrakt tyzyy
signature	кол тамга	kol tamga
to sign (vt)	кол коюу	kol kojɥu
seal (stamp)	мөөр	møør

subject of the contract	келишимдин предмети	keliʃimdin predmeti
clause	пункт	punkt
parties (in contract)	тараптар	taraptar
legal address	юридикалык дарек	jɥridikalık darek
to violate the contract	контрактты бузуу	kontrakttı buzuu
commitment (obligation)	милдеттенме	mildettenme

responsibility	жоопкерчилик	dʒoopkertʃilik
force majeure	форс-мажор	fors-madʒor
dispute	талаш	talaʃ
penalties	жаза чаралары	dʒaza tʃaraları

108. Import & Export

import	импорт	import
importer	импорттоочу	importtootʃu
to import (vt)	импорттоо	importtoo
import (as adj.)	импорт	import

export (exportation)	экспорт	eksport
exporter	экспорттоочу	eksporttootʃu
to export (vi, vt)	экспорттоо	eksporttoo
export (as adj.)	экспорт	eksport

| goods (merchandise) | товар | tovar |
| consignment, lot | жүк тобу | dʒyk tobu |

weight	салмак	salmak
volume	көлөм	køløm
cubic metre	куб метр	kub metr

manufacturer	өндүрүүчү	øndyryytʃy
transport company	транспорттук компания	transporttuk kompanija
container	контейнер	kontejner

border	чек ара	tʃek ara
customs	бажыкана	badʒıkana
customs duty	бажы салык	badʒı salık
customs officer	бажы кызматкери	badʒı kızmatkeri
smuggling	контрабанда	kontrabanda
contraband (smuggled goods)	контрабанда	kontrabanda

109. Finances

share, stock	акция	aktsija
bond (certificate)	баалуу кагаздар	baaluu kagazdar
promissory note	вексель	vekselʲ

| stock exchange | биржа | birdʒa |
| stock price | акциялар курсу | aktsijalar kursu |

| to go down (become cheaper) | арзандоо | arzandoo |
| to go up (become more expensive) | кымбаттоо | kımbattoo |

| share | үлүш | ylyʃ |
| controlling interest | башкаруучу пакет | baʃkaruutʃu paket |

investment	салым	salım
to invest (vt)	салым кылуу	salım kıluu
percent	пайыз	pajız
interest (on investment)	пайыз менен пайда	pajız menen pajda

profit	пайда	pajda
profitable (adj)	майнаптуу	majnaptuu
tax	салык	salık

currency (foreign ~)	валюта	valuta
national (adj)	улуттук	uluttuk
exchange (currency ~)	алмаштыруу	almaʃtıruu

| accountant | бухгалтер | buχgalter |
| accounting | бухгалтерия | buχgalterija |

bankruptcy	кудуретсиздик	kuduretsizdik
collapse, ruin	кыйроо	kıjroo
ruin	жакырдануу	dʒakırdanuu
to be ruined (financially)	жакырдануу	dʒakırdanuu
inflation	инфляция	inflʲatsija
devaluation	девальвация	devalʲvatsija

capital	капитал	kapital
income	киреше	kireʃe
turnover	жүгүртүлүш	dʒygyrtylyʃ
resources	такоолдор	takooldor
monetary resources	акча каражаттары	aktʃa karadʒattarı

| overheads | кошумча чыгашалар | koʃumtʃa tʃıgaʃalar |
| to reduce (expenses) | кыскартуу | kıskartuu |

110. Marketing

marketing	базар таануу	bazar taanuu
market	базар	bazar
market segment	базар сегменти	bazar segmenti
product	өнүм	ønym
goods (merchandise)	товар	tovar

brand	соода маркасы	sooda markası
trademark	соода маркасы	sooda markası
logotype	фирмалык белги	firmalık belgi
logo	логотип	logotip

demand	талап	talap
supply	сунуш	sunuʃ
need	керек	kerek
consumer	керектөөчү	kerektøøtʃy

analysis	талдоо	taldoo
to analyse (vt)	талдоо	taldoo
positioning	турак табуу	turak tabuu
to position (vt)	турак табуу	turak tabuu

price	баа	baa
pricing policy	баа саясаты	baa sajasatı
price formation	баа чыгаруу	baa tʃıgaruu

111. Advertising

advertising	жарнама	dʒarnama
to advertise (vt)	жарнамалоо	dʒarnamaloo
budget	бюджет	budʒet

ad, advertisement	жарнама	dʒarnama
TV advertising	теле жарнама	tele dʒarnama
radio advertising	радио жарнама	radio dʒarnama
outdoor advertising	сырткы жарнама	sırtkı dʒarnama

mass medias	масс медия	mass medija
periodical (n)	мезгилдүү басылма	mezgildyy basılma
image (public appearance)	имидж	imidʒ

slogan	лозунг	lozung
motto (maxim)	ураан	uraan

campaign	кампания	kampanija
advertising campaign	жарнамалык кампания	dʒarnamalık kampanija
target group	максаттуу топ	maksattuu top

business card	таанытма	taanıtma
leaflet (promotional ~)	баракча	baraktʃa
brochure (e.g. 12 pages ~)	китепче	kiteptʃe
pamphlet	кат-кат китепче	kat-kat kiteptʃe
newsletter	бюллетень	bulletenʲ

signboard (store sign, etc.)	көрнөк	kørnøk
poster	көрнөк	kørnøk
hoarding	жарнамалык такта	dʒarnamalık takta

112. Banking

bank	банк	bank
branch (of bank, etc.)	бөлүм	bølym

consultant	кеңешчи	keŋeʃtʃi
manager (director)	башкаруучу	baʃkaruutʃu

bank account	эсеп	esep
account number	эсеп номери	esep nomeri
current account	учурдагы эсеп	utʃurdagı esep
deposit account	топтолмо эсеп	toptolmo esep

to open an account	эсеп ачуу	esep atʃuu
to close the account	эсеп жабуу	esep dʒabuu
to deposit into the account	эсепке акча салуу	esepke aktʃa saluu

to withdraw (vt)	эсептен акча чыгаруу	esepten aktʃa tʃɨgaruu
deposit	аманат	amanat
to make a deposit	аманат кылуу	amanat kɨluu
wire transfer	акча которуу	aktʃa kotoruu
to wire, to transfer	акча которуу	aktʃa kotoruu

| sum | сумма | summa |
| How much? | Канча? | kantʃa? |

| signature | кол тамга | kol tamga |
| to sign (vt) | кол коюу | kol kojʉu |

credit card	насыя картасы	nasɨja kartasɨ
code (PIN code)	код	kod
credit card number	насыя картанын номери	nasɨja kartanɨn nomeri
cashpoint	банкомат	bankomat

cheque	чек	tʃek
to write a cheque	чек жазып берүү	tʃek dʒazɨp beryy
chequebook	чек китепчеси	tʃek kiteptʃesi

loan (bank ~)	насыя	nasɨja
to apply for a loan	насыя үчүн кайрылуу	nasɨja ytʃyn kajrɨluu
to get a loan	насыя алуу	nasɨja aluu
to give a loan	насыя берүү	nasɨja beryy
guarantee	кепилдик	kepildik

113. Telephone. Phone conversation

telephone	телефон	telefon
mobile phone	мобилдик	mobildik
answerphone	автоматтык жооп берүүчү	avtomattɨk dʒoop beryytʃy

| to call (by phone) | чалуу | tʃaluu |
| call, ring | чакыруу | tʃakɨruu |

to dial a number	номер терүү	nomer teryy
Hello!	Алло!	allo!
to ask (vt)	суроо	suroo
to answer (vi, vt)	жооп берүү	dʒoop beryy

to hear (vt)	угуу	uguu
well (adv)	жакшы	dʒakʃɨ
not well (adv)	жаман	dʒaman
noises (interference)	ызы-чуу	ɨzɨ-tʃuu

receiver	трубка	trubka
to pick up (~ the phone)	трубканы алуу	trubkanɨ aluu
to hang up (~ the phone)	трубканы коюу	trubkanɨ kojʉu

busy (engaged)	бош эмес	boʃ emes
to ring (ab. phone)	шыңгыроо	ʃɨŋgɨroo
telephone book	телефондук китепче	telefonduk kiteptʃe
local (adj)	жергиликтүү	dʒergiliktyy

local call	жергиликтүү чакыруу	dʒergiliktyy tʃakıruu
trunk (e.g. ~ call)	шаар аралык	ʃaar aralık
trunk call	шаар аралык чакыруу	ʃaar aralık tʃakıruu
international (adj)	эл аралык	el aralık
international call	эл аралык чакыруу	el aralık tʃakıruu

114. Mobile telephone

mobile phone	мобилдик	mobildik
display	дисплей	displej
button	баскыч	baskıtʃ
SIM card	SIM-карта	sim-karta

battery	батарея	batareja
to be flat (battery)	зарядканын түгөнүүсү	zarʲadkanın tygønyysy
charger	заряддоочу шайман	zarʲaddootʃu ʃajman

menu	меню	menʉ
settings	орнотуулар	ornotuular
tune (melody)	обон	obon
to select (vt)	тандоо	tandoo

calculator	калькулятор	kalʲkulʲator
voice mail	автоматтык жооп бергич	avtomattık dʒoop bergitʃ
alarm clock	ойготкуч	ojgotkutʃ
contacts	байланыштар	bajlanıʃtar

| SMS (text message) | SMS-кабар | esemes-kabar |
| subscriber | абонент | abonent |

115. Stationery

| ballpoint pen | калем сап | kalem sap |
| fountain pen | калем уч | kalem utʃ |

pencil	карандаш	karandaʃ
highlighter	маркер	marker
felt-tip pen	фломастер	flomaster

| notepad | дептерче | deptertʃe |
| diary | күндөлүк | kyndølyk |

ruler	сызгыч	sızgıtʃ
calculator	калькулятор	kalʲkulʲator
rubber	өчүргүч	øtʃyrgytʃ
drawing pin	кнопка	knopka
paper clip	кыскыч	kıskıtʃ

glue	желим	dʒelim
stapler	степлер	stepler
hole punch	тешкич	teʃkitʃ
pencil sharpener	учтагыч	utʃtagıtʃ

116. Various kinds of documents

account (report)	отчет	ottʃet
agreement	макулдашуу	makuldaʃuu
application form	билдирме	bildirme
authentic (adj)	көзү	køzy
badge (identity tag)	төшбелги	tøʃbelgi
business card	тааныtry	taanıtma

certificate (~ of quality)	сертификат	sertifikat
cheque (e.g. draw a ~)	чек	tʃek
bill (in restaurant)	эсеп	esep
constitution	конституция	konstitutsija

contract (agreement)	келишим	keliʃim
copy	көчүрмө	køtʃyrmø
copy (of contract, etc.)	нуска	nuska

customs declaration	бажы декларациясы	badʒı deklaratsijası
document	документ	dokument
driving licence	айдоочу күбөлүгү	ajdootʃu kybølygy
addendum	тиркеме	tirkeme
form	форма	forma

ID card (e.g., warrant card)	өздүк билдиргичи	øzdyk bildirgitʃi
inquiry (request)	суроо-талап	suroo-talap
invitation card	чакыруу билет	tʃakıruu bilet
invoice	фактура	faktura

law	мыйзам	mıjzam
letter (mail)	кат	kat
letterhead	бланк	blank
list (of names, etc.)	тизме	tizme
manuscript	кол жазма	kol dʒazma
newsletter	бюллетень	bulletenʲ
note (short letter)	кыскача жазуу	kıskatʃa dʒazuu

pass (for worker, visitor)	өткөрмө	øtkørmø
passport	паспорт	pasport
permit	уруксат кагазы	uruksat kagazı
curriculum vitae, CV	таржымал	tardʒımal
debt note, IOU	тил кат	til kat
receipt (for purchase)	дүмүрчөк	dymyrtʃøk
till receipt	чек	tʃek
report (mil.)	рапорт	raport

to show (ID, etc.)	көрсөтүү	kørsøtyy
to sign (vt)	кол коюу	kol kojuu
signature	кол тамга	kol tamga
seal (stamp)	мөөр	møør
text	текст	tekst
ticket (for entry)	билет	bilet

to cross out	чийип салуу	tʃijip saluu
to fill in (~ a form)	толтуруу	tolturuu

| waybill (shipping invoice) | коштомо кагаз | koʃtomo kagaz |
| will (testament) | керээз | kereez |

117. Kinds of business

accounting services	бухгалтердик кызмат	buxgalterdik kızmat
advertising	жарнама	dʒarnama
advertising agency	жарнама агенттиги	dʒarnama agenttigi
air-conditioners	аба желдеткичтер	aba dʒeldetkitʃter
airline	авиакомпания	aviakompanija

alcoholic beverages	алкоголь ичимдиктери	alkogolʲ itʃimdikteri
antiques (antique dealers)	антиквариат	antikvariat
art gallery (contemporary ~)	арт-галерея	art-galereja
audit services	аудиторлук кызмат	auditorluk kızmat

banking industry	банк бизнеси	bank biznesi
beauty salon	сулуулук салону	suluuluk salonu
bookshop	китеп дүкөнү	kitep dykøny
brewery	сыра чыгаруучу жай	sıra tʃıgaruutʃu dʒaj
business centre	бизнес-борбор	biznes-borbor
business school	бизнес-мектеп	biznes-mektep

casino	казино	kazino
chemist, pharmacy	дарыкана	darıkana
cinema	кинотеатр	kinoteatr
construction	курулуш	kuruluʃ
consulting	консалтинг	konsalting

dental clinic	стоматология	stomatologija
design	дизайн	dizajn
dry cleaners	химиялык тазалоо	ximijalık tazaloo

employment agency	кадрдык агенттиги	kadrdık agenttigi
financial services	каржылык кызматтар	kardʒılık kızmattar
food products	азык-түлүк	azık-tylyk
furniture (e.g. house ~)	эмерек	emerek
clothing, garment	кийим	kijim
hotel	мейманкана	mejmankana

ice-cream	бал муздак	bal muzdak
industry (manufacturing)	өнөр-жай	ønør-dʒaj
insurance	камсыздандыруу	kamsızdandıruu
Internet	интернет	internet
investments (finance)	салымдар	salımdar
jeweller	зергер	zerger
jewellery	зер буюмдар	zer bujumdar

laundry (shop)	кир жуу ишканасы	kir dʒuu iʃkanası
legal adviser	юридикалык кызматтар	juridikalık kızmattar
light industry	жеңил өнөр-жай	dʒeŋil ønør-dʒaj
magazine	журнал	dʒurnal
mail order selling	каталог боюнча соода-сатык	katalog bojuntʃa sooda-satık

medicine	медицина	meditsina
museum	музей	muzej
news agency	жаңылыктар агенттиги	dʒaŋılıktar agenttigi
newspaper	гезит	gezit
nightclub	түнкү клуб	tyŋky klub
oil (petroleum)	мунайзат	munajzat
courier services	чабармандык кызматы	tʃabarmandık kızmatı
pharmaceutics	фармацевтика	farmatsevtika
printing (industry)	полиграфия	poligrafija
pub	бар	bar
publishing house	басмакана	basmakana
radio (~ station)	үналгы	ynalgı
real estate	кыймылсыз мүлк	kıjmılsız mylk
restaurant	ресторан	restoran
security company	күзөт агенттиги	kyzøt agenttigi
shop	дүкөн	dykøn
sport	спорт	sport
stock exchange	биржа	birdʒa
supermarket	супермаркет	supermarket
swimming pool (public ~)	бассейн	bassejn
tailor shop	ателье	atelje
television	телекөрсөтүү	telekørsøtyy
theatre	театр	teatr
trade (commerce)	соода	sooda
transport companies	ташып жеткирүү	taʃıp dʒetkiryy
travel	туризм	turizm
undertakers	ырасым бүросу	ırasım bürosu
veterinary surgeon	мал доктуру	mal dokturu
warehouse	кампа	kampa
waste collection	таштанды чыгаруу	taʃtandı tʃıgaruu

Job. Business. Part 2

118. Show. Exhibition

exhibition, show	көргөзмө	kørgøzmø
trade show	соода көргөзмөсү	sooda kørgøzmøsy
participation	катышуу	katıʃuu
to participate (vi)	катышуу	katıʃuu
participant (exhibitor)	катышуучу	katıʃuutʃu
director	директор	direktor
organizers' office	уюштуруу комитети	ujuʃturuu komiteti
organizer	уюштуруучу	ujuʃturuutʃu
to organize (vt)	уюштуруу	ujuʃturuu
participation form	катышууга ынта билдирмеси	katıʃuuga ınta bildirmesi
to fill in (vt)	толтуруу	tolturuu
details	ийне-жиби	ijne-dʒibi
information	маалымат	maalımat
price (cost, rate)	баа	baa
including	кошуп	koʃup
to include (vt)	кошулган	koʃulgan
to pay (vi, vt)	төлөө	tøløø
registration fee	каттоо төгүмү	kattoo tøgymy
entrance	кирүү	kiryy
pavilion, hall	павильон	pavilʲon
to register (vt)	каттоо	kattoo
badge (identity tag)	төшбелги	tøʃbelgi
stand	көргөзмө стенди	kørgøzmø stendi
to reserve, to book	камдык буйрутмалоо	kamdık bujrutmaloo
display case	айнек стенд	ajnek stend
spotlight	чырак	tʃırak
design	дизайн	dizajn
to place (put, set)	жайгаштыруу	dʒajgaʃtıruu
to be placed	жайгашуу	dʒajgaʃuu
distributor	дистрибьютор	distribjutor
supplier	жеткирип берүүчү	dʒetkirip beryytʃy
to supply (vt)	жеткирип берүү	dʒetkirip beryy
country	өлкө	ølkø
foreign (adj)	чет өлкөлүк	tʃet ølkølyk
product	өнүм	ønym
association	ассоциация	assotsiatsija

conference hall	конференц-зал	konferents-zal
congress	конгресс	kongress
contest (competition)	жарыш	dʒarıʃ

visitor (attendee)	келүүчү	kelyytʃy
to visit (attend)	баш багуу	baʃ baguu
customer	кардар	kardar

119. Mass Media

newspaper	гезит	gezit
magazine	журнал	dʒurnal
press (printed media)	пресса	pressa
radio	үналгы	ynalgı
radio station	радио толкуну	radio tolkunu
television	телекөрсөтүү	telekørsøtyy

presenter, host	алып баруучу	alıp baruutʃu
newsreader	диктор	diktor
commentator	баяндамачы	bajandamatʃı

journalist	журналист	dʒurnalist
correspondent (reporter)	кабарчы	kabartʃı
press photographer	фотокорреспондент	fotokorrespondent
reporter	репортёр	reportʲor

| editor | редактор | redaktor |
| editor-in-chief | башкы редактор | baʃkı redaktor |

to subscribe (to ...)	жазылуу	dʒazıluu
subscription	жазылуу	dʒazıluu
subscriber	жазылуучу	dʒazıluutʃu
to read (vi, vt)	окуу	okuu
reader	окурман	okurman

circulation (of newspaper)	нуска	nuska
monthly (adj)	ай сайын	aj sajın
weekly (adj)	жума сайын	dʒuma sajın
issue (edition)	номер	nomer
new (~ issue)	жаңы	dʒaŋı

headline	баш аты	baʃ atı
short article	кыскача макала	kıskatʃa makala
column (regular article)	рубрика	rubrika
article	макала	makala
page	бет	bet

reportage, report	репортаж	reportadʒ
event (happening)	окуя	okuja
sensation (news)	дүң салуу	dyŋ saluu
scandal	жаңжал	dʒaŋdʒal
scandalous (adj)	жаңжалчы	dʒaŋdʒaltʃı
great (~ scandal)	чуулгандуу	tʃuulganduu
programme (e.g. cooking ~)	көрсөтүү	kørsøtyy

interview	интервью	intervjʉ
live broadcast	түз берүү	tyz beryy
channel	канал	kanal

120. Agriculture

agriculture	дыйкан чарбачылык	dıjkan ʧarbaʧılık
peasant (masc.)	дыйкан	dıjkan
peasant (fem.)	дыйкан аял	dıjkan ajal
farmer	фермер	fermer

| tractor | трактор | traktor |
| combine, harvester | комбайн | kombajn |

plough	соко	soko
to plough (vi, vt)	жер айдоо	ʤer ajdoo
ploughland	айдоо жер	ajdoo ʤer
furrow (in field)	жөөк	ʤøøk

to sow (vi, vt)	себүү	sebyy
seeder	сеялка	sejalka
sowing (process)	эгүү	egyy

| scythe | чалгы | ʧalgı |
| to mow, to scythe | чабуу | ʧabuu |

| spade (tool) | күрөк | kyrøk |
| to till (vt) | казуу | kazuu |

hoe	кетмен	ketmen
to hoe, to weed	отоо	otoo
weed (plant)	отоо чөп	otoo ʧøp

watering can	гүл челек	gyl ʧelek
to water (plants)	сугаруу	sugaruu
watering (act)	сугат	sugat

| pitchfork | айры | ajrı |
| rake | тырмоо | tırmoo |

fertiliser	жер семирткич	ʤer semirtkiʧ
to fertilise (vt)	жер семиртүү	ʤer semirtyy
manure (fertiliser)	кык	kık

field	талаа	talaa
meadow	шалбаа	ʃalbaa
vegetable garden	чарбак	ʧarbak
orchard (e.g. apple ~)	бакча	bakʧa

to graze (vt)	жаюу	ʤaʤʉu
herdsman	чабан	ʧaban
pasture	жайыт	ʤajıt
cattle breeding	мал чарбачылык	mal ʧarbaʧılık
sheep farming	кой чарбачылык	koj ʧarbaʧılık

plantation	плантация	plantatsija
row (garden bed ~s)	жөөк	dʒøøk
hothouse	күнөскана	kynøskana
drought (lack of rain)	кургакчылык	kurgaktʃılık
dry (~ summer)	кургак	kurgak
grain	дан эгиндери	dan eginderi
cereal crops	дан эгиндери	dan eginderi
to harvest, to gather	чаап алуу	tʃaap aluu
miller (person)	тегирменчи	tegirmentʃi
mill (e.g. gristmill)	тегирмен	tegirmen
to grind (grain)	майдалоо	majdaloo
flour	ун	un
straw	саман	saman

121. Building. Building process

building site	курулуш	kuruluʃ
to build (vt)	куруу	kuruu
building worker	куруучу	kuruutʃu
project	долбоор	dolboor
architect	архитектор	arχitektor
worker	жумушчу	dʒumuʃtʃu
foundations (of a building)	пайдубал	pajdubal
roof	чатыр	tʃatır
foundation pile	казык	kazık
wall	дубал	dubal
reinforcing bars	арматура	armatura
scaffolding	куруучу тепкичтер	kuruutʃu tepkitʃter
concrete	бетон	beton
granite	гранит	granit
stone	таш	taʃ
brick	кыш	kıʃ
sand	кум	kum
cement	цемент	tsement
plaster (for walls)	шыбак	ʃıbak
to plaster (vt)	шыбоо	ʃıboo
paint	сыр	sır
to paint (~ a wall)	боео	boeo
barrel	бочка	botʃka
crane	кран	kran
to lift, to hoist (vt)	көтөрүү	køtøryy
to lower (vt)	түшүрүү	tyʃyryy
bulldozer	бульдозер	bulʲdozer
excavator	экскаватор	ekskavator

scoop, bucket	ковш	kovʃ
to dig (excavate)	казуу	kazuu
hard hat	каска	kaska

122. Science. Research. Scientists

science	илим	ilim
scientific (adj)	илимий	ilimij
scientist	илимпоз	ilimpoz
theory	теория	teorija

axiom	аксиома	aksioma
analysis	талдоо	taldoo
to analyse (vt)	талдоо	taldoo
argument (strong ~)	далил	dalil
substance (matter)	зат	zat

hypothesis	гипотеза	gipoteza
dilemma	дилемма	dilemma
dissertation	диссертация	dissertatsija
dogma	догма	dogma

doctrine	доктрина	doktrina
research	изилдөө	izildøø
to research (vt)	изилдөө	izildøø
tests (laboratory ~)	сынак	sınak
laboratory	лаборатория	laboratorija

method	ыкма	ıkma
molecule	молекула	molekula
monitoring	бейлөө	bejløø
discovery (act, event)	таап ачуу	taap atʃuu

postulate	постулат	postulat
principle	усул	usul
forecast	божомол	bodʒomol
to forecast (vt)	алдын ала айтуу	aldın ala ajtuu

synthesis	синтез	sintez
trend (tendency)	умтулуу	umtuluu
theorem	теорема	teorema

| teachings | окуу | okuu |
| fact | далил | dalil |

| expedition | экспедиция | ekspeditsija |
| experiment | тажрыйба | tadʒrıjba |

academician	академик	akademik
bachelor (e.g. ~ of Arts)	бакалавр	bakalavr
doctor (PhD)	доктор	doktor
Associate Professor	доцент	dotsent
Master (e.g. ~ of Arts)	магистр	magistr
professor	профессор	professor

Professions and occupations

123. Job search. Dismissal

job	иш	iʃ
staff (work force)	жамаат	dʒamaat
personnel	жамаат курамы	dʒamaat kuramı
career	мансап	mansap
prospects (chances)	перспектива	perspektiva
skills (mastery)	чеберчилик	tʃebertʃilik
selection (screening)	тандоо	tandoo
employment agency	кадрдык агенттиги	kadrdık agenttigi
curriculum vitae, CV	таржымал	tardʒımal
job interview	аңгемелешүү	aŋgemeleʃyy
vacancy	жумуш орун	dʒumuʃ orun
salary, pay	эмгек акы	emgek akı
fixed salary	маяна	majana
pay, compensation	акысын төлөө	akısın tøløø
position (job)	кызмат орун	kızmat orun
duty (of employee)	милдет	mildet
range of duties	милдеттенмелер	mildettenmeler
busy (I'm ~)	бош эмес	boʃ emes
to fire (dismiss)	бошотуу	boʃotuu
dismissal	бошотуу	boʃotuu
unemployment	жумушсуздук	dʒumuʃsuzduk
unemployed (n)	жумушсуз	dʒumuʃsuz
retirement	бааракы	baarakı
to retire (from job)	ардактуу эс алууга чыгуу	ardaktuu es aluuga tʃıguu

124. Business people

director	директор	direktor
manager (director)	башкаруучу	baʃkaruutʃu
boss	башкаруучу	baʃkaruutʃu
superior	башчы	baʃtʃı
superiors	башчылар	baʃtʃılar
president	президент	prezident
chairman	төрага	tøraga
deputy (substitute)	орун басар	orun basar
assistant	жардамчы	dʒardamtʃı

secretary	катчы	kattʃı
personal assistant	жеке катчы	dʒeke kattʃı
businessman	бизнесмен	biznesmen
entrepreneur	ишкер	iʃker
founder	негиздөөчү	negizdøøtʃy
to found (vt)	негиздөө	negizdøø
founding member	уюмдаштыруучу	ujɯmdaʃtıruutʃu
partner	өнөктөш	ønøktøʃ
shareholder	акция кармоочу	aktsija karmootʃu
millionaire	миллионер	millioner
billionaire	миллиардер	milliarder
owner, proprietor	ээси	eesi
landowner	жер ээси	dʒer eesi
client	кардар	kardar
regular client	туруктуу кардар	turuktuu kardar
buyer (customer)	сатып алуучу	satıp aluutʃu
visitor	келүүчү	kelyytʃy
professional (n)	кесипкөй	kesipkøj
expert	ишбилги	iʃbilgi
specialist	адис	adis
banker	банкир	bankir
broker	далдалчы	daldaltʃı
cashier	кассир	kassir
accountant	бухгалтер	buxgalter
security guard	кароолчу	karooltʃu
investor	салым кошуучу	salım koʃuutʃu
debtor	карыздар	karızdar
creditor	насыя алуучу	nasıja aluutʃu
borrower	карызга алуучу	karızga aluutʃu
importer	импорттоочу	importtootʃu
exporter	экспорттоочу	eksporttootʃu
manufacturer	өндүрүүчү	øndyryytʃy
distributor	дистрибьютор	distribjɯtor
middleman	ортомчу	ortomtʃu
consultant	кеңешчи	keŋeʃtʃi
sales representative	сатуу агенти	satuu agenti
agent	агент	agent
insurance agent	камсыздандыруучу агент	kamsızdandıruutʃu agent

125. Service professions

cook	ашпозчу	aʃpoztʃu
chef (kitchen chef)	башкы ашпозчу	baʃkı aʃpoztʃu

baker	навайчы	navajʧı
barman	бармен	barmen
waiter	официант	ofitsiant
waitress	официант кыз	ofitsiant kız

lawyer, barrister	жактоочу	ʤaktooʧu
lawyer (legal expert)	юрист	jurist
notary public	нотариус	notarius

electrician	электрик	elektrik
plumber	сантехник	santeχnik
carpenter	жыгач уста	ʤıgatʃ usta

masseur	укалоочу	ukalooʧu
masseuse	укалоочу	ukalooʧu
doctor	доктур	doktur

taxi driver	такси айдоочу	taksi ajdooʧu
driver	айдоочу	ajdooʧu
delivery man	жеткирүүчү	ʤetkiryyʧy

chambermaid	үй кызматкери	yj kızmatkeri
security guard	кароолчу	karoolʧu
flight attendant (fem.)	стюардесса	stuardessa

schoolteacher	мугалим	mugalim
librarian	китепканачы	kitepkanaʧı
translator	котормочу	kotormoʧu
interpreter	оозеки котормочу	oozeki kotormoʧu
guide	гид	gid

hairdresser	чач тарач	ʧaʧ taratʃ
postman	кат ташуучу	kat taʃuuʧu
salesman (store staff)	сатуучу	satuutʃu

gardener	багбанчы	bagbanʧı
domestic servant	үй кызматчы	yj kızmatʧı
maid (female servant)	үй кызматчы аял	yj kızmatʧı ajal
cleaner (cleaning lady)	тазалагыч	tazalagıʧ

126. Military professions and ranks

private	катардагы жоокер	katardagı ʤooker
sergeant	сержант	serʤant
lieutenant	лейтенант	lejtenant
captain	капитан	kapitan

major	майор	major
colonel	полковник	polkovnik
general	генерал	general
marshal	маршал	marʃal
admiral	адмирал	admiral
military (n)	аскер кызматчысы	asker kızmatʧısı
soldier	аскер	asker

| officer | офицер | ofitser |
| commander | командир | komandir |

border guard	чек арачы	ʧek araʧı
radio operator	радист	radist
scout (searcher)	чалгынчы	ʧalgınʧı
pioneer (sapper)	сапёр	sapʲor
marksman	аткыч	atkıʧ
navigator	штурман	ʃturman

127. Officials. Priests

| king | король, падыша | korolʲ, padıʃa |
| queen | ханыша | χanıʃa |

| prince | канзаада | kanzaada |
| princess | ханбийке | χanbijke |

| czar | падыша | padıʃa |
| czarina | ханыша | χanıʃa |

president	президент	prezident
Secretary (minister)	министр	ministr
prime minister	премьер-министр	premjer-ministr
senator	сенатор	senator

diplomat	дипломат	diplomat
consul	консул	konsul
ambassador	элчи	elʧi
counsellor (diplomatic officer)	кеңешчи	keŋeʃʧi

official, functionary (civil servant)	аткаминер	atkaminer
prefect	префект	prefekt
mayor	мэр	mer

| judge | сот | sot |
| prosecutor | прокурор | prokuror |

missionary	миссионер	missioner
monk	кечил	keʧil
abbot	аббат	abbat
rabbi	раввин	ravvin

vizier	визирь	vizirʲ
shah	шах	ʃaχ
sheikh	шейх	ʃejχ

128. Agricultural professions

| beekeeper | балчы | balʧı |
| shepherd | чабан | ʧaban |

agronomist	агроном	agronom
cattle breeder	малчы	maltʃı
veterinary surgeon	мал доктуру	mal dokturu

farmer	фермер	fermer
winemaker	вино жасоочу	vino dʒasootʃu
zoologist	зоолог	zoolog
cowboy	ковбой	kovboj

129. Art professions

| actor | актёр | aktʲor |
| actress | актриса | aktrisa |

| singer (masc.) | ырчы | ırtʃı |
| singer (fem.) | ырчы кыз | ırtʃı kız |

| dancer (masc.) | бийчи жигит | bijtʃi dʒigit |
| dancer (fem.) | бийчи кыз | bijtʃi kız |

| performer (masc.) | аткаруучу | atkaruutʃu |
| performer (fem.) | аткаруучу | atkaruutʃu |

musician	музыкант	muzıkant
pianist	пианист	pianist
guitar player	гитарист	gitarist

conductor (orchestra ~)	дирижёр	diridʒʲor
composer	композитор	kompozitor
impresario	импресарио	impresario

film director	режиссёр	redʒissʲor
producer	продюсер	produser
scriptwriter	сценарист	stsenarist
critic	сынчы	sıntʃı

writer	жазуучу	dʒazuutʃu
poet	акын	akın
sculptor	бедизчи	bediztʃi
artist (painter)	сүрөтчү	syrøttʃy

juggler	жонглёр	dʒonglʲor
clown	маскарапоз	maskarapoz
acrobat	акробат	akrobat
magician	көз боечу	køz boetʃu

130. Various professions

doctor	доктур	doktur
nurse	медсестра	medsestra
psychiatrist	психиатр	psiχiatr
dentist	тиш доктур	tiʃ doktur

114

surgeon	хирург	χirurg
astronaut	астронавт	astronavt
astronomer	астроном	astronom
pilot	учкуч	uʧkuʧ

driver (of taxi, etc.)	айдоочу	ajdooʧu
train driver	машинист	maʃinist
mechanic	механик	meχanik

miner	кенчи	kenʧi
worker	жумушчу	ʤumuʃʧu
locksmith	слесарь	slesarⁱ
joiner (carpenter)	жыгач уста	ʤɪgaʧ usta
turner (lathe operator)	токарь	tokarⁱ
building worker	куруучу	kuruuʧu
welder	ширеткич	ʃiretkiʧ

professor (title)	профессор	professor
architect	архитектор	arχitektor
historian	тарыхчы	tarɪχʧɪ
scientist	илимпоз	ilimpoz
physicist	физик	fizik
chemist (scientist)	химик	χimik

archaeologist	археолог	arχeolog
geologist	геолог	geolog
researcher (scientist)	изилдөөчү	izildøøʧy

| babysitter | бала баккыч | bala bakkɪʧ |
| teacher, educator | мугалим | mugalim |

editor	редактор	redaktor
editor-in-chief	башкы редактор	baʃkɪ redaktor
correspondent	кабарчы	kabarʧɪ
typist (fem.)	машинистка	maʃinistka

designer	дизайнер	dizajner
computer expert	компьютер адиси	kompjuter adisi
programmer	программист	programmist
engineer (designer)	инженер	inʤener

sailor	деңизчи	deŋizʧi
seaman	матрос	matros
rescuer	куткаруучу	kutkaruuʧu

firefighter	өрт өчүргүч	ørt øʧyrgyʧ
police officer	полиция кызматкери	politsija kɪzmatkeri
watchman	кароолчу	karoolʧu
detective	аңдуучу	aŋduuʧu

customs officer	бажы кызматкери	baʤɪ kɪzmatkeri
bodyguard	жан сакчы	ʤan sakʧɪ
prison officer	күзөтчү	kyzøtʧy
inspector	инспектор	inspektor
sportsman	спортчу	sportʧu
trainer, coach	машыктыруучу	maʃɪktɪruuʧu

butcher	касапчы	kasapʧı
cobbler (shoe repairer)	өтүкчү	øtykʧy
merchant	жеке соодагер	ʤeke soodager
loader (person)	жүк ташуучу	ʤyk taʃuuʧu

| fashion designer | модельер | modeljer |
| model (fem.) | модель | modelⁱ |

131. Occupations. Social status

| schoolboy | окуучу | okuuʧu |
| student (college ~) | студент | student |

philosopher	философ	filosof
economist	экономист	ekonomist
inventor	ойлоп табуучу	ojlop tabuuʧu

unemployed (n)	жумушсуз	ʤumuʃsuz
pensioner	бааргер	baarger
spy, secret agent	тыңчы	tıŋʧı

prisoner	камактагы адам	kamaktagı adam
striker	иш калтыргыч	iʃ kaltırgıʧ
bureaucrat	бюрократ	bʉrokrat
traveller (globetrotter)	саякатчы	sajakatʧı

gay, homosexual (n)	гомосексуалист	gomoseksualist
hacker	хакер	χaker
hippie	хиппи	χippi

bandit	ууру-кески	uuru-keski
hit man, killer	жалданма киши өлтүргүч	ʤaldanma kiʃi øltyrgyʧ
drug addict	баңги	baŋgi
drug dealer	баңгизат сатуучу	baŋgizat satuuʧu
prostitute (fem.)	сойку	sojku
pimp	жан бакты	ʤan baktı

sorcerer	жадыгөй	ʤadıgøj
sorceress (evil ~)	жадыгөй	ʤadıgøj
pirate	деңиз каракчысы	deŋiz karakʧısı
slave	кул	kul
samurai	самурай	samuraj
savage (primitive)	жапайы	ʤapajı

Sports

132. Kinds of sports. Sportspersons

sportsman	спортчу	sporttʃu
kind of sport	спорттун түрү	sporttun tyry
basketball	баскетбол	basketbol
basketball player	баскетбол ойноочу	basketbol ojnootʃu
baseball	бейсбол	bejsbol
baseball player	бейсбол ойноочу	bejsbol ojnootʃu
football	футбол	futbol
football player	футбол ойноочу	futbol ojnootʃu
goalkeeper	дарбазачы	darbazatʃı
ice hockey	хоккей	χokkej
ice hockey player	хоккей ойноочу	χokkej ojnootʃu
volleyball	волейбол	volejbol
volleyball player	волейбол ойноочу	volejbol ojnootʃu
boxing	бокс	boks
boxer	бокс мушташуучу	boks muʃtaʃuutʃu
wrestling	күреш	kyrøʃ
wrestler	күрешчү	kyrøʃtʃy
karate	карате	karate
karate fighter	карате мушташуучу	karate muʃtaʃuutʃu
judo	дзюдо	dzʉdo
judo athlete	дзюдо чалуучу	dzʉdo tʃaluutʃu
tennis	теннис	tennis
tennis player	теннис ойноочу	tennis ojnootʃu
swimming	сүзүү	syzyy
swimmer	сүзүүчү	syzyytʃy
fencing	кылычташуу	kılıtʃtaʃuu
fencer	кылычташуучу	kılıtʃtaʃuutʃu
chess	шахмат	ʃaχmat
chess player	шахмат ойноочу	ʃaχmat ojnootʃu
alpinism	альпинизм	alʲpinizm
alpinist	альпинист	alʲpinist
running	чуркоо	tʃurkoo

runner	жөө күлүк	dʒøø kylyk
athletics	жеңил атлетика	dʒeŋil atletika
athlete	атлет	atlet

| horse riding | ат спорту | at sportu |
| horse rider | чабандес | tʃabandes |

figure skating	муз бийи	muz biji
figure skater (masc.)	муз бийчи	muz bijtʃi
figure skater (fem.)	муз бийчи	muz bijtʃi

| powerlifting | оор атлетика | oor atletika |
| powerlifter | оор атлет | oor atlet |

| car racing | авто жарыш | avto dʒarıʃ |
| racer (driver) | гонщик | gonʃtʃik |

| cycling | велоспорт | velosport |
| cyclist | велосипед тебүүчү | velosiped tebyytʃy |

long jump	узундукка секирүү	uzundukka sekiryy
pole vaulting	шырык менен секирүү	ʃırık menen sekiryy
jumper	секирүүчү	sekiryytʃy

133. Kinds of sports. Miscellaneous

American football	американский футбол	amerikanskij futbol
badminton	бадминтон	badminton
biathlon	биатлон	biatlon
billiards	бильярд	biljard

bobsleigh	бобслей	bobslej
bodybuilding	бодибилдинг	bodibilding
water polo	суу полосу	suu polosu
handball	гандбол	gandbol
golf	гольф	golʲf

rowing	калакты уруу	kalaktı uruu
scuba diving	сууга чөмүүчү	suuga tʃømyytʃy
cross-country skiing	чаңгы жарышы	tʃaŋgı dʒarıʃı
table tennis (ping-pong)	стол тенниси	stol tennisi

sailing	парус астында сызуу	parus astında sızuu
rally	ралли	ralli
rugby	регби	regbi
snowboarding	сноуборд	snoubord
archery	жаа атуу	dʒaa atuu

134. Gym

| barbell | штанга | ʃtanga |
| dumbbells | гантелдер | gantelder |

training machine	машыгуу машине	maʃɪguu maʃine
exercise bicycle	велотренажёр	velotrenadʒʲor
treadmill	тегеретме	tegeretme

horizontal bar	көпүрө жыгач	køpyrø dʒɪgatʃ
parallel bars	брусдар	brusdar
vault (vaulting horse)	ат	at
mat (exercise ~)	мат	mat

skipping rope	секиргич	sekirgitʃ
aerobics	аэробика	aerobika
yoga	йога	joga

135. Ice hockey

ice hockey	хоккей	χokkej
ice hockey player	хоккей ойноочу	χokkej ojnootʃu
to play ice hockey	хоккей ойноо	χokkej ojnoo
ice	муз	muz

puck	шайба	ʃajba
ice hockey stick	иймек таяк	ijmek tajak
ice skates	коньки	konʲki

| board (ice hockey rink ~) | тосмо | tosmo |
| shot | сокку | sokku |

goaltender	дарбазачы	darbazatʃı
goal (score)	гол	gol
to score a goal	гол киргизүү	gol kirgizyy

period	мезгил	mezgil
second period	экинчи мезгил	ekintʃi mezgil
substitutes bench	кезек отургучу	kezek oturgutʃu

136. Football

football	футбол	futbol
football player	футбол ойноочу	futbol ojnootʃu
to play football	футбол ойноо	futbol ojnoo

major league	жогорку лига	dʒogorku liga
football club	футбол клубу	futbol klubu
coach	машыктыруучу	maʃıktıruutʃu
owner, proprietor	ээси	eesi

team	топ	top
team captain	топтун капитаны	toptun kapitanı
player	оюнчу	ojʉntʃu
substitute	кезектеги оюнчу	kezektegi ojʉntʃu
forward	чабуулчу	tʃabuultʃu
centre forward	бордордук чабуулчу	borborduk tʃabuultʃu

scorer	жаадыргыч	dʒaadırgıtʃ
defender, back	коргоочу	korgootʃu
midfielder, halfback	жарым коргоочу	dʒarım korgootʃu

match	матч	mattʃ
to meet (vi, vt)	жолугушуу	dʒologuʃuu
final	финал	final
semi-final	жарым финал	dʒarım final
championship	чемпионат	tʃempionat

period, half	тайм	tajm
first period	биринчи тайм	birintʃi tajm
half-time	тыныгуу	tınıguu

goal	дарбаза	darbaza
goalkeeper	дарбазачы	darbazatʃı
goalpost	штанга	ʃtanga
crossbar	көпүрө жыгач	køpyrø dʒıgatʃ
net	тор	tor
to concede a goal	гол киргизип алуу	gol kirgizip aluu

ball	топ	top
pass	топ узатуу	top uzatuu
kick	сокку	sokku
to kick (~ the ball)	сокку берүү	sokku beryy
free kick (direct ~)	жаза сокку	dʒaza sokku
corner kick	бурчтан сокку	burtʃtan sokku

attack	чабуул	tʃabuul
counterattack	каршы чабуул	karʃı tʃabuul
combination	комбинация	kombinatsija

referee	арбитр	arbitr
to blow the whistle	ышкыруу	ıʃkıruu
whistle (sound)	ышкырык	ıʃkırık
foul, misconduct	бузуу	buzuu
to commit a foul	бузуу	buzuu
to send off	оюн талаасынан чыгаруу	ojun talaasınan tʃıgaruu

yellow card	сары карточка	sarı kartotʃka
red card	кызыл карточка	kızıl kartotʃka
disqualification	дисквалификация	diskvalifikatsija
to disqualify (vt)	дисквалифициялоо	diskvalifitsijaloo

penalty kick	пенальти	penalʲti
wall	дубал	dubal
to score (vi, vt)	жаадыруу	dʒaadıruu
goal (score)	гол	gol
to score a goal	гол киргизүү	gol kirgizyy

substitution	алмаштыруу	almaʃtıruu
to replace (a player)	алмаштыруу	almaʃtıruu
rules	эрежелер	eredʒeler
tactics	тактика	taktika
stadium	стадион	stadion
terrace	трибуна	tribuna

| fan, supporter | күйөрман | kyjørman |
| to shout (vi) | кыйкыруу | kıjkıruu |

| scoreboard | табло | tablo |
| score | эсеп | esep |

defeat	утулуу	utuluu
to lose (not win)	жеңилүү	dʒeŋilyy
draw	теңме-тең	teŋme-teŋ
to draw (vi)	теңме-тең бүтүрүү	teŋme-teŋ bytyryy

| victory | жеңиш | dʒeŋiʃ |
| to win (vi, vt) | жеңүү | dʒeŋyy |

champion	чемпион	tʃempion
best (adj)	эң жакшы	eŋ dʒakʃı
to congratulate (vt)	куттуктоо	kuttuktoo

commentator	баяндамачы	bajandamatʃı
to commentate (vt)	баяндоо	bajandoo
broadcast	берүү	beryy

137. Alpine skiing

skis	чаңгы	tʃaŋgı
to ski (vi)	чаңгы тебүү	tʃaŋgı tebyy
mountain-ski resort	тоо лыжа курорту	too lıdʒa kurortu
ski lift	көтөргүч	køtørgytʃ

ski poles	таякчалар	tajaktʃalar
slope	эңкейиш	eŋkejiʃ
slalom	слалом	slalom

138. Tennis. Golf

golf	гольф	golʲf
golf club	гольф-клуб	golʲf-klub
golfer	гольф оюнчу	golʲf ojuntʃu

hole	тешикче	teʃiktʃe
club	иймек таяк	ijmek tajak
golf trolley	иймек таяк үчүн арабача	ijmek tajak ytʃyn arabatʃa

| tennis | теннис | tennis |
| tennis court | корт | kort |

| serve | кийирүү | kijiryy |
| to serve (vt) | кийирүү | kijiryy |

racket	ракетка	raketka
net	тор	tor
ball	топ	top

139. Chess

chess	шахмат	ʃaχmat
chessmen	шахмат фигурасы	ʃaχmat figurası
chess player	шахмат ойноочу	ʃaχmat ojnootʃu
chessboard	шахмат тактасы	ʃaχmat taktası
chessman	фигура	figura
White (white pieces)	актар	aktar
Black (black pieces)	каралар	karalar
pawn	пешка	peʃka
bishop	пил	pil
knight	ат	at
rook	ладья	ladja
queen	ферзь	ferzⁱ
king	король	korolʲ
move	жүрүш	dʒyryʃ
to move (vi, vt)	жүрүү	dʒyryy
to sacrifice (vt)	курман кылуу	kurman kıluu
castling	рокировка	rokirovka
check	шах	ʃaχ
checkmate	мат	mat
chess tournament	шахмат турнири	ʃaχmat turniri
Grand Master	гроссмейстер	grossmejster
combination	комбинация	kombinatsija
game (in chess)	партия	partija
draughts	шашкалар	ʃaʃkalar

140. Boxing

boxing	бокс	boks
fight (bout)	мушташ	muʃtaʃ
boxing match	жекеме-жеке мушташ	dʒekeme-dʒeke muʃtaʃ
round (in boxing)	раунд	raund
ring	ринг	ring
gong	гонг	gong
punch	сокку	sokku
knockdown	нокдаун	nokdaun
knockout	нокаут	nokaut
to knock out	нокаутка жиберүү	nokautka dʒiberyy
boxing glove	бокс колкабы	boks kolkabı
referee	рефери	referi
lightweight	жеңил салмак	dʒeŋil salmak
middleweight	орто салмак	orto salmak
heavyweight	оор салмак	oor salmak

141. Sports. Miscellaneous

Olympic Games	Олимпиада Оюндары	olimpiada ojɵndarı
winner	жеңүүчү	ʤeŋyyʧy
to be winning	жеңүү	ʤeŋyy
to win (vi)	утуу	utuu
leader	топ башы	top baʃı
to lead (vi)	топ башында болуу	top baʃında boluu
first place	биринчи орун	birinʧi orun
second place	экинчи орун	ekinʧi orun
third place	үчүнчү орун	yʧynʧy orun
medal	медаль	medalʲ
trophy	трофей	trofej
prize cup (trophy)	кубок	kubok
prize (in game)	байге	bajge
main prize	баш байге	baʃ bajge
record	рекорд	rekord
to set a record	рекорд коюу	rekord kojɵu
final	финал	final
final (adj)	финалдык	finaldık
champion	чемпион	ʧempion
championship	чемпионат	ʧempionat
stadium	стадион	stadion
terrace	трибуна	tribuna
fan, supporter	күйөрман	kyjɵrman
opponent, rival	каршылаш	karʃılaʃ
start (start line)	старт	start
finish line	маара	maara
defeat	утулуу	utuluu
to lose (not win)	жеңилүү	ʤeŋilyy
referee	судья	sudja
jury (judges)	калыстар	kalıstar
score	эсеп	esep
draw	теңме-тең	teŋme-teŋ
to draw (vi)	теңме-тең бүтүрүү	teŋme-teŋ bytyryy
point	упай	upaj
result (final score)	натыйжа	natıjʤa
period	убак	ubak
half-time	тыныгуу	tınıguu
doping	допинг	doping
to penalise (vt)	жазалоо	ʤazaloo
to disqualify (vt)	дисквалификациялоо	diskvalifitsijaloo
apparatus	снаряд	snarʲad

javelin	найза	najza
shot (metal ball)	ядро	jadro
ball (snooker, etc.)	бильярд шары	biljard ʃarı

aim (target)	бута	buta
target	бута	buta
to shoot (vi)	атуу	atuu
accurate (~ shot)	таамай	taamaj

trainer, coach	машыктыруучу	maʃıktıruuʧu
to train (sb)	машыктыруу	maʃıktıruu
to train (vi)	машыгуу	maʃıguu
training	машыгуу	maʃıguu

gym	спортзал	sportzal
exercise (physical)	көнүгүү	kønygyy
warm-up (athlete ~)	дене көрүү	dene keryy

Education

142. School

school	мектеп	mektep
headmaster	мектеп директору	mektep direktoru
pupil (boy)	окуучу бала	okuutʃu bala
pupil (girl)	окуучу кыз	okuutʃu kız
schoolboy	окуучу	okuutʃu
schoolgirl	окуучу кыз	okuutʃu kız
to teach (sb)	окутуу	okutuu
to learn (language, etc.)	окуу	okuu
to learn by heart	жаттоо	dʒattoo
to learn (~ to count, etc.)	үйрөнүү	yjrønyy
to be at school	мектепке баруу	mektepke baruu
to go to school	окууга баруу	okuuga baruu
alphabet	алфавит	alfavit
subject (at school)	сабак	sabak
classroom	класс	klass
lesson	сабак	sabak
playtime, break	танапис	tanapis
school bell	коңгуроо	koŋguroo
school desk	парта	parta
blackboard	такта	takta
mark	баа	baa
good mark	жакшы баа	dʒakʃı baa
bad mark	жаман баа	dʒaman baa
to give a mark	баа коюу	baa kojʉu
mistake, error	ката	kata
to make mistakes	ката кетирүү	kata ketiryy
to correct (an error)	түзөтүү	tyzøtyy
crib	шпаргалка	ʃpargalka
homework	үй иши	yj iʃi
exercise (in education)	көнүгүү	kønygyy
to be present	катышуу	katıʃuu
to be absent	келбей калуу	kelbej kaluu
to miss school	сабактарды калтыруу	sabaktardı kaltıruu
to punish (vt)	жазалоо	dʒazaloo
punishment	жаза	dʒaza
conduct (behaviour)	жүрүм-турум	dʒyrym-turum

school report	күндөлүк	kyndølyk
pencil	карандаш	karandaʃ
rubber	өчүргүч	øʧyrgyʧ
chalk	бор	bor
pencil case	калем салгыч	kalem salgıʧ

schoolbag	портфель	portfelʲ
pen	калем сап	kalem sap
exercise book	дептер	depter
textbook	китеп	kitep
compasses	циркуль	tsırkulʲ

| to make technical drawings | чийүү | ʧijyy |
| technical drawing | чийме | ʧijme |

poem	ыр сап	ır sap
by heart (adv)	жатка	dʒatka
to learn by heart	жаттоо	dʒattoo

school holidays	эс алуу	es aluu
to be on holiday	эс алууда болуу	es aluuda boluu
to spend holidays	эс алууну өткөзүү	es aluunu øtkøzyy

test (at school)	текшерүү иш	tekʃeryy iʃ
essay (composition)	дил баян	dil bajan
dictation	жат жаздыруу	dʒat dʒazdıruu
exam (examination)	экзамен	ekzamen
to do an exam	экзамен тапшыруу	ekzamen tapʃıruu
experiment (e.g., chemistry ~)	тажрыйба	tadʒrıjba

143. College. University

academy	академия	akademija
university	университет	universitet
faculty (e.g., ~ of Medicine)	факультет	fakulʲtet

student (masc.)	студент бала	student bala
student (fem.)	студент кыз	student kız
lecturer (teacher)	мугалим	mugalim

| lecture hall, room | дарскана | darskana |
| graduate | окуу жайды бүтүрүүчү | okuu dʒajdı bytyryyʧy |

| diploma | диплом | diplom |
| dissertation | диссертация | dissertatsija |

| study (report) | изилдөө | izildøø |
| laboratory | лаборатория | laboratorija |

lecture	лекция	lektsija
coursemate	курсташ	kurstaʃ
scholarship, bursary	стипендия	stipendija
academic degree	илимий даража	ilimij daradʒa

144. Sciences. Disciplines

mathematics	математика	matematika
algebra	алгебра	algebra
geometry	геометрия	geometrija
astronomy	астрономия	astronomija
biology	биология	biologija
geography	география	geografija
geology	геология	geologija
history	тарых	tarıχ
medicine	медицина	meditsina
pedagogy	педагогика	pedagogika
law	укук	ukuk
physics	физика	fizika
chemistry	химия	χimija
philosophy	философия	filosofija
psychology	психология	psiχologija

145. Writing system. Orthography

grammar	грамматика	grammatika
vocabulary	лексика	leksika
phonetics	фонетика	fonetika
noun	зат атооч	zat atootʃ
adjective	сын атооч	sın atootʃ
verb	этиш	etiʃ
adverb	тактооч	taktootʃ
pronoun	ат атооч	at atootʃ
interjection	сырдык сөз	sırdık søz
preposition	препозиция	prepozitsija
root	сөздүн уңгусу	søzdyn uŋgusu
ending	жалгоо	dʒalgoo
prefix	префикс	prefiks
syllable	муун	muun
suffix	суффикс	suffiks
stress mark	басым	basım
apostrophe	апостроф	apostrof
full stop	чекит	tʃekit
comma	үтүр	ytyr
semicolon	чекитүү үтүр	tʃekityy ytyr
colon	кош чекит	koʃ tʃekit
ellipsis	көп чекит	køp tʃekit
question mark	суроо белгиси	suroo belgisi
exclamation mark	илеп белгиси	ilep belgisi

inverted commas	тырмакча	tɪrmakʧa
in inverted commas	тырмакчага алынган	tɪrmakʧaga alɪngan
parenthesis	кашаа	kaʃaa
in parenthesis	кашаага алынган	kaʃaaga alɪngan

hyphen	дефис	defis
dash	тире	tire
space (between words)	аралык	aralɪk

| letter | тамга | tamga |
| capital letter | баш тамга | baʃ tamga |

| vowel (n) | үндүү тыбыш | yndyy tɪbɪʃ |
| consonant (n) | үнсүз тыбыш | ynsyz tɪbɪʃ |

sentence	сүйлөм	syjløm
subject	сүйлөмдүн ээси	syjlømdyn eesi
predicate	баяндооч	bajandooʧ

line	сап	sap
on a new line	жаңы сап	ʤaŋɪ sap
paragraph	абзац	abzaʦ

word	сөз	søz
group of words	сөз айкашы	søz ajkaʃɪ
expression	туюнтма	tujʉntma
synonym	синоним	sinonim
antonym	антоним	antonim

rule	эреже	ereʤe
exception	чектен чыгаруу	ʧekten ʧɪgaruu
correct (adj)	туура	tuura

conjugation	жактоо	ʤaktoo
declension	жөндөлүш	ʤøndølyʃ
nominal case	жөндөмө	ʤøndømø
question	суроо	suroo
to underline (vt)	баса белгилөө	basa belgiløø
dotted line	пунктир	punktir

146. Foreign languages

language	тил	til
foreign (adj)	чет	ʧet
foreign language	чет тил	ʧet til
to study (vt)	окуу	okuu
to learn (language, etc.)	үйрөнүү	yjrønyy

to read (vi, vt)	окуу	okuu
to speak (vi, vt)	сүйлөө	syjløø
to understand (vt)	түшүнүү	tyʃynyy
to write (vt)	жазуу	ʤazuu
fast (adv)	тез	tez
slowly (adv)	жай	ʤaj

128

fluently (adv)	эркин	erkin
rules	эрежелер	eredʒeler
grammar	грамматика	grammatika
vocabulary	лексика	leksika
phonetics	фонетика	fonetika

textbook	китеп	kitep
dictionary	сөздүк	søzdyk
teach-yourself book	өзү үйрөткүч	øzy yjrøtkytʃ
phrasebook	тилачар	tilatʃar

cassette, tape	кассета	kasseta
videotape	видеокассета	videokasseta
CD, compact disc	CD, компакт-диск	sidi, kompakt-disk
DVD	DVD-диск	dividi-disk

alphabet	алфавит	alfavit
to spell (vt)	эжелеп айтуу	edʒelep ajtuu
pronunciation	айтылышы	ajtılıʃı

accent	акцент	aktsent
with an accent	акцент менен	aktsent menen
without an accent	акцентсиз	aktsentsiz

| word | сөз | søz |
| meaning | маани | maani |

course (e.g. a French ~)	курстар	kurstar
to sign up	курска жазылуу	kurska dʒazıluu
teacher	окутуучу	okutuutʃu

translation (process)	которуу	kotoruu
translation (text, etc.)	кормо	kotormo
translator	кормочу	kotormotʃu
interpreter	оозеки кормочу	oozeki kotormotʃu

| polyglot | полиглот | poliglot |
| memory | эс тутум | es tutum |

147. Fairy tale characters

Santa Claus	Санта Клаус	santa klaus
Cinderella	Күлала кыз	kylala kız
mermaid	суу периси	suu perisi
Neptune	Нептун	neptun

magician, wizard	сыйкырчы	sıjkırtʃı
fairy	сыйкырчы	sıjkırtʃı
magic (adj)	сыйкырдуу	sıjkırduu
magic wand	сыйкырлуу таякча	sıjkırluu tajaktʃa

fairy tale	жомок	dʒomok
miracle	керемет	keremet
dwarf	эргежээл	ergedʒeel

129

to turn into …	…га айлануу	…ga ajlanuu
ghost	арбак	arbak
phantom	көрүнчү	køryntʃy
monster	желмогуз	dʒelmoguz
dragon	ажыдаар	adʒıdaar
giant	дөө	døø

148. Zodiac Signs

Aries	Кой	koj
Taurus	Букачар	bukatʃar
Gemini	Эгиздер	egizder
Cancer	Рак	rak
Leo	Арстан	arstan
Virgo	Суу пери	suu peri
Libra	Тараза	taraza
Scorpio	Чаян	tʃajan
Sagittarius	Жаачы	dʒaatʃı
Capricorn	Текечер	teketʃer
Aquarius	Суу куяр	suu kujar
Pisces	Балыктар	balıktar
character	мүнөз	mynøz
character traits	мүнөздүн түрү	mynøzdyn tyry
behaviour	жүрүм-турум	dʒyrym-turum
to tell fortunes	төлгө ачуу	tølgø atʃuu
fortune-teller	көз ачык	køz atʃık
horoscope	жылдыз төлгө	dʒıldız tølgø

Arts

149. Theatre

theatre	театр	teatr
opera	опера	opera
operetta	оперетта	operetta
ballet	балет	balet
theatre poster	афиша	afiʃa
theatre company	труппа	truppa
tour	гастрольго чыгуу	gastrolʲgo tʃɪguu
to be on tour	гастрольдо жүрүү	gastrolʲdo dʒyryy
to rehearse (vi, vt)	репетиция кылуу	repetitsija kɪluu
rehearsal	репетиция	repetitsija
repertoire	репертуар	repertuar
performance	көрсөтүү	kørsøtyy
theatrical show	спектакль	spektaklʲ
play	пьеса	pjesa
ticket	билет	bilet
booking office	билет кассасы	bilet kassasɪ
lobby, foyer	холл	χoll
coat check (cloakroom)	гардероб	garderob
cloakroom ticket	номерок	nomerok
binoculars	дүрбү	dyrby
usher	текшерүүчү	tekʃeryytʃy
stalls (orchestra seats)	партер	parter
balcony	балкон	balkon
dress circle	бельэтаж	beljetadʒ
box	ложа	lodʒa
row	катар	katar
seat	орун	orun
audience	эл	el
spectator	көрүүчү	køryytʃy
to clap (vi, vt)	кол чабуу	kol tʃabuu
applause	кол чабуулар	kol tʃabuular
ovation	дүркүрөгөн кол чабуулар	dyrkyrøgøn kol tʃabuular
stage	сахна	saχna
curtain	көшөгө	køʃøgø
scenery	декорация	dekoratsija
backstage	көшөгө артында	køʃøgø artɪnda
scene (e.g. the last ~)	көрсөтмө	kørsøtmø
act	окуя	okuja
interval	антракт	antrakt

150. Cinema

actor	актёр	aktᵘor
actress	актриса	aktrisa
cinema (industry)	кино	kino
film	тасма	tasma
episode	серия	serija
detective film	детектив	detektiv
action film	салгылаш тасмасы	salgılaʃ tasması
adventure film	укмуштуу окуялуу тасма	ukmuʃtuu okujaluu tasma
science fiction film	билим-жалган аралаш тасмасы	bilim-dʒalgan aralaʃ tasması
horror film	коркутуу тасмасы	korkutuu tasması
comedy film	күлкүлүү кино	kylkylyy kino
melodrama	ый менен кайгы аралаш	ıy menen kajgı aralaʃ
drama	драма	drama
fictional film	көркөм тасма	kørkøm tasma
documentary	документүү тасма	dokumentyy tasma
cartoon	мультфильм	mulᵗfilᵐm
silent films	үнсүз кино	ynsyz kino
role (part)	роль	rolʲ
leading role	башкы роль	baʃkı rolʲ
to play (vi, vt)	ойноо	ojnoo
film star	кино жылдызы	kino dʒıldızı
well-known (adj)	белгилүү	belgilyy
famous (adj)	атактуу	ataktuu
popular (adj)	даңазалуу	daŋazaluu
script (screenplay)	сценарий	stsenarij
scriptwriter	сценарист	stsenarist
film director	режиссёр	redʒissʲor
producer	продюсер	prodᵘser
assistant	ассистент	assistent
cameraman	оператор	operator
stuntman	айлагер	ajlager
double (stuntman)	кейпин кийүүчү	kejpin kijyyʧy
to shoot a film	тасма тартуу	tasma tartuu
audition, screen test	сыноо	sınoo
shooting	тартуу	tartuu
film crew	тартуу группасы	tartuu gruppası
film set	тартуу аянты	tartuu ajantı
camera	кинокамера	kinokamera
cinema	кинотеатр	kinoteatr
screen (e.g. big ~)	экран	ekran
to show a film	тасманы көрсөтүү	tasmanı kørsøtyy
soundtrack	үн нугу	yn nugu
special effects	атайын эффектер	atajın effekter

subtitles	субтитрлер	subtitrler
credits	титрлер	titrler
translation	которуу	kotoruu

151. Painting

art	керкем енер	kørkøm ønør
fine arts	керкем чеберчилик	kørkøm tʃebertʃilik
art gallery	арт-галерея	art-galereja
art exhibition	сүрөт керезмесү	syrøt kørgøzmøsy

painting (art)	живопись	dʒivopisʲ
graphic art	графика	grafika
abstract art	абстракционизм	abstraktsionizm
impressionism	импрессионизм	impressionizm

picture (painting)	сүрөт	syrøt
drawing	сүрөт	syrøt
poster	кернек	kørnøk

illustration (picture)	иллюстрация	illustratsija
miniature	миниатюра	miniatura
copy (of painting, etc.)	кечүрме	køtʃyrmø
reproduction	репродукция	reproduktsija

mosaic	мозаика	mozaika
stained glass window	витраж	vitradʒ
fresco	фреска	freska
engraving	гравюра	gravura

bust (sculpture)	бюст	bust
sculpture	айкел	ajkel
statue	айкел	ajkel
plaster of Paris	гипс	gips
plaster (as adj)	гипстен	gipsten

portrait	портрет	portret
self-portrait	автопортрет	avtoportret
landscape painting	теребел сүрөтү	terebel syrøty
still life	буюмдар сүрөтү	bujumdar syrøty
caricature	карикатура	karikatura
sketch	сомо	somo

paint	боек	boek
watercolor paint	акварель	akvarelʲ
oil (paint)	майбоёк	majbojok
pencil	карандаш	karandaʃ
Indian ink	тушь	tuʃ
charcoal	кемур	kømyr

to draw (vi, vt)	тартуу	tartuu
to paint (vi, vt)	боёк менен тартуу	bojok menen tartuu
to pose (vi)	атайын туруу	atajın turuu
artist's model (masc.)	атайын туруучу	atajın turuutʃu

artist's model (fem.)	атайын туруучу	atajın turuutʃu
artist (painter)	сүрөтчү	syrøttʃy
work of art	чыгарма	tʃıgarma
masterpiece	чеберчиликтин чокусу	tʃebertʃiliktin tʃokusu
studio (artist's workroom)	устакана	ustakana
canvas (cloth)	кендир	kendir
easel	мольберт	molʲbert
palette	палитра	palitra
frame (picture ~, etc.)	алкак	alkak
restoration	калыбына келтирүү	kalıbına keltiryy
to restore (vt)	калыбына келтирүү	kalıbına keltiryy

152. Literature & Poetry

literature	адабият	adabijat
author (writer)	автор	avtor
pseudonym	лакап ат	lakap at
book	китеп	kitep
volume	том	tom
table of contents	мазмун	mazmun
page	бет	bet
main character	башкы каарман	baʃkı kaarman
autograph	кол тамга	kol tamga
short story	окуя	okuja
story (novella)	аңгеме	aŋgeme
novel	роман	roman
work (writing)	дил баян	dil bajan
fable	тамсил	tamsil
detective novel	детектив	detektiv
poem (verse)	ыр сап	ır sap
poetry	поэзия	poezija
poem (epic, ballad)	поэма	poema
poet	акын	akın
fiction	сулуулатып жазуу	suluulatıp dʒazuu
science fiction	билим-жалган аралаш	bilim-dʒalgan aralaʃ
adventures	укмуштуу окуялар	ukmuʃtuu okujalar
educational literature	билим берүү адабияты	bilim beryy adabijatı
children's literature	балдар адабияты	baldar adabijatı

153. Circus

circus	цирк	tsırk
travelling circus	цирк-шапито	tsırk-ʃapito
programme	программа	programma
performance	көрсөтүү	kørsøtyy
act (circus ~)	номер	nomer

circus ring	арена	arena
pantomime (act)	пантомима	pantomima
clown	маскарапоз	maskarapoz

acrobat	акробат	akrobat
acrobatics	акробатика	akrobatika
gymnast	гимнаст	gimnast
acrobatic gymnastics	гимнастика	gimnastika
somersault	тоңкочуктап атуу	toŋkotʃuktap atuu

strongman	атлет	atlet
tamer (e.g., lion ~)	ыкка көндүрүүчү	ɪkka køndyryytʃy
rider (circus horse ~)	чабандес	tʃabandes
assistant	жардамчы	dʒardamtʃɪ

stunt	ыкма	ɪkma
magic trick	көз боемо	køz boemo
conjurer, magician	көз боемочу	køz boemotʃu

juggler	жонглёр	dʒonglʲor
to juggle (vi, vt)	жонглёрлук кылуу	dʒonglʲorluk kɪluu
animal trainer	үйрөтүүчү	yjrøtyytʃy
animal training	үйрөтүү	yjrøtyy
to train (animals)	үйрөтүү	yjrøtyy

154. Music. Pop music

music	музыка	muzɪka
musician	музыкант	muzɪkant
musical instrument	музыка аспабы	muzɪka aspabɪ
to play …	…да ойноо	…da ojnoo

guitar	гитара	gitara
violin	скрипка	skripka
cello	виолончель	violontʃelʲ
double bass	контрабас	kontrabas
harp	арфа	arfa

piano	пианино	pianino
grand piano	рояль	rojalʲ
organ	орган	organ

wind instruments	үйлө аспаптары	yjlø aspaptarɪ
oboe	гобой	goboj
saxophone	саксофон	saksofon
clarinet	кларнет	klarnet
flute	флейта	flejta
trumpet	сурнай	surnaj

| accordion | аккордеон | akkordeon |
| drum | добулбас | dobulbas |

| duo | дуэт | duet |
| trio | трио | trio |

quartet	квартет	kvartet
choir	хор	χor
orchestra	оркестр	orkestr

pop music	поп-музыка	pop-muzıka
rock music	рок-музыка	rok-muzıka
rock group	рок-группа	rok-gruppa
jazz	джаз	dʒaz

| idol | аздек | azdek |
| admirer, fan | күйөрман | kyjørman |

concert	концерт	kontsert
symphony	симфония	simfonija
composition	чыгарма	tʃıgarma
to compose (write)	чыгаруу	tʃıgaruu

singing (n)	ырдоо	ırdoo
song	ыр	ır
tune (melody)	обон	obon
rhythm	ыргак	ırgak
blues	блюз	blʉz

sheet music	ноталар	notalar
baton	таякча	tajaktʃa
bow	кылдуу таякча	kılduu tajaktʃa
string	кыл	kıl
case (e.g. guitar ~)	куту	kutu

Rest. Entertainment. Travel

155. Trip. Travel

tourism, travel	туризм	turizm
tourist	турист	turist
trip, voyage	саякат	sajakat
adventure	укмуштуу окуя	ukmuʃtuu okuja
trip, journey	сапар	sapar
holiday	дем алыш	dem alıʃ
to be on holiday	дем алышка чыгуу	dem alıʃka tʃıguu
rest	эс алуу	es aluu
train	поезд	poezd
by train	поезд менен	poezd menen
aeroplane	учак	utʃak
by aeroplane	учакта	utʃakta
by car	автомобилде	avtomobilde
by ship	кемеде	kemede
luggage	жүк	dʒyk
suitcase	чемодан	tʃemodan
luggage trolley	араба	araba
passport	паспорт	pasport
visa	виза	viza
ticket	билет	bilet
air ticket	авиабилет	aviabilet
guidebook	жол көрсөткүч	dʒol kørsøtkytʃ
map (tourist ~)	карта	karta
area (rural ~)	жай	dʒaj
place, site	жер	dʒer
exotica (n)	экзотика	ekzotika
exotic (adj)	экзотикалуу	ekzotikaluu
amazing (adj)	ажайып	adʒajıp
group	топ	top
excursion, sightseeing tour	экскурсия	ekskursija
guide (person)	экскурсия жетекчиси	ekskursija dʒetektʃisi

156. Hotel

hotel	мейманкана	mejmankana
motel	мотель	motelʲ
three-star (~ hotel)	үч жылдыздуу	ytʃ dʒıldızduu

| five-star | беш жылдыздуу | beʃ dʒıldızduu |
| to stay (in a hotel, etc.) | токтоо | toktoo |

room	номер	nomer
single room	бир орундуу	bir orunduu
double room	эки орундуу	eki orunduu
to book a room	номерди камдык буйрутмалоо	nomerdi kamdık bujrutmaloo

| half board | жарым пансион | dʒarım pansion |
| full board | толук пансион | toluk pansion |

with bath	ваннасы менен	vannası menen
with shower	душ менен	duʃ menen
satellite television	спутник	sputnik
air-conditioner	аба желдеткич	aba dʒeldetkiʧ
towel	сүлгү	sylgy
key	ачкыч	aʧkıʧ

administrator	администратор	administrator
chambermaid	үй кызматкери	yj kızmatkeri
porter	жүк ташуучу	dʒyk taʃuuʧu
doorman	эшик ачуучу	eʃik aʧuuʧu

restaurant	ресторан	restoran
pub, bar	бар	bar
breakfast	таңкы тамак	taŋkı tamak
dinner	кечки тамак	keʧki tamak
buffet	шведче стол	ʃvedʧe stol

| lobby | вестибюль | vestibɥlʲ |
| lift | лифт | lift |

| DO NOT DISTURB | ТЫНЧЫБЫЗДЫ АЛБАГЫЛА! | tınʧıbızdı albagıla! |
| NO SMOKING | ТАМЕКИ ЧЕГҮҮГӨ БОЛБОЙТ! | tameki ʧegyygø bolbojt! |

157. Books. Reading

book	китеп	kitep
author	автор	avtor
writer	жазуучу	dʒazuuʧu
to write (~ a book)	жазуу	dʒazuu

reader	окурман	okurman
to read (vi, vt)	окуу	okuu
reading (activity)	окуу	okuu

| silently (to oneself) | үн чыгарбай | yn ʧıgarbaj |
| aloud (adv) | үн чыгарып | yn ʧıgarıp |

| to publish (vt) | басып чыгаруу | basıp ʧıgaruu |
| publishing (process) | басып чыгаруу | basıp ʧıgaruu |

| publisher | басып чыгаруучу | basıp ʧıgaruutʃu |
| publishing house | басмакана | basmakana |

to come out (be released)	жарык көрүү	dʒarık køryy
release (of a book)	чыгуу	ʧıguu
print run	нуска	nuska

| bookshop | китеп дүкөнү | kitep dykøny |
| library | китепкана | kitepkana |

story (novella)	аңгеме	aŋeme
short story	окуя	okuja
novel	роман	roman
detective novel	детектив	detektiv

memoirs	эсте калгандары	este kalgandarı
legend	уламыш	ulamıʃ
myth	миф	mif

poetry, poems	ыр	ır
autobiography	автобиография	avtobiografija
selected works	тандалма	tandalma
science fiction	билим-жалган аралаш	bilim-dʒalgan aralaʃ

title	аталышы	atalıʃı
introduction	кириш сөз	kiriʃ søz
title page	наам барагы	naam baragı

chapter	бөлум	bølum
extract	үзүндү	yzyndy
episode	эпизод	epizod

plot (storyline)	сюжет	sudʒet
contents	мазмун	mazmun
table of contents	мазмун	mazmun
main character	башкы каарман	baʃkı kaarman

volume	том	tom
cover	мукаба	mukaba
binding	мукабалоо	mukabaloo
bookmark	чөп кат	ʧøp kat

page	бет	bet
to page through	барактоо	baraktoo
margins	талаа	talaa
annotation (marginal note, etc.)	белги	belgi
footnote	эскертүү	eskertyy

text	текст	tekst
type, fount	шрифт	ʃrift
misprint, typo	ката	kata

translation	котормо	kotormo
to translate (vt)	которуу	kotoruu
original (n)	түпнуска	typnuska

famous (adj)	атактуу	ataktuu
unknown (not famous)	белгисиз	belgisiz
interesting (adj)	кызыктуу	kızıktuu
bestseller	талашып сатып алынган	talaʃıp satıp alıngan

dictionary	сөздүк	søzdyk
textbook	китеп	kitep
encyclopedia	энциклопедия	entsiklopedija

158. Hunting. Fishing

hunting	аңчылык	aŋʧılık
to hunt (vi, vt)	аңчылык кылуу	aŋʧılık kıluu
hunter	аңчы	aŋʧı

to shoot (vi)	атуу	atuu
rifle	мылтык	mıltık
bullet (shell)	ок	ok
shot (lead balls)	чачма	ʧaʧma

steel trap	капкан	kapkan
snare (for birds, etc.)	тузак	tuzak
to fall into the steel trap	капканга түшүү	kapkanga tyʃyy
to lay a steel trap	капкан коюу	kapkan kojʉu

poacher	браконьер	brakonjer
game (in hunting)	илбээсин	ilbeesin
hound dog	тайган	tajgan
safari	сафари	safari
mounted animal	кеп	kep
fisherman	балыкчы	balıkʧı
fishing (angling)	балык улоо	balık uloo
to fish (vi)	балык улоо	balık uloo

fishing rod	кайырмак	kajırmak
fishing line	кайырмак жиби	kajırmak dʒibi
hook	илгич	ilgiʧ
float	калкыма	kalkıma
bait	жем	dʒem

to cast a line	кайырмак таштоо	kajırmak taʃtoo
to bite (ab. fish)	чокулоо	ʧokuloo
catch (of fish)	кармалган балык	karmalgan balık
ice-hole	муздагы оюк	muzdagı ojʉk

fishing net	тор	tor
boat	кайык	kajık
to net (to fish with a net)	тор менен кармоо	tor menen karmoo
to cast[throw] the net	тор таштоо	tor taʃtoo
to haul the net in	торду чыгаруу	tordu ʧıgaruu
to fall into the net	торго түшүү	torgo tyʃyy
whaler (person)	кит уулоочу	kit uulooʧu
whaleboat	кит уулоочу кеме	kit uulooʧu keme
harpoon	гарпун	garpun

159. Games. Billiards

billiards	бильярд	biljard
billiard room, hall	бильярдкана	biljardkana
ball (snooker, etc.)	бильярд шары	biljard ʃarı
to pocket a ball	шарды киргизүү	ʃardı kirgizyy
cue	кий	kij
pocket	луза	luza

160. Games. Playing cards

diamonds	момун	momun
spades	карга	karga
hearts	кызыл ача	kızıl atʃa
clubs	чырым	tʃırım
ace	туз	tuz
king	король	korolʲ
queen	матке	matke
jack, knave	балта	balta
playing card	оюн картасы	ojʉn kartası
cards	карталар	kartalar
trump	көзүр	køzyr
pack of cards	колода	koloda
point	очко	otʃko
to deal (vi, vt)	таратуу	taratuu
to shuffle (cards)	аралаштыруу	aralaʃtıruu
lead, turn (n)	жүрүү	dʒyryy
cardsharp	шумпай	ʃumpaj

161. Casino. Roulette

casino	казино	kazino
roulette (game)	рулетка	ruletka
bet	коюм	kojʉm
to place bets	коюм коюу	kojʉm kojʉu
red	кызыл	kızıl
black	кара	kara
to bet on red	кызылга коюу	kızılga kojʉu
to bet on black	карага коюу	karaga kojʉu
croupier (dealer)	крупье	krupje
to spin the wheel	барабанды айлантуу	barabandı ajlantuu
rules (of game)	оюн эрежеси	ojʉn eredʒesi
chip	фишка	fiʃka
to win (vi, vt)	утуу	utuu
win (winnings)	утуу	utuu

| to lose (~ 100 dollars) | жеңилүү | dʒeŋilyy |
| loss (losses) | уткузуу | utkuzuu |

player	оюнчу	ojʉntʃu
blackjack (card game)	блэк джек	blek dʒek
craps (dice game)	сөөк оюну	søøk ojʉnu
dice (a pair of ~)	сөөктөр	søøktør
fruit machine	оюн автоматы	ojʉn avtomatı

162. Rest. Games. Miscellaneous

to stroll (vi, vt)	сейилдөө	sejildøø
stroll (leisurely walk)	жөө сейилдөө	dʒøø sejildøø
car ride	саякат	sajakat
adventure	укмуштуу окуя	ukmuʃtuu okuja
picnic	пикник	piknik

game (chess, etc.)	оюн	ojʉn
player	оюнчу	ojʉntʃu
game (one ~ of chess)	партия	partija

collector (e.g. philatelist)	жыйнакчы	dʒıjnaktʃı
to collect (stamps, etc.)	жыйноо	dʒıjnoo
collection	жыйнак	dʒıjnak

crossword puzzle	кроссворд	krossvord
racecourse (hippodrome)	ат майданы	at majdanı
disco (discotheque)	дискотека	diskoteka

| sauna | сауна | sauna |
| lottery | лотерея | lotereja |

camping trip	жөө сапар	dʒøø sapar
camp	лагерь	lagerⁱ
tent (for camping)	чатыр	tʃatır
compass	компас	kompas
camper	турист	turist

to watch (film, etc.)	көрүү	køryy
viewer	телекөрүүчү	telekøryytʃy
TV show (TV program)	теле көрсөтүү	tele kørsøtyy

163. Photography

| camera (photo) | фотоаппарат | fotoapparat |
| photo, picture | фото | foto |

photographer	сүрөтчү	syrøttʃy
photo studio	фотостудия	fotostudija
photo album	фотоальбом	fotoalⁱbom
camera lens	объектив	obʰjektiv
telephoto lens	телеобъектив	teleobʰjektiv

| filter | фильтр | filʲtr |
| lens | линза | linza |

optics (high-quality ~)	оптика	optika
diaphragm (aperture)	диафрагма	diafragma
exposure time (shutter speed)	тушугуу	tuʃuguu
viewfinder	көрүнүш табуучу	kørynyʃ tabuutʃu

digital camera	санарип камерасы	sanarip kamerası
tripod	үч бут	ytʃ but
flash	жарк этүү	dʒark etyy

to photograph (vt)	сүрөткө тартуу	syrøtkø tartuu
to take pictures	тартуу	tartuu
to have one's picture taken	сүрөткө түшүү	syrøtkø tyʃyy

focus	фокус	fokus
to focus	фокусту оңдоо	fokustu oŋdoo
sharp, in focus (adj)	фокуста	fokusta
sharpness	дааналык	daanalık

| contrast | контраст | kontrast |
| contrast (as adj) | контрасттагы | kontrasttagı |

picture (photo)	сүрөт	syrøt
negative (n)	негатив	negativ
film (a roll of ~)	фотоплёнка	fotoplʲonka
frame (still)	кадр	kadr
to print (photos)	басып чыгаруу	basıp tʃıgaruu

164. Beach. Swimming

beach	суу жээги	suu dʒeegi
sand	кум	kum
deserted (beach)	ээн суу жээги	een suu dʒeegi

suntan	күнгө күйүү	kyngø kyjyy
to get a tan	күнгө кактануу	kyngø kaktanuu
tanned (adj)	күнгө күйгөн	kyngø kyjgøn
sunscreen	күнгө күйүш үчүн крем	kyngø kyjyʃ ytʃyn krem

bikini	бикини	bikini
swimsuit, bikini	купальник	kupalʲnik
swim trunks	плавки	plavki

swimming pool	бассейн	bassejn
to swim (vi)	сүзүү	syzyy
shower	душ	duʃ
to change (one's clothes)	кийим алмаштыруу	kijim almaʃtıruu
towel	сүлгү	sylgy

| boat | кайык | kajık |
| motorboat | катер | kater |

water ski	суу чаңгысы	suu ʧaŋgısı
pedalo	суу велосипеди	suu velosipedi
surfing	тактай тебүү	taktaj tebyy
surfer	тактай тебүүчү	taktaj tebyyʧy

scuba set	акваланг	akvalang
flippers (swim fins)	ласты	lastı
mask (diving ~)	маска	maska
diver	сууга сүңгүү	suuga syngyy
to dive (vi)	сүңгүү	syngyy
underwater (adv)	суу астында	suu astında

beach umbrella	зонт	zont
beach chair (sun lounger)	шезлонг	ʃezlong
sunglasses	көз айнек	køz ajnek
air mattress	сүзүү үчүн матрас	syzyy yʧyn matras

| to play (amuse oneself) | ойноо | ojnoo |
| to go for a swim | сууга түшүү | suuga tyʃyy |

beach ball	топ	top
to inflate (vt)	үйлөө	yjløø
inflatable, air (adj)	үйлөнмө	yjlønmø

wave	толкун	tolkun
buoy (line of ~s)	буй	buj
to drown (ab. person)	чөгүү	ʧøgyy

to save, to rescue	куткаруу	kutkaruu
life jacket	куткаруучу күрмө	kutkaruuʧu kyrmø
to observe, to watch	байкоо	bajkoo
lifeguard	куткаруучу	kutkaruuʧu

TECHNICAL EQUIPMENT. TRANSPORT

Technical equipment

165. Computer

computer	компьютер	kompjʉter
notebook, laptop	ноутбук	noutbuk
to turn on	күйгүзүү	kyjgyzyy
to turn off	өчүрүү	øʧyryy
keyboard	ариптакта	ariptakta
key	баскыч	baskıʧ
mouse	чычкан	ʧıʧkan
mouse mat	килемче	kilemʧe
button	баскыч	baskıʧ
cursor	курсор	kursor
monitor	монитор	monitor
screen	экран	ekran
hard disk	катуу диск	katuu disk
hard disk capacity	катуу дисктин көлөмү	katuu disktin kølømy
memory	эс тутум	es tutum
random access memory	оперативдик эс тутум	operativdik es tutum
file	файл	fajl
folder	папка	papka
to open (vt)	ачуу	aʧuu
to close (vt)	жабуу	ʤabuu
to save (vt)	сактоо	saktoo
to delete (vt)	жок кылуу	ʤok kıluu
to copy (vt)	көчүрүү	køʧyryy
to sort (vt)	иреттөө	irettøø
to transfer (copy)	өткөрүү	øtkøryy
programme	программа	programma
software	программалык	programmalık
programmer	программист	programmist
to program (vt)	программалаштыруу	programmalaʃtıruu
hacker	хакер	χaker
password	сырсөз	sırsøz
virus	вирус	virus
to find, to detect	издеп табуу	izdep tabuu
byte	байт	bajt

megabyte	мегабайт	megabajt
data	маалыматтар	maalımattar
database	маалымат базасы	maalımat bazası

cable (USB, etc.)	кабель	kabelʲ
to disconnect (vt)	ажыратуу	adʒıratuu
to connect (sth to sth)	туташтыруу	tutaʃtıruu

166. Internet. E-mail

Internet	интернет	internet
browser	браузер	brauzer
search engine	издөө аспабы	izdøø aspabı
provider	провайдер	provajder

webmaster	веб-мастер	web-master
website	веб-сайт	web-sajt
webpage	веб-баракча	web-baraktʃa

| address (e-mail ~) | дарек | darek |
| address book | дарек китепчеси | darek kiteptʃesi |

postbox	почта ящиги	potʃta jaʃtʃigi
post	почта	potʃta
full (adj)	толуп калган	tolup kalgan

message	кабар	kabar
incoming messages	келген кабарлар	kelgen kabarlar
outgoing messages	жөнөтүлгөн кабарлар	dʒønøtylgøn kabarlar

sender	жөнөтүүчү	dʒønøtyytʃy
to send (vt)	жөнөтүү	dʒønøtyy
sending (of mail)	жөнөтүү	dʒønøtyy

| receiver | алуучу | aluutʃu |
| to receive (vt) | алуу | aluu |

| correspondence | жазышуу | dʒazıʃuu |
| to correspond (vi) | жазышуу | dʒazıʃuu |

file	файл	fajl
to download (vt)	жүктөө	dʒyktøø
to create (vt)	жаратуу	dʒaratuu
to delete (vt)	жок кылуу	dʒok kıluu
deleted (adj)	жок кылынган	dʒok kılıngan

connection (ADSL, etc.)	байланыш	bajlanıʃ
speed	ылдамдык	ıldamdık
modem	модем	modem
access	жеткирилүү	dʒetkirilyy
port (e.g. input ~)	порт	port

| connection (make a ~) | туташуу | tutaʃuu |
| to connect to ... (vi) | ... туташуу | ... tutaʃuu |

| to select (vt) | тандоо | tandoo |
| to search (for ...) | ... издөө | ... izdøø |

167. Electricity

electricity	электр кубаты	elektr kubatı
electric, electrical (adj)	электрикалык	elektrikalık
electric power station	электростанция	elektrostantsija
energy	энергия	energija
electric power	электр кубаты	elektr kubatı

light bulb	лампочка	lampotʃka
torch	шам	ʃam
street light	шам	ʃam

light	жарык	dʒarık
to turn on	күйгүзүү	kyjgyzyy
to turn off	өчүрүү	øtʃyryy
to turn off the light	жарыкты өчүрүү	dʒarıktı øtʃyryy

to burn out (vi)	күйүп кетүү	kyjyp ketyy
short circuit	кыска туташуу	kıska tutaʃuu
broken wire	үзүлүү	yzylyy
contact (electrical ~)	контакт	kontakt

light switch	өчүргүч	øtʃyrgytʃ
socket outlet	розетка	rozetka
plug	сайгыч	sajgıtʃ
extension lead	узарткыч	uzartkıtʃ

fuse	эриме сактагыч	erime saktagıtʃ
cable, wire	зым	zım
wiring	электр зымы	elektr zımı

ampere	ампер	amper
amperage	токтун күчү	toktun kytʃy
volt	вольт	volʲt
voltage	чыңалуу	tʃıŋaluu

| electrical device | электр алет | elektr alet |
| indicator | көрсөткүч | kørsøtkytʃ |

electrician	электрик	elektrik
to solder (vt)	кандоо	kaŋdoo
soldering iron	кандагыч аспап	kaŋdagıtʃ aspap
electric current	электр тогу	elektr togu

168. Tools

tool, instrument	аспап	aspap
tools	аспаптар	aspaptar
equipment (factory ~)	жабдуу	dʒabduu

hammer	балка	balka
screwdriver	бурагыч	buragıtʃ
axe	балта	balta

saw	араа	araa
to saw (vt)	аралоо	araloo
plane (tool)	тактай сүргүч	taktaj syrgytʃ
to plane (vt)	сүрүү	syryy
soldering iron	кандагыч аспап	kaŋdagıtʃ aspap
to solder (vt)	кандоо	kaŋdoo

file (tool)	егее	øgøø
carpenter pincers	аттиш	attiʃ
combination pliers	жалпак тиштүү кычкач	dʒalpak tiʃtyy kıtʃkatʃ
chisel	тешкич	teʃkitʃ

drill bit	бургу	burgu
electric drill	үшкү	yʃky
to drill (vi, vt)	бургулап тешүү	burgulap teʃyy

knife	бычак	bıtʃak
pocket knife	чөнтөк бычак	tʃøntøk bıtʃak
blade	миз	miz

sharp (blade, etc.)	курч	kurtʃ
dull, blunt (adj)	мокок	mokok
to get blunt (dull)	мокотулуу	mokotuluu
to sharpen (vt)	курчутуу	kurtʃutuu

bolt	буроо	buroo
nut	бурама	burama
thread (of a screw)	бураманын сайы	buramanın sajı
wood screw	буроо мык	buroo mık

| nail | мык | mık |
| nailhead | баш | baʃ |

ruler (for measuring)	сызгыч	sızgıtʃ
tape measure	рулетка	ruletka
spirit level	деңгээл	deŋgeel
magnifying glass	чоңойтуч	tʃoŋojtutʃ

measuring instrument	ченөөчү аспап	tʃenøøtʃy aspap
to measure (vt)	ченөө	tʃenøø
scale (of thermometer, etc.)	шкала	ʃkala
readings	көрсөтүү ченем	kørsøtyy tʃenem

| compressor | компрессор | kompressor |
| microscope | микроскоп | mikroskop |

pump (e.g. water ~)	соргу	sorgu
robot	робот	robot
laser	лазер	lazer

| spanner | гайка ачкычы | gajka atʃkıtʃı |
| adhesive tape | жабышкак тасма | dʒabıʃkak tasma |

glue	желим	ʤelim
sandpaper	кум кагаз	kum kagaz
spring	серпилгич	serpilgiʧ
magnet	магнит	magnit
gloves	колкап	kolkap

rope	аркан	arkan
cord	жип	ʤip
wire (e.g. telephone ~)	зым	zım
cable	кабель	kabelʲ

sledgehammer	барскан	barskan
prybar	лом	lom
ladder	шаты	ʃatı
stepladder	кичинекей шаты	kiʧinekej ʃatı

to screw (tighten)	бурап бекитүү	burap bekityy
to unscrew (lid, filter, etc.)	бурап чыгаруу	burap ʧıgaruu
to tighten (e.g. with a clamp)	кысуу	kısuu
to glue, to stick	жабыштыруу	ʤabıʃtıruu
to cut (vt)	кесүү	kesyy

malfunction (fault)	бузулгандык	buzulgandık
repair (mending)	оңдоо	oŋdoo
to repair, to fix (vt)	оңдоо	oŋdoo
to adjust (machine, etc.)	тууралоо	tuuraloo

to check (to examine)	текшерүү	tekʃeryy
checking	текшерүү	tekʃeryy
readings	көрсөтүү ченем	kørsøtyy ʧenem

| reliable, solid (machine) | ишеничтүү | iʃeniʧtyy |
| complex (adj) | кыйын | kıjın |

to rust (get rusted)	дат басуу	dat basuu
rusty (adj)	дат баскан	dat baskan
rust	дат	dat

Transport

169. Aeroplane

aeroplane	учак	uʧak
air ticket	авиабилет	aviabilet
airline	авиакомпания	aviakompanija
airport	аэропорт	aeroport
supersonic (adj)	сверхзвуковой	sverχzvukovoj
captain	кеме командири	keme komandiri
crew	экипаж	ekipadʒ
pilot	учкуч	uʧkuʧ
stewardess	стюардесса	stʉardessa
navigator	штурман	ʃturman
wings	канаттар	kanattar
tail	куйрук	kujruk
cockpit	кабина	kabina
engine	кыймылдаткыч	kɪjmɪldatkɪʧ
undercarriage (landing gear)	шасси	ʃassi
turbine	турбина	turbina
propeller	пропеллер	propeller
black box	кара куту	kara kutu
yoke (control column)	штурвал	ʃturval
fuel	күйүүчү май	kyjyyʧy may
safety card	коопсуздук көрсөтмөсү	koopsuzduk kørsøtmøsy
oxygen mask	кислород чүмбөтү	kislorod ʧymbøty
uniform	бир беткей кийим	bir betkey kijim
lifejacket	куткаруучу күрмө	kutkaruuʧu kyrmø
parachute	парашют	paraʃʉt
takeoff	учуп көтөрүлүү	uʧup køtørylyy
to take off (vi)	учуп көтөрүлүү	uʧup køtørylyy
runway	учуп чыгуу тилкеси	uʧup ʧɪguu tilkesi
visibility	көрүнүш	kørynyʃ
flight (act of flying)	учуу	uʧuu
altitude	бийиктик	bijiktik
air pocket	аба чүңкуру	aba ʧyŋkuru
seat	орун	orun
headphones	кулакчын	kulakʧın
folding tray (tray table)	бүктөлмө стол	byktølmø stol
airplane window	иллюминатор	illʉminator
aisle	өтмөк	øtmøk

170. Train

train	поезд	poezd
commuter train	электричка	elektritʃka
express train	бат жүрүүчү поезд	bat dʒyryytʃy poezd
diesel locomotive	тепловоз	teplovoz
steam locomotive	паровоз	parovoz
coach, carriage	вагон	vagon
buffet car	вагон-ресторан	vagon-restoran
rails	рельсалар	relʲsalar
railway	темир жолу	temir dʒolu
sleeper (track support)	шпала	ʃpala
platform (railway ~)	платформа	platforma
platform (~ 1, 2, etc.)	жол	dʒol
semaphore	семафор	semafor
station	бекет	beket
train driver	машинист	maʃinist
porter (of luggage)	жук ташуучу	dʒuk taʃuutʃu
carriage attendant	проводник	provodnik
passenger	жүргүнчү	dʒyrgyntʃy
ticket inspector	текшерүүчү	tekʃeryytʃy
corridor (in train)	коридор	koridor
emergency brake	стоп-кран	stop-kran
compartment	купе	kupe
berth	текче	tektʃe
upper berth	үстүнкү текче	ystyŋky tektʃe
lower berth	ылдыйкы текче	ıldıjkı tektʃe
bed linen, bedding	жууркан-төшөк	dʒuurkan-tøʃøk
ticket	билет	bilet
timetable	ырааттама	ıraattama
information display	табло	tablo
to leave, to depart	жөнөө	dʒønøø
departure (of train)	жөнөө	dʒønøø
to arrive (ab. train)	келүү	kelyy
arrival	келүү	kelyy
to arrive by train	поезд менен келүү	poezd menen kelyy
to get on the train	поездге отуруу	poezdge oturuu
to get off the train	поездден түшүү	poezdden tyʃyy
train crash	кыйроо	kıjroo
to derail (vi)	рельсадан чыгып кетүү	relʲsadan tʃıgıp ketyy
steam locomotive	паровоз	parovoz
stoker, fireman	от жагуучу	ot dʒaguutʃu
firebox	меш	meʃ
coal	көмүр	kømyr

171. Ship

ship	кеме	keme
vessel	кеме	keme
steamship	пароход	paroχod
riverboat	теплоход	teploχod
cruise ship	лайнер	lajner
cruiser	крейсер	krejser
yacht	яхта	jaχta
tugboat	буксир	buksir
barge	баржа	bardʒa
ferry	паром	parom
sailing ship	парус	parus
brigantine	бригантина	brigantina
ice breaker	муз жаргыч кеме	muz dʒargıtʃ keme
submarine	суу астында жүрүүчү кеме	suu astında dʒyryytʃy keme
boat (flat-bottomed ~)	кайык	kajık
dinghy	шлюпка	ʃлɯpka
lifeboat	куткаруу шлюпкасы	kutkaruu ʃлɯpkası
motorboat	катер	kater
captain	капитан	kapitan
seaman	матрос	matros
sailor	деңизчи	deŋiztʃi
crew	экипаж	ekipadʒ
boatswain	боцман	botsman
ship's boy	юнга	jɯnga
cook	кок	kok
ship's doctor	кеме доктуру	keme dokturu
deck	палуба	paluba
mast	мачта	matʃta
sail	парус	parus
hold	трюм	trɯm
bow (prow)	тумшук	tumʃuk
stern	кеменин арткы бөлүгү	kemenin artkı bølygy
oar	калак	kalak
screw propeller	винт	vint
cabin	каюта	kajɯta
wardroom	кают-компания	kajɯt-kompanija
engine room	машина бөлүгү	maʃina bølygy
bridge	капитан мостиги	kapitan mostigi
radio room	радиорубка	radiorubka
wave (radio)	толкун	tolkun
logbook	кеме журналы	keme dʒurnalı
spyglass	дүрбү	dyrby

| bell | коңгуроо | konguroo |
| flag | байрак | bajrak |

| hawser (mooring ~) | аркан | arkan |
| knot (bowline, etc.) | түйүн | tyjyn |

| deckrails | туткуч | tutkuʧ |
| gangway | трап | trap |

anchor	кеме казык	keme kazık
to weigh anchor	кеме казыкты көтөрүү	keme kazıktı kotoryy
to drop anchor	кеме казыкты таштоо	keme kazıktı taʃtoo
anchor chain	казык чынжыры	kazık ʧindʒırı

port (harbour)	порт	port
quay, wharf	причал	priʧal
to berth (moor)	келип токтоо	kelip toktoo
to cast off	жээктен алыстоо	dʒeekten alıstoo

trip, voyage	саякат	sajakat
cruise (sea trip)	деңиз саякаты	deŋiz sajakatı
course (route)	курс	kurs
route (itinerary)	каттам	kattam

fairway (safe water channel)	фарватер	farvater
shallows	тайыз жер	tajız dʒer
to run aground	тайыз жерге отуруу	tajız dʒerge oturuu

storm	бороон чапкын	boroon ʧapkın
signal	сигнал	signal
to sink (vi)	чөгүү	ʧøgyy
Man overboard!	Сууда адам бар!	suuda adam bar!
SOS (distress signal)	SOS	sos
ring buoy	куткаруучу тегерек	kutkaruuʧu tegerek

172. Airport

airport	аэропорт	aeroport
aeroplane	учак	uʧak
airline	авиакомпания	aviakompanija
air traffic controller	авиадиспетчер	aviadispetʧer

departure	учуп кетүү	uʧup ketyy
arrival	учуп келүү	uʧup kelyy
to arrive (by plane)	учуп келүү	uʧup kelyy

| departure time | учуп кетүү убактысы | uʧup ketyy ubaktısı |
| arrival time | учуп келүү убактысы | uʧup kelyy ubaktısı |

| to be delayed | кармалуу | karmaluu |
| flight delay | учуп кетүүнүн кечигиши | uʧup ketyynyn keʧigiʃi |

| information board | маалымат таблосу | maalımat tablosu |
| information | маалымат | maalımat |

| to announce (vt) | кулактандыруу | kulaktandıruu |
| flight (e.g. next ~) | рейс | rejs |

| customs | бажыкана | badʒıkana |
| customs officer | бажы кызматкери | badʒı kızmatkeri |

customs declaration	бажы декларациясы	badʒı deklaratsijası
to fill in (vt)	толтуруу	tolturuu
to fill in the declaration	декларация толтуруу	deklaratsija tolturuu
passport control	паспорт текшерүү	pasport tekʃeryy

luggage	жүк	dʒyk
hand luggage	кол жүгү	kol dʒygy
luggage trolley	араба	araba

landing	конуу	konuu
landing strip	конуу тилкеси	konuu tilkesi
to land (vi)	конуу	konuu
airstair (passenger stair)	трап	trap

check-in	катталуу	kattaluu
check-in counter	каттоо стойкасы	kattoo stojkası
to check-in (vi)	катталуу	kattaluu
boarding card	отуруу үчүн талон	oturuu ytʃyn talon
departure gate	чыгуу	tʃıguu

transit	транзит	tranzit
to wait (vt)	күтүү	kytyy
departure lounge	күтүү залы	kutyy zalı
to see off	узатуу	uzatuu
to say goodbye	коштошуу	koʃtoʃuu

173. Bicycle. Motorcycle

bicycle	велосипед	velosiped
scooter	мотороллер	motoroller
motorbike	мотоцикл	mototsikl

to go by bicycle	велосипедде жүрүү	velosipedde dʒyryy
handlebars	руль	rulʲ
pedal	педаль	pedalʲ
brakes	тормоз	tormoz
bicycle seat (saddle)	отургуч	oturgutʃ

| pump | соркыскыч | sorkıskıtʃ |
| pannier rack | багажник | bagadʒnik |

| front lamp | фонарь | fonarʲ |
| helmet | шлем | ʃlem |

wheel	дөңгөлөк	døŋgøløk
mudguard	калкан	kalkan
rim	дөңгөлөктүн алкагы	døŋgøløktyn alkagı
spoke	чабак	tʃabak

Cars

174. Types of cars

car	автоунаа	avtounaa
sports car	спорттук автоунаа	sporttuk avtounaa
limousine	лимузин	limuzin
off-road vehicle	жолтандабас	dʒoltandabas
drophead coupé (convertible)	кабриолет	kabriolet
minibus	микроавтобус	mikroavtobus
ambulance	тез жардам	tez dʒardam
snowplough	кар күрөөчү машина	kar kyrøøtʃy maʃina
lorry	жүк ташуучу машина	dʒyk taʃuutʃu maʃina
road tanker	бензовоз	benzovoz
van (small truck)	фургон	furgon
tractor unit	тягач	tʲagatʃ
trailer	чиркегич	tʃirkegitʃ
comfortable (adj)	жайлуу	dʒajluu
used (adj)	колдонулган	koldonulgan

175. Cars. Bodywork

bonnet	капот	kapot
wing	калкан	kalkan
roof	үстү	ysty
windscreen	шамалдан тоскон айнек	ʃamaldan toskon ajnek
rear-view mirror	арткы күзгү	artkı kyzgy
windscreen washer	айнек жуугуч	ajnek dʒuugutʃ
windscreen wipers	щётка	ʃtʃʲotka
side window	каптал айнек	kaptal ajnek
electric window	айнек көтөргүч	ajnek køtørgytʃ
aerial	антенна	antenna
sunroof	люк	lʉk
bumper	бампер	bamper
boot	жүк салгыч	dʒyk salgıtʃ
roof luggage rack	жүк салгыч	dʒyk salgıtʃ
door	эшик	eʃik
door handle	кармагыч	karmagıtʃ
door lock	кулпу	kulpu
number plate	номер	nomer
silencer	глушитель	gluʃitelʲ

155

| petrol tank | бензобак | benzobak |
| exhaust pipe | калдыктар түтүгү | kaldıktar tytygy |

accelerator	газ	gaz
pedal	педаль	pedalʲ
accelerator pedal	газ педали	gaz pedali

brake	тормоз	tormoz
brake pedal	тормоздун педалы	tormozdun pedalı
to brake (use the brake)	тормоз басуу	tormoz basuu
handbrake	токтомо тормозу	toktomo tormozu

clutch	илиштирүү	iliʃtiryy
clutch pedal	илиштирүү педали	iliʃtiryy pedali
clutch disc	илиштирүү диски	iliʃtiryy diski
shock absorber	амортизатор	amortizator

wheel	дөңгөлөк	døŋgøløk
spare tyre	запас дөңгөлөгү	zapas døŋgøløgy
tyre	покрышка	pokrıʃka
wheel cover (hubcap)	жапкыч	dʒapkıʧ

driving wheels	салма дөңгөлөктөр	salma døŋgøløktør
front-wheel drive (as adj)	алдыңкы дөңгөлөк салмалуу	aldıŋkı døŋgøløk salmaluu
rear-wheel drive (as adj)	арткы дөңгөлөк салмалуу	artkı døŋgøløk salmaluu
all-wheel drive (as adj)	бардык дөңгөлөк салмалуу	bardık døŋgøløk salmaluu

gearbox	бергилик куту	bergilik kutu
automatic (adj)	автоматтык	avtomattık
mechanical (adj)	механикалуу	meχanikaluu
gear lever	бергилик кутунун жылышуусу	bergilik kutunun dʒılıʃuusu

| headlamp | фара | fara |
| headlights | фаралар | faralar |

dipped headlights	жакынкы чырак	dʒakınkı ʧırak
full headlights	алыскы чырак	alıskı ʧırak
brake light	стоп-сигнал	stop-signal

sidelights	габарит чырактары	gabarit ʧıraktarı
hazard lights	авария чырактары	avarija ʧıraktarı
fog lights	туманга каршы чырактар	tumanga karʃı ʧıraktar
turn indicator	бурулуш чырагы	buruluʃ ʧıragı
reversing light	арткы чырак	artkı ʧırak

176. Cars. Passenger compartment

car inside (interior)	салон	salon
leather (as adj)	тери	teri
velour (as adj)	велюр	velʉr
upholstery	каптоо	kaptoo

instrument (gage)	алет	alet
dashboard	алет панели	alet paneli
speedometer	спидометр	spidometr
needle (pointer)	жебе	dʒebe

mileometer	эсептегич	eseptegitʃ
indicator (sensor)	көрсөткүч	kørsøtkytʃ
level	деңгээл	deŋgeel
warning light	көрсөткүч	kørsøtkytʃ

steering wheel	руль	rulⁱ
horn	сигнал	signal
button	баскыч	baskıtʃ
switch	которгуч	kotorgutʃ

seat	орун	orun
backrest	жөлөнгүч	dʒøløngytʃ
headrest	баш жөлөгүч	baʃ dʒøløgytʃ
seat belt	орундук куру	orunduk kuru
to fasten the belt	курду тагынуу	kurdu tagınuu
adjustment (of seats)	жөндөө	dʒøndøø

| airbag | аба жаздыкчасы | aba dʒazdıktʃası |
| air-conditioner | аба желдеткич | aba dʒeldetkitʃ |

radio	үналгы	ynalgı
CD player	CD-ойноткуч	sidi-ojnotkutʃ
to turn on	жүргүзүү	dʒyrgyzyy
aerial	антенна	antenna
glove box	колкап бөлүмү	kolkap bølymy
ashtray	күл салгыч	kyl salgıtʃ

177. Cars. Engine

engine	кыймылдаткыч	kıjmıldatkıtʃ
motor	мотор	motor
diesel (as adj)	дизель менен	dizelⁱ menen
petrol (as adj)	бензин менен	benzin menen

engine volume	кыймылдаткычтын көлөмү	kıjmıldatkıtʃtın kølømy
power	кубатуулугу	kubatuulugu
horsepower	ат күчү	at kytʃy
piston	бишкек	biʃkek
cylinder	цилиндр	tsılindr
valve	сарпкапкак	sarpkapkak

injector	бүрккүч	byrkkytʃ
generator (alternator)	генератор	generator
carburettor	карбюратор	karburator
motor oil	мотор майы	motor majı

| radiator | радиатор | radiator |
| coolant | суутуучу суюктук | suutuutʃu sujuktuk |

cooling fan	желдеткич	dʒeldetkiʧ
battery (accumulator)	аккумулятор	akkumulʲator
starter	стартер	starter
ignition	от алдыруу	ot aldıruu
sparking plug	от алдыруу шамы	ot aldıruu ʃamı

terminal (of battery)	клемма	klemma
positive terminal	плюс	plʉs
negative terminal	минус	minus
fuse	эриме сактагыч	erime saktagıʧ

air filter	аба чыпкасы	aba ʧıpkası
oil filter	май чыпкасы	maj ʧıpkası
fuel filter	күйүүчү май чыпкасы	kyjyyʧy may ʧıpkası

178. Cars. Crash. Repair

car crash	авто урунушу	avto urunuʃu
traffic accident	жол кырсыгы	dʒol kırsıgı
to crash (into the wall, etc.)	урунуу	urunuu
to get smashed up	талкалануу	talkalanuu
damage	бузулуу	buzuluu
intact (unscathed)	бүтүн	bytyn

breakdown	бузулуу	buzuluu
to break down (vi)	бузулуп калуу	buzulup kaluu
towrope	сүйрөө арканы	syjrøø arkanı

puncture	тешилип калуу	teʃilip kaluu
to have a puncture	желин чыгаруу	dʒelin ʧıgaruu
to pump up	үйлөтүү	yjløtyy
pressure	басым	basım
to check (to examine)	текшерүү	tekʃeryy

repair	оңдоо	oŋdoo
auto repair shop	автосервис	avtoservis
spare part	белен тетик	belen tetik
part	тетик	tetik

bolt (with nut)	буроо	buroo
screw (fastener)	буралма	buralma
nut	бурама	burama
washer	эбелек	ebelek
bearing (e.g. ball ~)	мунакжаздам	munakdʒazdam

tube	түтүк	tytyk
gasket (head ~)	төшөм	tøʃøm
cable, wire	зым	zım

jack	домкрат	domkrat
spanner	гайка ачкычы	gajka aʧkıʧı
hammer	балка	balka
pump	соркыскыч	sorkıskıʧ
screwdriver	бурагыч	buragıʧ

| fire extinguisher | өрт өчүргүч | ørt øtʃyrgytʃ |
| warning triangle | эскертүү үчбурчтук | eskertyy ytʃburtʃtuk |

to stall (vi)	өчүп калуу	øtʃyp kaluu
stall (n)	иштебей калуу	iʃtebej kaluu
to be broken	бузулуп калуу	buzulup kaluu

to overheat (vi)	кайнап кетүү	kajnap ketyy
to be clogged up	тыгылуу	tıgıluu
to freeze up (pipes, etc.)	тоңуп калуу	toŋup kaluu
to burst (vi, ab. tube)	жарылып кетүү	dʒarılıp ketyy

pressure	басым	basım
level	деңгээл	deŋgeel
slack (~ belt)	бош	boʃ

dent	кабырылуу	kabırıluu
knocking noise (engine)	такылдоо	takıldoo
crack	жарака	dʒaraka
scratch	чийилип калуу	tʃijilip kaluu

179. Cars. Road

road	жол	dʒol
motorway	кан жол	kan dʒol
highway	шоссе	ʃosse
direction (way)	багыт	bagıt
distance	аралык	aralık

bridge	көпүрө	køpyrø
car park	унаа токтоочу жай	unaa toktootʃu dʒaj
square	аянт	ajant
road junction	баштан өйдө өткөн жол	baʃtan øjdø øtkøn dʒol
tunnel	тоннель	tonnelʲ

petrol station	май куюучу станция	maj kujuutʃu stantsija
car park	унаа токтоочу жай	unaa toktootʃu dʒaj
petrol pump	колонка	kolonka
auto repair shop	автосервис	avtoservis
to fill up	май куюу	maj kujuu
fuel	күйүүчү май	kyjyytʃy may
jerrycan	канистра	kanistra

asphalt, tarmac	асфальт	asfalʲt
road markings	салынган тамга	salıngan tamga
kerb	бордюр	bordur
crash barrier	тосмо	tosmo
ditch	арык	arık
roadside (shoulder)	жол чети	dʒol tʃeti
lamppost	чырак мамы	tʃırak mamı

to drive (a car)	айдоо	ajdoo
to turn (e.g., ~ left)	бурулуу	buruluu
to make a U-turn	артка кайтуу	artka kajtuu

reverse (~ gear)	артка айдоо	artka ajdoo
to honk (vi)	сигнал берүү	signal beryy
honk (sound)	дабыш сигналы	dabıʃ signalı
to get stuck (in the mud, etc.)	тыгылып калуу	tıgılıp kaluu
to spin the wheels	сүйрөө	syjrøø
to cut, to turn off (vt)	басаңдатуу	basaŋdatuu

speed	ылдамдык	ıldamdık
to exceed the speed limit	ылдамдыктан ашуу	ıldamdıktan aʃuu
to give a ticket	айып салуу	ajıp saluu
traffic lights	светофор	svetofor
driving licence	айдоочу күбөлүгү	ajdootʃu kybølygy

level crossing	кесип өтмө	kesip øtmø
crossroads	кесилиш	kesiliʃ
zebra crossing	жөө жүрүүчүлөр жолу	dʒøø dʒyryytʃylør dʒolu
bend, curve	бурулуш	buruluʃ
pedestrian precinct	жөө жүрүүчүлөр алкагы	dʒøø dʒyryytʃylør alkagı

180. Signs

Highway Code	жол эрежеси	dʒol eredʒesi
road sign (traffic sign)	белги	belgi
overtaking	озуп өтүү	ozup øtyy
curve	бурулуш	buruluʃ
U-turn	артка кайтуу	artka kajtuu
roundabout	айланма кыймыл	ajlanma kıjmıl

No entry	кирүүгө болбойт	kiryygø bolbojt
All vehicles prohibited	жол кыймылы жок	dʒol kıjmılı dʒok
No overtaking	озуп өтүү жок	ozup øtyy dʒok
No parking	унаа токтотуу жок	unaa toktotuu dʒok
No stopping	токтолуу жок	toktoluu dʒok

dangerous curve	кескин бурулуш	keskin buruluʃ
steep descent	тик эңкейиш	tik eŋkejiʃ
one-way traffic	бир тараптуу	bir taraptuu
zebra crossing	жөө жүрүүчүлөр жолу	dʒøø dʒyryytʃylør dʒolu
slippery road	тайгалак жол	tajgalak dʒol
GIVE WAY	жолду бер	dʒoldu ber

PEOPLE. LIFE EVENTS

Life events

181. Holidays. Event

celebration, holiday	майрам	majram
national day	улуттук	uluttuk
public holiday	майрам күнү	majram kyny
to commemorate (vt)	майрамдоо	majramdoo
event (happening)	окуя	okuja
event (organized activity)	иш-чара	iʃ-tʃara
banquet (party)	банкет	banket
reception (formal party)	кабыл алуу	kabıl aluu
feast	той	toj
anniversary	жылдык	dʒıldık
jubilee	юбилей	jʉbilej
to celebrate (vt)	белгилөө	belgilөө
New Year	Жаны жыл	dʒanı dʒıl
Happy New Year!	Жаны Жылыңар менен!	dʒanı dʒılıŋar menen!
Father Christmas	Аяз ата, Санта Клаус	ajaz ata, santa klaus
Christmas	Рождество	rodʒdestvo
Merry Christmas!	Рождество майрамыңыз менен!	rodʒdestvo majramıŋız menen!
Christmas tree	Жаңы жылдык балаты	dʒaŋı dʒıldık balatı
fireworks (fireworks show)	салют	salʉt
wedding	үйлөнүү той	yjlөnyy toy
groom	күйөө	kyjөө
bride	колукту	koluktu
to invite (vt)	чакыруу	tʃakıruu
invitation card	чакыруу	tʃakıruu
guest	конок	konok
to visit (~ your parents, etc.)	конокко баруу	konokko baruu
to meet the guests	конок тосуу	konok tosuu
gift, present	белек	belek
to give (sth as present)	белек берүү	belek beryy
to receive gifts	белек алуу	belek aluu
bouquet (of flowers)	десте	deste
congratulations	куттуктоо	kuttuktoo
to congratulate (vt)	куттуктоо	kuttuktoo

greetings card	куттуктоо ачык каты	kuttuktoo atʃık katı
to send a postcard	ачык катты жөнөтүү	atʃık kattı dʒønøtyy
to get a postcard	ачык катты алуу	atʃık kattı aluu

toast	каалоо тилек	kaaloo tilek
to offer (a drink, etc.)	ооз тийгизүү	ooz tijgizyy
champagne	шампан	ʃampan

to enjoy oneself	көңүл ачуу	køŋyl atʃuu
merriment (gaiety)	көңүлдүүлүк	køŋyldyylyk
joy (emotion)	кубаныч	kubanıtʃ

| dance | бий | bij |
| to dance (vi, vt) | бийлөө | bijløø |

| waltz | вальс | valʲs |
| tango | танго | tango |

182. Funerals. Burial

cemetery	мүрзө	myrzø
grave, tomb	мүрзө	myrzø
cross	крест	krest
gravestone	мүрзө үстүндөгү жазуу	myrzø ystyndøgy dʒazuu
fence	тосмо	tosmo
chapel	кичинекей чиркөө	kitʃinekej tʃirkøø

death	өлүм	ølym
to die (vi)	өлүү	ølyy
the deceased	маркум	markum
mourning	аза	aza

to bury (vt)	көмүү	kømyy
undertakers	ырасым бюросу	ırasım bʉrosu
funeral	сөөк узатуу жана көмүү	søøk uzatuu dʒana kømyy
wreath	гүлчамбар	gyltʃambar
coffin	табыт	tabıt
hearse	катафалк	katafalk
shroud	кепин	kepin

funeral procession	узатуу жүрүшү	uzatuu dʒyryʃy
funerary urn	сөөк күлдүн кутусу	søøk kyldyn kutusu
crematorium	крематорий	krematorij

obituary	некролог	nekrolog
to cry (weep)	ыйлоо	ıjloo
to sob (vi)	боздоп ыйлоо	bozdop ıjloo

183. War. Soldiers

| platoon | взвод | vzvod |
| company | рота | rota |

regiment	полк	polk
army	армия	armija
division	дивизия	divizija

| section, squad | отряд | otrˈad |
| host (army) | куралдуу аскер | kuralduu asker |

| soldier | аскер | asker |
| officer | офицер | ofitser |

private	катардагы жоокер	katardagı dʒooker
sergeant	сержант	serdʒant
lieutenant	лейтенант	lejtenant
captain	капитан	kapitan
major	майор	major
colonel	полковник	polkovnik
general	генерал	general

sailor	деңизчи	deŋiztʃi
captain	капитан	kapitan
boatswain	боцман	botsman

artilleryman	артиллерист	artillerist
paratrooper	десантник	desantnik
pilot	учкуч	utʃkutʃ
navigator	штурман	ʃturman
mechanic	механик	meχanik

pioneer (sapper)	сапёр	sapˈor
parachutist	парашютист	paraʃutist
reconnaissance scout	чалгынчы	tʃalgıntʃı
sniper	көзатар	køzatar

patrol (group)	жол-күзөт	dʒol-kyzøt
to patrol (vt)	жол-күзөткө чыгуу	dʒol-kyzøtkø tʃıguu
sentry, guard	сакчы	saktʃı

| warrior | жоокер | dʒooker |
| patriot | мекенчил | mekentʃil |

| hero | баатыр | baatır |
| heroine | баатыр айым | baatır ajım |

| traitor | чыккынчы | tʃıkkıntʃı |
| to betray (vt) | кыянаттык кылуу | kıjanattık kıluu |

| deserter | качкын | katʃkın |
| to desert (vi) | качуу | katʃuu |

mercenary	жалданма	dʒaldanma
recruit	жаңы алынган аскер	dʒaŋı alıngan asker
volunteer	ыктыярчы	ıktıjartʃı

dead (n)	өлтүрүлгөн	øltyrylgøn
wounded (n)	жарадар	dʒaradar
prisoner of war	туткун	tutkun

163

184. War. Military actions. Part 1

war	согуш	soguʃ
to be at war	согушуу	soguʃuu
civil war	жарандык согуш	dʒarandık soguʃ
treacherously (adv)	жүзү каралык менен кол салуу	dʒyzy karalık menen kol saluu
declaration of war	согушту жарыялоо	soguʃtu dʒarıjaloo
to declare (~ war)	согуш жарыялоо	soguʃ dʒarıjaloo
aggression	агрессия	agressija
to attack (invade)	кол салуу	kol saluu
to invade (vt)	басып алуу	basıp aluu
invader	баскынчы	baskıntʃı
conqueror	басып алуучу	basıp aluutʃu
defence	коргонуу	korgonuu
to defend (a country, etc.)	коргоо	korgoo
to defend (against ...)	коргонуу	korgonuu
enemy	душман	duʃman
foe, adversary	каршылаш	karʃılaʃ
enemy (as adj)	душмандын	duʃmandın
strategy	стратегия	strategija
tactics	тактика	taktika
order	буйрук	bujruk
command (order)	команда	komanda
to order (vt)	буйрук берүү	bujruk beryy
mission	тапшырма	tapʃırma
secret (adj)	жашыруун	dʒaʃıruun
battle	салгылаш	salgılaʃ
battle	согуш	soguʃ
combât	салгылаш	salgılaʃ
attack	чабуул	tʃabuul
charge (assault)	чабуул	tʃabuul
to storm (vt)	чабуул жасоо	tʃabuul dʒasoo
siege (to be under ~)	тегеректеп курчоо	tegerektep kurtʃoo
offensive (n)	чабуул	tʃabuul
to go on the offensive	чабуул салуу	tʃabuul saluu
retreat	чегинүү	tʃeginyy
to retreat (vi)	чегинүү	tʃeginyy
encirclement	курчоо	kurtʃoo
to encircle (vt)	курчоого алуу	kurtʃoogo aluu
bombing (by aircraft)	бомба жаадыруу	bomba dʒaadıruu
to drop a bomb	бомба таштоо	bomba taʃtoo
to bomb (vt)	бомба жаадыруу	bomba dʒaadıruu

explosion	жарылуу	dʒarıluu
shot	атылуу	atıluu
to fire (~ a shot)	атуу	atuu
firing (burst of ~)	атуу	atuu

to aim (to point a weapon)	мээлөө	meeløø
to point (a gun)	мээлөө	meeløø
to hit (the target)	тийүү	tijyy

to sink (~ a ship)	чөктүрүү	tʃøktyryy
hole (in a ship)	тешик	teʃik
to founder, to sink (vi)	суу астына кетүү	suu astına ketyy

front (war ~)	майдан	majdan
evacuation	эвакуация	evakuatsija
to evacuate (vt)	эвакуациялоо	evakuatsijaloo

trench	окоп	okop
barbed wire	тикендүү зым	tikendyy zım
barrier (anti tank ~)	тосмо	tosmo
watchtower	мунара	munara

military hospital	госпиталь	gospitalʲ
to wound (vt)	жарадар кылуу	dʒaradar kıluu
wound	жара	dʒara
wounded (n)	жарадар	dʒaradar
to be wounded	жаракат алуу	dʒarakat aluu
serious (wound)	оор жаракат	oor dʒarakat

185. War. Military actions. Part 2

captivity	туткун	tutkun
to take captive	туткунга алуу	tutkunga aluu
to be held captive	туткунда болуу	tutkunda boluu
to be taken captive	туткунга түшүү	tutkunga tyʃyy

concentration camp	концлагерь	kontslagerʲ
prisoner of war	туткун	tutkun
to escape (vi)	качуу	katʃuu

to betray (vt)	кыянаттык кылуу	kıjanattık kıluu
betrayer	чыккынчы	tʃıkkıntʃı
betrayal	чыккынчылык	tʃıkkıntʃılık

to execute (by firing squad)	атып өлтүрүү	atıp øltyryy
execution (by firing squad)	атып өлтүрүү	atıp øltyryy

equipment (military gear)	аскер кийими	asker kijimi
shoulder board	погон	pogon
gas mask	противогаз	protivogaz

field radio	рация	ratsija
cipher, code	шифр	ʃifr
secrecy	жекеликте сактоо	dʒekelikte saktoo

password	сырсөз	sırsøz
land mine	мина	mina
to mine (road, etc.)	миналоо	minaloo
minefield	мина талаасы	mina talaası

air-raid warning	аба айгайы	aba ajgajı
alarm (alert signal)	айгай	ajgaj
signal	сигнал	signal
signal flare	сигнал ракетасы	signal raketası

headquarters	штаб	ʃtab
reconnaissance	чалгын	tʃalgın
situation	кырдаал	kırdaal
report	рапорт	raport
ambush	буктурма	bukturma
reinforcement (of army)	кошумча күч	koʃumtʃa kytʃ
target	бута	buta
training area	полигон	poligon
military exercise	манервлер	manervler

panic	дүрбөлөң	dyrbøløŋ
devastation	кыйроо	kıjroo
destruction, ruins	кыйроо	kıjroo
to destroy (vt)	кыйратуу	kıjratuu

to survive (vi, vt)	тирүү калуу	tiryy kaluu
to disarm (vt)	куралсыздандыруу	kuralsızdandıruu
to handle (~ a gun)	мамиле кылуу	mamile kıluu

| Attention! | Түз тур! | tyz tur! |
| At ease! | Эркин! | erkin! |

feat, act of courage	эрдик	erdik
oath (vow)	ант	ant
to swear (an oath)	ант берүү	ant beryy

decoration (medal, etc.)	сыйлык	sıjlık
to award (give medal to)	сыйлоо	sıjloo
medal	медаль	medalʲ
order (e.g. ~ of Merit)	орден	orden

victory	жеңиш	dʒeŋiʃ
defeat	жеңилүү	dʒeŋilyy
armistice	жарашуу	dʒaraʃuu

standard (battle flag)	байрак	bajrak
glory (honour, fame)	даңк	daŋk
parade	парад	parad
to march (on parade)	маршта басуу	marʃta basuu

186. Weapons

| weapons | курал | kural |
| firearms | курал жарак | kural dʒarak |

cold weapons (knives, etc.)	атылбас курал	atılbas kural
chemical weapons	химиялык курал	χimijalık kural
nuclear (adj)	ядерлүү	jaderlyy
nuclear weapons	ядерлүү курал	jaderlyy kural

| bomb | бомба | bomba |
| atomic bomb | атом бомбасы | atom bombası |

pistol (gun)	тапанча	tapantʃa
rifle	мылтык	mıltık
submachine gun	автомат	avtomat
machine gun	пулемёт	pulemʲot

muzzle	мылтыктын оозу	mıltıktın oozu
barrel	ствол	stvol
calibre	калибр	kalibr

trigger	курок	kurok
sight (aiming device)	кароолго алуу	karoolgo aluu
magazine	магазин	magazin
butt (shoulder stock)	күндак	kyndak

| hand grenade | граната | granata |
| explosive | жарылуучу зат | dʒarıluutʃu zat |

bullet	ок	ok
cartridge	патрон	patron
charge	дүрмөк	dyrmøk
ammunition	ок-дары	ok-darı

bomber (aircraft)	бомбалоочу	bombalootʃu
fighter	кыйраткыч учак	kıjratkıtʃ utʃak
helicopter	вертолёт	vertolʲot

anti-aircraft gun	зенитка	zenitka
tank	танк	tank
tank gun	замбирек	zambirek

artillery	артиллерия	artillerija
gun (cannon, howitzer)	замбирек	zambirek
to lay (a gun)	мээлөө	meeløø

shell (projectile)	снаряд	snarʲad
mortar bomb	мина	mina
mortar	миномёт	minomʲot
splinter (shell fragment)	сыныктар	sınıktar

submarine	суу астында жүрүүчү кеме	suu astında dʒyryytʃy keme
torpedo	торпеда	torpeda
missile	ракета	raketa

to load (gun)	октоо	oktoo
to shoot (vi)	атуу	atuu
to point at (the cannon)	мээлөө	meeløø
bayonet	найза	najza

rapier	шпага	ʃpaga
sabre (e.g. cavalry ~)	кылыч	kılıtʃ
spear (weapon)	найза	najza
bow	жаа	dʒaa
arrow	жебе	dʒebe
musket	мушкет	muʃket
crossbow	арбалет	arbalet

187. Ancient people

primitive (prehistoric)	алгачкы	algatʃkı
prehistoric (adj)	тарыхтан илгери	tarıχtan ilgeri
ancient (~ civilization)	байыркы	bajırkı

Stone Age	Таш доору	taʃ dooru
Bronze Age	Коло доору	kolo dooru
Ice Age	Муз доору	muz dooru

tribe	уруу	uruu
cannibal	адам жегич	adam dʒegitʃ
hunter	аңчы	aŋtʃı
to hunt (vi, vt)	аңчылык кылуу	aŋtʃılık kıluu
mammoth	мамонт	mamont

cave	үңкүр	yŋkyr
fire	от	ot
campfire	от	ot
cave painting	ташка чегерилген сүрөт	taʃka tʃegerilgen syrøt

tool (e.g. stone axe)	эмгек куралы	emgek kuralı
spear	найза	najza
stone axe	таш балта	taʃ balta
to be at war	согушуу	soguʃuu
to domesticate (vt)	колго көндүрүү	kolgo køndyryy

idol	бут	but
to worship (vt)	сыйынуу	sıjınuu
superstition	жок нерсеге ишенүү	dʒok nersege iʃenyy
rite	ырым-жырым	ırım-dʒırım

| evolution | эволюция | evolʉtsija |
| development | өнүгүү | ønygyy |

| disappearance (extinction) | жок болуу | dʒok boluu |
| to adapt oneself | ылайыкташуу | ılajıktaʃuu |

archaeology	археология	arχeologija
archaeologist	археолог	arχeolog
archaeological (adj)	археологиялык	arχeologijalık

excavation site	казуу жери	kazuu dʒeri
excavations	казуу иштери	kazuu iʃteri
find (object)	табылга	tabılga
fragment	фрагмент	fragment

188. Middle Ages

people (ethnic group)	эл	el
peoples	элдер	elder
tribe	уруу	uruu
tribes	уруулар	uruular
barbarians	варварлар	varvarlar
Gauls	галлдар	galldar
Goths	готтор	gottor
Slavs	славяндар	slavʲandar
Vikings	викингдер	vikingder
Romans	римдиктер	rimdikter
Roman (adj)	римдик	rimdik
Byzantines	византиялыктар	vizantijalıktar
Byzantium	Византия	vizantija
Byzantine (adj)	византиялык	vizantijalık
emperor	император	imperator
leader, chief (tribal ~)	башчы	baʃʧı
powerful (~ king)	кудуреттүү	kudurettyy
king	король, падыша	korolʲ, padıʃa
ruler (sovereign)	башкаруучу	baʃkaruutʃu
knight	рыцарь	rıtsarʲ
feudal lord	феодал	feodal
feudal (adj)	феодалдуу	feodalduu
vassal	вассал	vassal
duke	герцог	gertsog
earl	граф	graf
baron	барон	baron
bishop	епископ	episkop
armour	курал жана соот-шайман	kural dʒana soot-ʃajman
shield	калкан	kalkan
sword	кылыч	kılıtʃ
visor	туулганын бет калканы	tuulganın bet kalkanı
chainmail	зоот	zoot
Crusade	крест астындагы черүү	krest astındagı tʃeryy
crusader	черүүгө чыгуучу	tʃeryygø tʃıguutʃu
territory	аймак	ajmak
to attack (invade)	кол салуу	kol saluu
to conquer (vt)	ээ болуу	ee boluu
to occupy (invade)	басып алуу	basıp aluu
siege (to be under ~)	тегеректеп курчоо	tegerektep kurtʃoo
besieged (adj)	курчалган	kurtʃalgan
to besiege (vt)	курчоого алуу	kurtʃoogo aluu
inquisition	инквизиция	inkvizitsija
inquisitor	инквизитор	inkvizitor

torture	кыйноо	kıjnoo
cruel (adj)	ырайымсыз	ırajımsız
heretic	еретик	eretik
heresy	ересь	eresʲ

seafaring	деңизде сүзүү	deŋizde syzyy
pirate	деңиз каракчысы	deŋiz karakʧısı
piracy	деңиз каракчылыгы	deŋiz karakʧılıgı
boarding (attack)	абордаж	abordadʒ
loot, booty	олжо	oldʒo
treasures	казына	kazına

discovery	ачылыш	atʃılıʃ
to discover (new land, etc.)	таап ачуу	taap atʃuu
expedition	экспедиция	ekspeditsija

musketeer	мушкетёр	muʃketʲor
cardinal	кардинал	kardinal
heraldry	геральдика	geralʲdika
heraldic (adj)	гералдык	geraldık

189. Leader. Chief. Authorities

king	король, падыша	korolʲ, padıʃa
queen	ханыша	χanıʃa
royal (adj)	падышалык	padıʃalık
kingdom	падышалык	padıʃalık

| prince | канзаада | kanzaada |
| princess | ханбийке | χanbijke |

president	президент	prezident
vice-president	вице-президент	vitse-prezident
senator	сенатор	senator

monarch	монарх	monarχ
ruler (sovereign)	башкаруучу	baʃkaruutʃu
dictator	диктатор	diktator
tyrant	зулум	zulum
magnate	магнат	magnat

director	директор	direktor
chief	башчы	baʃʧı
manager (director)	башкаруучу	baʃkaruutʃu
boss	шеф	ʃef
owner	кожоюн	kodʒodʒun

leader	алдыңкы катардагы	aldıŋkı katardagı
head (~ of delegation)	башчы	baʃʧı
authorities	бийликтер	bijlikter
superiors	башчылар	baʃʧılar

| governor | губернатор | gubernator |
| consul | консул | konsul |

diplomat	дипломат	diplomat
mayor	мэр	mer
sheriff	шериф	ʃerif

emperor	император	imperator
tsar, czar	падыша	padıʃa
pharaoh	фараон	faraon
khan	хан	χan

190. Road. Way. Directions

| road | жол | dʒol |
| way (direction) | жол | dʒol |

highway	шоссе	ʃosse
motorway	кан жол	kan dʒol
trunk road	улуттук жол	uluttuk dʒol

| main road | негизги жол | negizgi dʒol |
| dirt road | кыштактар арасындагы жол | kıʃtaktar arasındagı dʒol |

| pathway | чыйыр жол | tʃıjır dʒol |
| footpath (troddenpath) | чыйыр жол | tʃıjır dʒol |

Where?	Каерде?	kaerde?
Where (to)?	Каяка?	kajaka?
From where?	Каяктан?	kajaktan?

| direction (way) | багыт | bagıt |
| to point (~ the way) | көрсөтүү | kørsøtyy |

to the left	солго	solgo
to the right	оңго	oŋgo
straight ahead (adv)	түз	tyz
back (e.g. to turn ~)	артка	artka

bend, curve	бурулуш	buruluʃ
to turn (e.g., ~ left)	бурулуу	buruluu
to make a U-turn	артка кайтуу	artka kajtuu

| to be visible (mountains, castle, etc.) | көрүнүп туруу | kørynyp turuu |
| to appear (come into view) | көрүнүү | kørynyy |

stop, halt (e.g., during a trip)	токтоо	toktoo
to rest, to pause (vi)	эс алуу	es aluu
rest (pause)	эс алуу	es aluu

to lose one's way	адашып кетүү	adaʃıp ketyy
to lead to ... (ab. road)	...га алып баруу	...ga alıp baruu
to came out (e.g., on the highway)	...га чыгуу	...ga tʃıguu
stretch (of road)	жолдун бир бөлүгү	dʒoldun bir bølygy

asphalt	асфальт	asfalʲt
kerb	бордюр	bordʉr
ditch	арык	arık
manhole	люк	lʉk
roadside (shoulder)	жол чети	dʒol ʧeti
pit, pothole	чуңкур	ʧuŋkur

| to go (on foot) | жөө басуу | dʒøø basuu |
| to overtake (vt) | ашып кетүү | aʃıp ketyy |

| step (footstep) | кадам | kadam |
| on foot (adv) | жөө | dʒøø |

to block (road)	тосуу	tosuu
boom gate	шлагбаум	ʃlagbaum
dead end	туюк көчө	tujʉk køʧø

191. Breaking the law. Criminals. Part 1

bandit	ууру-кески	uuru-keski
crime	кылмыш	kılmıʃ
criminal (person)	кылмышкер	kılmıʃker

thief	ууру	uuru
to steal (vi, vt)	уурдоо	uurdoo
stealing (larceny)	уруулук	uruuluk
theft	уурдоо	uurdoo

to kidnap (vt)	ала качуу	ala kaʧuu
kidnapping	ала качуу	ala kaʧuu
kidnapper	ала качуучу	ala kaʧuuʧu

ransom	кутказуу акчасы	kutkazuu akʧası
to demand ransom	кутказуу акчага	kutkazuu akʧaga
	талап коюу	talap kojʉu

to rob (vt)	тоноо	tonoo
robbery	тоноо	tonoo
robber	тоноочу	tonooʧu

to extort (vt)	опузалоо	opuzaloo
extortionist	опузалоочу	opuzalooʧu
extortion	опуза	opuza

to murder, to kill	өлтүрүү	øltyryy
murder	өлтүрүү	øltyryy
murderer	киши өлтүргүч	kiʃi øltyrgyʧ

gunshot	атылуу	atıluu
to fire (~ a shot)	атуу	atuu
to shoot to death	атып салуу	atıp saluu
to shoot (vi)	атуу	atuu
shooting	атышуу	atıʃuu
incident (fight, etc.)	окуя	okuja

fight, brawl	уруш	uruʃ
Help!	Жардамга!	dʒardamga!
victim	жапа чеккен	dʒapa ʧekken

to damage (vt)	зыян келтирүү	zıjan keltiryy
damage	залал	zalal
dead body, corpse	өлүк	ølyk
grave (~ crime)	оор	oor

to attack (vt)	кол салуу	kol saluu
to beat (to hit)	уруу	uruu
to beat up	ур-токмокко алуу	ur-tokmokko aluu
to take (rob of sth)	тартып алуу	tartıp aluu
to stab to death	союп өлтүрүү	sojꭐp øltyryy
to maim (vt)	майып кылуу	majıp kıluu
to wound (vt)	жарадар кылуу	dʒaradar kıluu

blackmail	шантаж кылуу	ʃantadʒ kıluu
to blackmail (vt)	шантаждоо	ʃantadʒdoo
blackmailer	шантажист	ʃantadʒist

protection racket	рэкет	reket
racketeer	рэкетир	reketir
gangster	гангстер	gangster
mafia	мафия	mafija

pickpocket	чөнтөк ууру	ʧøntøk uuru
burglar	бузуп алуучу ууру	buzup aluuʧu uuru
smuggling	контрабанда	kontrabanda
smuggler	контрабандачы	kontrabandaʧı

forgery	окшотуп жасоо	okʃotup dʒasoo
to forge (counterfeit)	жасалмалоо	dʒasalmaloo
fake (forged)	жасалма	dʒasalma

192. Breaking the law. Criminals. Part 2

rape	зордуктоо	zorduktoo
to rape (vt)	зордуктоо	zorduktoo
rapist	зордукчул	zorduktʃul
maniac	маньяк	manjak

prostitute (fem.)	сойку	sojku
prostitution	сойкучулук	sojkuʧuluk
pimp	жак бакты	dʒak baktı

| drug addict | баңги | baŋgi |
| drug dealer | баңгизат сатуучу | baŋgizat satuuʧu |

to blow up (bomb)	жардыруу	dʒardıruu
explosion	жарылуу	dʒarıluu
to set fire	өрттөө	ørttøø
arsonist	өрттөөчү	ørttøøʧy
terrorism	терроризм	terrorizm

| terrorist | террорист | terrorist |
| hostage | заложник | zaloʤnik |

to swindle (deceive)	алдоо	aldoo
swindle, deception	алдамчылык	aldamʧılık
swindler	алдамчы	aldamʧı

to bribe (vt)	сатып алуу	satıp aluu
bribery	сатып алуу	satıp aluu
bribe	пара	para

poison	уу	uu
to poison (vt)	ууландыруу	uulandıruu
to poison oneself	уулануу	uulanuu

| suicide (act) | жанын кыюу | ʤanın kıʤuu |
| suicide (person) | жанын кыйгыч | ʤanın kıjgıʧ |

to threaten (vt)	коркутуу	korkutuu
threat	коркунуч	korkunuʧ
to make an attempt	кол салуу	kol saluu
attempt (attack)	кол салуу	kol saluu

| to steal (a car) | айдап кетүү | ajdap ketyy |
| to hijack (a plane) | ала качуу | ala kaʧuu |

| revenge | кек | kek |
| to avenge (get revenge) | өч алуу | øʧ aluu |

to torture (vt)	кыйноо	kıjnoo
torture	кыйноо	kıjnoo
to torment (vt)	азапка салуу	azapka saluu

pirate	деңиз каракчысы	deŋiz karakʧısı
hooligan	бейбаш	bejbaʃ
armed (adj)	куралданган	kuraldangan
violence	зордук	zorduk
illegal (unlawful)	мыйзамдан тыш	mıjzamdan tıʃ

| spying (espionage) | тыңчылык | tıŋʧılık |
| to spy (vi) | тыңчылык кылуу | tıŋʧılık kıluu |

193. Police. Law. Part 1

| justice | адилеттүү сот | adilettyy sot |
| court (see you in ~) | сот | sot |

judge	сот	sot
jurors	сот калыстары	sot kalıstarı
jury trial	калыстар соту	sot
to judge, to try (vt)	сотко тартуу	sotko tartuu
lawyer, barrister	жактоочу	ʤaktooʧu
defendant	сот жообуна тартылган киши	sot ʤoobuna tartılgan kiʃi

dock	соттуулар отуруучу орун	sottuular oturuutʃu orun
charge	айыптоо	ajıptoo
accused	айыпталуучу	ajıptaluutʃu
sentence	өкүм	økym
to sentence (vt)	өкүм чыгаруу	økym tʃıgaruu
guilty (culprit)	күнөөкөр	kynøøkør
to punish (vt)	жазалоо	dʒazaloo
punishment	жаза	dʒaza
fine (penalty)	айып	ajıp
life imprisonment	өмүр бою	ømyr bojʉ
death penalty	өлүм жазасы	ølym dʒazası
electric chair	электр столу	elektr stolu
gallows	дарга	darga
to execute (vt)	өлүм жазасын аткаруу	ølym dʒazasın atkaruu
execution	өлүм жазасын аткаруу	ølym dʒazasın atkaruu
prison	түрмө	tyrmø
cell	камера	kamera
escort (convoy)	конвой	konvoj
prison officer	түрмө сакчысы	tyrmø saktʃısı
prisoner	камактагы адам	kamaktagı adam
handcuffs	кишен	kiʃen
to handcuff (vt)	кишен кийгизүү	kiʃen kijgizyy
prison break	качуу	katʃuu
to break out (vi)	качуу	katʃuu
to disappear (vi)	жоголуп кетүү	dʒogolup ketyy
to release (from prison)	бошотуу	boʃotuu
amnesty	амнистия	amnistija
police	полиция	politsija
police officer	полиция кызматкери	politsija kızmatkeri
police station	полиция бөлүмү	politsija bølymy
truncheon	резина союлчасы	rezina sojultʃası
megaphone (loudhailer)	керней	kernej
patrol car	жол күзөт машинасы	dʒol kyzøt maʃinası
siren	сирена	sirena
to turn on the siren	сиренаны басуу	sirenanı basuu
siren call	сиренанын боздошу	sirenanın bozdoʃu
crime scene	кылмыш болгон жер	kılmıʃ bolgon dʒer
witness	күбө	kybø
freedom	эркиндик	erkindik
accomplice	шерик	ʃerik
to flee (vi)	из жашыруу	iz dʒaʃıruu
trace (to leave a ~)	из	iz

194. Police. Law. Part 2

search (investigation)	издөө	izdøø
to look for ...	... издөө	... izdøø
suspicion	шек	ʃek
suspicious (e.g., ~ vehicle)	шектүү	ʃektyy
to stop (cause to halt)	токтотуу	toktotuu
to detain (keep in custody)	кармоо	karmoo
case (lawsuit)	иш	iʃ
investigation	териштирүү	teriʃtiryy
detective	аңдуучу	aŋduutʃu
investigator	тергөөчү	tergøøtʃy
hypothesis	жоромол	dʒoromol
motive	себеп	sebep
interrogation	сурак	surak
to interrogate (vt)	суракка алуу	surakka aluu
to question	сураштыруу	suraʃtıruu
(~ neighbors, etc.)		
check (identity ~)	текшерүү	tekʃeryy
round-up (raid)	тегеректөө	tegerektøø
search (~ warrant)	тинтүү	tintyy
chase (pursuit)	куу	kuu
to pursue, to chase	изине түшүү	izine tyʃyy
to track (a criminal)	изине түшүү	izine tyʃyy
arrest	камак	kamak
to arrest (sb)	камакка алуу	kamakka aluu
to catch (thief, etc.)	кармоо	karmoo
capture	колго түшүрүү	kolgo tyʃyryy
document	документ	dokument
proof (evidence)	далил	dalil
to prove (vt)	далилдөө	dalildøø
footprint	из	iz
fingerprints	манжанын изи	mandʒanın izi
piece of evidence	далил	dalil
alibi	алиби	alibi
innocent (not guilty)	бейкүнөө	bejkynøø
injustice	адилетсиздик	adiletsizdik
unjust, unfair (adj)	адилетсиз	adiletsiz
criminal (adj)	кылмыштуу	kılmıʃtuu
to confiscate (vt)	тартып алуу	tartıp aluu
drug (illegal substance)	баңгизат	baŋgizat
weapon, gun	курал	kural
to disarm (vt)	куралсыздандыруу	kuralsızdandıruu
to order (command)	буйрук берүү	bujruk beryy
to disappear (vi)	жоголуп кетүү	dʒogolup ketyy
law	мыйзам	mıjzam
legal, lawful (adj)	мыйзамдуу	mıjzamduu

illegal, illicit (adj)	мыйзамдан тыш	mıjzamdan tıʃ
responsibility (blame)	жоопкерчилик	ʤoopkerʧilik
responsible (adj)	жоопкерчиликтүү	ʤoopkerʧiliktyy

NATURE

The Earth. Part 1

195. Outer space

space	космос	kosmos
space (as adj)	космос	kosmos
outer space	космос мейкиндиги	kosmos mejkindigi
world	дүйнө	dyjnø
universe	аалам	aalam
galaxy	галактика	galaktika
star	жылдыз	dʒɪldɪz
constellation	жылдыздар	dʒɪldɪzdar
planet	планета	planeta
satellite	жолдош	dʒoldoʃ
meteorite	метеорит	meteorit
comet	комета	kometa
asteroid	астероид	asteroid
orbit	орбита	orbita
to revolve (~ around the Earth)	айлануу	ajlanuu
atmosphere	атмосфера	atmosfera
the Sun	күн	kyn
solar system	күн системасы	kyn sistemasɪ
solar eclipse	күндүн тутулушу	kyndyn tutuluʃu
the Earth	Жер	dʒer
the Moon	Ай	aj
Mars	Марс	mars
Venus	Венера	venera
Jupiter	Юпитер	jupiter
Saturn	Сатурн	saturn
Mercury	Меркурий	merkurij
Uranus	Уран	uran
Neptune	Нептун	neptun
Pluto	Плутон	pluton
Milky Way	Саманчынын жолу	samantʃɪnɪn dʒolu
Great Bear (Ursa Major)	Чоң Жетиген	tʃoŋ dʒetigen
North Star	Полярдык Жылдыз	polʲardɪk dʒɪldɪz
Martian	марсианин	marsianin

extraterrestrial (n)	инопланетянин	inoplanet'anin
alien	келгин	kelgin
flying saucer	учуучу табак	utʃuutʃu tabak

spaceship	космос кемеси	kosmos kemesi
space station	орбитадагы станция	orbitadagı stantsija
blast-off	старт	start

engine	кыймылдаткыч	kıjmıldatkıtʃ
nozzle	сопло	soplo
fuel	күйүүчү май	kyjyytʃy may

cockpit, flight deck	кабина	kabina
aerial	антенна	antenna
porthole	иллюминатор	illʉminator
solar panel	күн батареясы	kyn batarejası
spacesuit	скафандр	skafandr

| weightlessness | салмаксыздык | salmaksızdık |
| oxygen | кислород | kislorod |

| docking (in space) | жалгаштыруу | dʒalgaʃtıruu |
| to dock (vi, vt) | жалгаштыруу | dʒalgaʃtıruu |

observatory	обсерватория	observatorija
telescope	телескоп	teleskop
to observe (vt)	байкоо	bajkoo
to explore (vt)	изилдөө	izildøø

196. The Earth

the Earth	Жер	dʒer
the globe (the Earth)	жер шары	dʒer ʃarı
planet	планета	planeta

atmosphere	атмосфера	atmosfera
geography	география	geografija
nature	табийгат	tabijgat

globe (table ~)	глобус	globus
map	карта	karta
atlas	атлас	atlas

Europe	Европа	evropa
Asia	Азия	azija
Africa	Африка	afrika
Australia	Австралия	avstralija

America	Америка	amerika
North America	Северная Америка	severnaja amerika
South America	Южная Америка	jʉdʒnaja amerika

| Antarctica | Антарктида | antarktida |
| the Arctic | Арктика | arktika |

197. Cardinal directions

north	түндүк	tyndyk
to the north	түндүккө	tyndykkø
in the north	түндүктө	tyndyktø
northern (adj)	түндүк	tyndyk
south	түштүк	tyʃtyk
to the south	түштүккө	tyʃtykkø
in the south	түштүктө	tyʃtyktø
southern (adj)	түштүк	tyʃtyk
west	батыш	batıʃ
to the west	батышка	batıʃka
in the west	батышта	batıʃta
western (adj)	батыш	batıʃ
east	чыгыш	ʧıgıʃ
to the east	чыгышка	ʧıgıʃka
in the east	чыгышта	ʧıgıʃta
eastern (adj)	чыгыш	ʧıgıʃ

198. Sea. Ocean

sea	деңиз	deŋiz
ocean	мухит	muχit
gulf (bay)	булуң	buluŋ
straits	кысык	kısık
land (solid ground)	жер	dʒer
continent (mainland)	материк	materik
island	арал	aral
peninsula	жарым арал	dʒarım aral
archipelago	архипелаг	arχipelag
bay, cove	булуң	buluŋ
harbour	гавань	gavanʲ
lagoon	лагуна	laguna
cape	тумшук	tumʃuk
atoll	атолл	atoll
reef	риф	rif
coral	маржан	mardʒan
coral reef	маржан рифи	mardʒan rifi
deep (adj)	терең	tereŋ
depth (deep water)	терेңдик	tereŋdik
abyss	түбү жок	tyby dʒok
trench (e.g. Mariana ~)	ойдуң	ojduŋ
current (Ocean ~)	агым	agım
to surround (bathe)	курчап туруу	kurʧap turuu

| shore | жээк | ʤeek |
| coast | жээк | ʤeek |

flow (flood tide)	суунун көтөрүлүшү	suunun køtørylyʃy
ebb (ebb tide)	суунун тартылуусу	suunun tartıluusu
shoal	тайыздык	tajızdık
bottom (~ of the sea)	суунун түбү	suunun tyby

wave	толкун	tolkun
crest (~ of a wave)	толкундун кыры	tolkundun kırı
spume (sea foam)	көбүк	købyk

storm (sea storm)	бороон чапкын	boroon ʧapkın
hurricane	бороон	boroon
tsunami	цунами	tsunami
calm (dead ~)	штиль	ʃtilʲ
quiet, calm (adj)	тынч	tınʧ

| pole | уюл | ujʉl |
| polar (adj) | полярдык | polʲardık |

latitude	кеңдик	keŋdik
longitude	узундук	uzunduk
parallel	параллель	parallelʲ
equator	экватор	ekvator

sky	асман	asman
horizon	горизонт	gorizont
air	аба	aba

lighthouse	маяк	majak
to dive (vi)	сүңгүү	syŋgyy
to sink (ab. boat)	чөгүп кетүү	ʧøgyp ketyy
treasures	казына	kazına

199. Seas & Oceans names

Atlantic Ocean	Атлантика мухити	atlantika muχiti
Indian Ocean	Индия мухити	indija muχiti
Pacific Ocean	Тынч мухити	tınʧ muχiti
Arctic Ocean	Түндүк Муз мухити	tyndyk muz muχiti

Black Sea	Кара деңиз	kara deŋiz
Red Sea	Кызыл деңиз	kızıl deŋiz
Yellow Sea	Сары деңиз	sarı deŋiz
White Sea	Ак деңиз	ak deŋiz

Caspian Sea	Каспий деңизи	kaspij deŋizi
Dead Sea	Өлүк деңиз	ølyk deŋiz
Mediterranean Sea	Жер Ортолук деңиз	ʤer ortoluk deŋiz

Aegean Sea	Эгей деңизи	egej deŋizi
Adriatic Sea	Адриатика деңизи	adriatika deŋizi
Arabian Sea	Аравия деңизи	aravija deŋizi

Sea of Japan	Япон деңизи	japon deŋizi
Bering Sea	Беринг деңизи	bering deŋizi
South China Sea	Түштүк-Кытай деңизи	tyʃtyk-kıtaj deŋizi
Coral Sea	Маржан деңизи	mardʒan deŋizi
Tasman Sea	Тасман деңизи	tasman deŋizi
Caribbean Sea	Кариб деңизи	karib deŋizi
Barents Sea	Баренц деңизи	barents deŋizi
Kara Sea	Карск деңизи	karsk deŋizi
North Sea	Түндүк деңиз	tyndyk deŋiz
Baltic Sea	Балтика деңизи	baltika deŋizi
Norwegian Sea	Норвегиялык деңизи	norvegijalık deŋizi

200. Mountains

mountain	тоо	too
mountain range	тоо тизмеги	too tizmegi
mountain ridge	тоо кыркалары	too kırkaları
summit, top	чоку	tʃoku
peak	чоку	tʃoku
foot (~ of the mountain)	тоо этеги	too etegi
slope (mountainside)	эңкейиш	eŋkejiʃ
volcano	вулкан	vulkan
active volcano	күйүп жаткан	kyjyp dʒatkan
dormant volcano	өчүп калган вулкан	øtʃyp kalgan vulkan
eruption	атырылып чыгуу	atırılıp tʃıguu
crater	кратер	krater
magma	магма	magma
lava	лава	lava
molten (~ lava)	кызыган	kızıgan
canyon	каньон	kanjon
gorge	капчыгай	kaptʃıgaj
crevice	жарака	dʒaraka
abyss (chasm)	жар	dʒar
pass, col	ашуу	aʃuu
plateau	дөңсөө	døŋsøø
cliff	зоока	zooka
hill	дөбө	døbø
glacier	муз	muz
waterfall	шаркыратма	ʃarkıratma
geyser	гейзер	gejzer
lake	көл	køl
plain	түздүк	tyzdyk
landscape	теребел	terebel
echo	жаңырык	dʒaŋırık

alpinist	альпинист	alʲpinist
rock climber	скалолаз	skalolaz
to conquer (in climbing)	багындыруу	bagındıruu
climb (an easy ~)	тоонун чокусуна чыгуу	toonun tʃokusuna tʃıguu

201. Mountains names

The Alps	Альп тоолору	alʲp tooloru
Mont Blanc	Монблан	monblan
The Pyrenees	Пиреней тоолору	pirenej tooloru

The Carpathians	Карпат тоолору	karpat tooloru
The Ural Mountains	Урал тоолору	ural tooloru
The Caucasus Mountains	Кавказ тоолору	kavkaz tooloru
Mount Elbrus	Эльбрус	elʲbrus

The Altai Mountains	Алтай тоолору	altaj tooloru
The Tian Shan	Тянь-Шань	tjanʲ-ʃanʲ
The Pamir Mountains	Памир тоолору	pamir tooloru
The Himalayas	Гималай тоолору	gimalaj tooloru
Mount Everest	Эверест	everest

| The Andes | Анд тоолору | and tooloru |
| Mount Kilimanjaro | Килиманджаро | kilimandʒaro |

202. Rivers

river	дарыя	darıja
spring (natural source)	булак	bulak
riverbed (river channel)	сай	saj
basin (river valley)	бассейн	bassejn
to flow into ...	... куюу	... kujɵu

| tributary | куйма | kujma |
| bank (of river) | жээк | dʒeek |

current (stream)	агым	agım
downstream (adv)	агым боюнча	agım bojɵntʃa
upstream (adv)	агымга каршы	agımga karʃı

inundation	ташкын	taʃkın
flooding	суу ташкыны	suu taʃkını
to overflow (vi)	дайранын ташышы	dajranın taʃıʃı
to flood (vt)	суу каптоо	suu kaptoo

| shallow (shoal) | тайыздык | tajızdık |
| rapids | босого | bosogo |

dam	тогоон	togoon
canal	канал	kanal
reservoir (artificial lake)	суу сактагыч	suu saktagıtʃ
sluice, lock	шлюз	ʃɵz

water body (pond, etc.)	көлмө	kølmø
swamp (marshland)	саз	saz
bog, marsh	баткак	batkak
whirlpool	айлампа	ajlampa

stream (brook)	суу	suu
drinking (ab. water)	ичилчү суу	itʃiltʃy suu
fresh (~ water)	тузсуз	tuzsuz

| ice | муз | muz |
| to freeze over (ab. river, etc.) | тоңуп калуу | toŋup kaluu |

203. Rivers names

| Seine | Сена | sena |
| Loire | Луара | luara |

Thames	Темза	temza
Rhine	Рейн	rejn
Danube	Дунай	dunaj

Volga	Волга	volga
Don	Дон	don
Lena	Лена	lena

Yellow River	Хуанхэ	χuanχe
Yangtze	Янцзы	jantszı
Mekong	Меконг	mekong
Ganges	Ганг	gang

Nile River	Нил	nil
Congo River	Конго	kongo
Okavango River	Окаванго	okavango
Zambezi River	Замбези	zambezi
Limpopo River	Лимпопо	limpopo
Mississippi River	Миссисипи	missisipi

204. Forest

| forest, wood | токой | tokoj |
| forest (as adj) | токойлуу | tokojluu |

thick forest	чытырман токой	tʃıtırman tokoj
grove	токойчо	tokojtʃo
forest clearing	аянт	ajant

| thicket | бадал | badal |
| scrubland | бадал | badal |

footpath (troddenpath)	чыйыр жол	tʃıjır dʒol
gully	жар	dʒar
tree	дарак	darak

| leaf | жалбырак | ʤalbırak |
| leaves (foliage) | жалбырак | ʤalbırak |

fall of leaves	жалбырак түшүү мезгили	ʤalbırak tyʃyy mezgili
to fall (ab. leaves)	түшүү	tyʃyy
top (of the tree)	чоку	ʧoku

branch	бутак	butak
bough	бутак	butak
bud (on shrub, tree)	бүчүр	byʧyr
needle (of pine tree)	ийне	ijne
fir cone	тобурчак	toburʧak

tree hollow	көңдөй	køŋdøj
nest	уя	uja
burrow (animal hole)	ийин	ijin

trunk	сөңгөк	søŋgøk
root	тамыр	tamır
bark	кыртыш	kırtıʃ
moss	мох	moχ

to uproot (remove trees or tree stumps)	дүмүрүн казуу	dymyryn kazuu
to chop down	кыюу	kıjʉu
to deforest (vt)	токойду кыюу	tokojdu kıjʉu
tree stump	дүмүр	dymyr

campfire	от	ot
forest fire	өрт	ørt
to extinguish (vt)	өчүрүү	øʧyryy

forest ranger	токойчу	tokojʧu
protection	өсүмдүктөрдү коргоо	øsymdyktørdy korgoo
to protect (~ nature)	сактоо	saktoo
poacher	браконьер	brakonjer
steel trap	капкан	kapkan

to pick (mushrooms)	терүү	teryy
to pick (berries)	терүү	teryy
to lose one's way	адашып кетүү	adaʃıp ketyy

205. Natural resources

natural resources	жаратылыш байлыктары	ʤaratılıʃ bajlıktarı
minerals	пайдалуу кендер	pajdaluu kender
deposits	кен	ken
field (e.g. oilfield)	кендүү жер	kendyy ʤer

to mine (extract)	казуу	kazuu
mining (extraction)	казуу	kazuu
ore	кен	ken
mine (e.g. for coal)	шахта	ʃaχta
shaft (mine ~)	шахта	ʃaχta

miner	кенчи	kentʃi
gas (natural ~)	газ	gaz
gas pipeline	газопровод	gazoprovod
oil (petroleum)	мунайзат	munajzat
oil pipeline	мунайзар түтүгү	munajzar tytygy
oil well	мунайзат скважинасы	munajzat skvadʒinası
derrick (tower)	мунайзат мунарасы	munajzat munarası
tanker	танкер	tanker
sand	кум	kum
limestone	акиташ	akitaʃ
gravel	шагыл	ʃagıl
peat	торф	torf
clay	ылай	ılaj
coal	көмүр	kømyr
iron (ore)	темир	temir
gold	алтын	altın
silver	күмүш	kymyʃ
nickel	никель	nikelʲ
copper	жез	dʒez
zinc	цинк	tsınk
manganese	марганец	marganets
mercury	сымап	sımap
lead	коргошун	korgoʃun
mineral	минерал	mineral
crystal	кристалл	kristall
marble	мрамор	mramor
uranium	уран	uran

The Earth. Part 2

206. Weather

weather	аба-ырайы	aba-ırajı
weather forecast	аба-ырайы боюнча маалымат	aba-ırajı bojunʧa maalımat
temperature	температура	temperatura
thermometer	термометр	termometr
barometer	барометр	barometr
humid (adj)	нымдуу	nımduu
humidity	ным	nım
heat (extreme ~)	ысык	ısık
hot (torrid)	кыйын ысык	kıjın ısık
it's hot	ысык	ısık
it's warm	жылуу	dʒıluu
warm (moderately hot)	жылуу	dʒıluu
it's cold	суук	suuk
cold (adj)	суук	suuk
sun	күн	kyn
to shine (vi)	күн тийүү	kyn tijyy
sunny (day)	күн ачык	kyn atʃık
to come up (vi)	чыгуу	ʧıguu
to set (vi)	батуу	batuu
cloud	булут	bulut
cloudy (adj)	булуттуу	buluttuu
rain cloud	булут	bulut
somber (gloomy)	күн бүркөк	kyn byrkøk
rain	жамгыр	dʒamgır
it's raining	жамгыр жаап жатат	dʒamgır dʒaap dʒatat
rainy (~ day, weather)	жаандуу	dʒaanduu
to drizzle (vi)	дыбыратуу	dıbıratuu
pouring rain	нөшөрлөгөн жаан	nøʃørløgøn dʒaan
downpour	нөшөр	nøʃør
heavy (e.g. ~ rain)	катуу	katuu
puddle	көлчүк	køltʃyk
to get wet (in rain)	суу болуу	suu boluu
fog (mist)	туман	tuman
foggy	тумандуу	tumanduu
snow	кар	kar
it's snowing	кар жаап жатат	kar dʒaap dʒatat

207. Severe weather. Natural disasters

thunderstorm	чагылгандуу жаан	ʧagılganduu ʤaan
lightning (~ strike)	чагылган	ʧagılgan
to flash (vi)	жарк этүү	ʤark etyy
thunder	күн күркүрөө	kyn kyrkyrøø
to thunder (vi)	күн күркүрөө	kyn kyrkyrøø
it's thundering	күн күркүрөп жатат	kyn kyrkyrøp ʤatat
hail	мөндүр	møndyr
it's hailing	мөндүр түшүп жатат	møndyr tyʃyp ʤatat
to flood (vt)	суу каптоо	suu kaptoo
flood, inundation	ташкын	taʃkın
earthquake	жер титирөө	ʤer titirøø
tremor, shoke	жердин силкиниши	ʤerdin silkiniʃi
epicentre	эпицентр	epiʦentr
eruption	атырылып чыгуу	atırılıp ʧıguu
lava	лава	lava
twister	куюн	kujʉn
tornado	торнадо	tornado
typhoon	тайфун	tajfun
hurricane	бороон	boroon
storm	бороон чапкын	boroon ʧapkın
tsunami	цунами	ʦunami
cyclone	циклон	ʦıklon
bad weather	жаан-чачындуу күн	ʤaan-ʧaʧınduu kyn
fire (accident)	өрт	ørt
disaster	кыйроо	kıjroo
meteorite	метеорит	meteorit
avalanche	көчкү	køʧky
snowslide	кар көчкүсү	kar køʧkysy
blizzard	кар бороону	kar boroonu
snowstorm	бурганак	burganak

208. Noises. Sounds

silence (quiet)	жымжырттык	ʤımʤırttık
sound	добуш	dobuʃ
noise	ызы-чуу	ızı-ʧuu
to make noise	чуулдоо	ʧuuldoo
noisy (adj)	дуулдаган	duuldagan
loudly (to speak, etc.)	катуу	katuu
loud (voice, etc.)	катуу	katuu
constant (e.g., ~ noise)	үзгүлтүксүз	yzgyltyksyz

cry, shout (n)	кыйкырык	kıjkırık
to cry, to shout (vi)	кыйкыруу	kıjkıruu
whisper	шыбыр	ʃɪbɪr
to whisper (vi, vt)	шыбырап айтуу	ʃɪbɪrap ajtuu

| barking (dog's ~) | үрүү | yryy |
| to bark (vi) | үрүү | yryy |

groan (of pain, etc.)	онтоо	ontoo
to groan (vi)	онтоо	ontoo
cough	жөтөл	dʒøtøl
to cough (vi)	жөтөлүү	dʒøtølyy

whistle	ышкырык	ɪʃkɪrɪk
to whistle (vi)	ышкыруу	ɪʃkɪruu
knock (at the door)	такылдатуу	takıldatuu
to knock (on the door)	такылдатуу	takıldatuu

| to crack (vi) | чыртылдоо | tʃɪrtɪldoo |
| crack (cracking sound) | чыртылдоо | tʃɪrtɪldoo |

siren	сирена	sirena
whistle (factory ~, etc.)	гудок	gudok
to whistle (ab. train)	гудок чалуу	gudok tʃaluu
honk (car horn sound)	сигнал	signal
to honk (vi)	сигнал басуу	signal basuu

209. Winter

winter (n)	кыш	kıʃ
winter (as adj)	кышкы	kıʃkı
in winter	кышында	kıʃɪnda

snow	кар	kar
it's snowing	кар жаап жатат	kar dʒaap dʒatat
snowfall	кар жаашы	kar dʒaaʃɪ
snowdrift	күрткү	kyrtky

snowflake	кар учкуну	kar utʃkunu
snowball	томолоктолгон кар	tomoloktolgon kar
snowman	кар адам	kar adam
icicle	тоңгон муз	toŋgon muz

December	декабрь	dekabrʲ
January	январь	janvarʲ
February	февраль	fevralʲ

| frost (severe ~, freezing cold) | аяз | ajaz |
| frosty (weather, air) | аяздуу | ajazduu |

below zero (adv)	нольдон төмөн	nolʲdon tømøn
first frost	үшүк	yʃyk
hoarfrost	кыроо	kıroo
cold (cold weather)	суук	suuk

189

it's cold	суук	suuk
fur coat	тон	ton
mittens	мээлей	meelej

to fall ill	ооруп калуу	oorup kaluu
cold (illness)	суук тийүү	suuk tijyy
to catch a cold	суук тийгизип алуу	suuk tijgizip aluu

ice	муз	muz
black ice	кара тоңголок	kara toŋgolok
to freeze over (ab. river, etc.)	тоңуп калуу	toŋup kaluu
ice floe	муздун чоң сыныгы	muzdun ʧoŋ sınıgı

skis	чаңгы	ʧaŋgı
skier	чаңычы	ʧaŋıʧı
to ski (vi)	чаңгы тебүү	ʧaŋgı tebyy
to skate (vi)	коньки тебүү	konʲki tebyy

Fauna

210. Mammals. Predators

predator	жырткыч	dʒɪrtkɪtʃ
tiger	жолборс	dʒolbors
lion	арстан	arstan
wolf	карышкыр	karıʃkır
fox	түлкү	tylky
jaguar	ягуар	jaguar
leopard	леопард	leopard
cheetah	гепард	gepard
black panther	пантера	pantera
puma	пума	puma
snow leopard	илбирс	ilbirs
lynx	сүлөөсүн	syløøsyn
coyote	койот	kojot
jackal	чөө	tʃøø
hyena	гиена	giena

211. Wild animals

animal	жаныбар	dʒanıbar
beast (animal)	жапайы жаныбар	dʒapajı dʒanıbar
squirrel	тыйын чычкан	tıjın tʃɪtʃkan
hedgehog	кирпичечен	kirpitʃetʃen
hare	коен	koen
rabbit	коен	koen
badger	кашкулак	kaʃkulak
raccoon	енот	enot
hamster	хомяк	χomʲak
marmot	суур	suur
mole	момолой	momoloj
mouse	чычкан	tʃɪtʃkan
rat	келемиш	kelemiʃ
bat	жарганат	dʒarganat
ermine	арс чычкан	ars tʃɪtʃkan
sable	киш	kiʃ
marten	суусар	suusar
weasel	ласка	laska
mink	норка	norka

beaver	кемчет	kemtʃet
otter	кундуз	kunduz
horse	жылкы	ʤɪlkɪ
moose	багыш	bagɪʃ
deer	бугу	bugu
camel	төө	tøø
bison	бизон	bizon
wisent	зубр	zubr
buffalo	буйвол	bujvol
zebra	зебра	zebra
antelope	антилопа	antilopa
roe deer	элик	elik
fallow deer	лань	lanʲ
chamois	жейрен	ʤejren
wild boar	каман	kaman
whale	кит	kit
seal	тюлень	tʉlenʲ
walrus	морж	morʤ
fur seal	деңиз мышыгы	deŋiz mɪʃɪgɪ
dolphin	дельфин	delʲfin
bear	аюу	ajʉu
polar bear	ак аюу	ak ajʉu
panda	панда	panda
monkey	маймыл	majmɪl
chimpanzee	шимпанзе	ʃimpanze
orangutan	орангутанг	orangutang
gorilla	горилла	gorilla
macaque	макака	makaka
gibbon	гиббон	gibbon
elephant	пил	pil
rhinoceros	керик	kerik
giraffe	жираф	ʤiraf
hippopotamus	бегемот	begemot
kangaroo	кенгуру	kenguru
koala (bear)	коала	koala
mongoose	мангуст	mangust
chinchilla	шиншилла	ʃinʃilla
skunk	скунс	skuns
porcupine	чүткөр	ʧytkør

212. Domestic animals

cat	ургаачы мышык	urgaaʧɪ mɪʃɪk
tomcat	эркек мышык	erkek mɪʃɪk
dog	ит	it

horse	жылкы	ʤılkı
stallion (male horse)	айгыр	ajgır
mare	бээ	bee

cow	уй	uj
bull	бука	buka
ox	өгүз	øgyz

sheep (ewe)	кой	koj
ram	кочкор	koʧkor
goat	эчки	eʧki
billy goat, he-goat	теке	teke

| donkey | эшек | eʃek |
| mule | качыр | kaʧır |

pig	чочко	ʧoʧko
piglet	торопой	toropoj
rabbit	коен	koen

| hen (chicken) | тоок | took |
| cock | короз | koroz |

duck	өрдөк	ørdøk
drake	эркек өрдөк	erkek ørdøk
goose	каз	kaz

| tom turkey, gobbler | күрп | kyrp |
| turkey (hen) | ургаачы күрп | urgaaʧı kyrp |

domestic animals	үй жаныбарлары	yj ʤanıbarları
tame (e.g. ~ hamster)	колго үйрөтүлгөн	kolgo yjrøtylgøn
to tame (vt)	колго үйрөтүү	kolgo yjrøtyy
to breed (vt)	өстүрүү	østyryy

farm	ферма	ferma
poultry	үй канаттулары	yj kanattuları
cattle	мал	mal
herd (cattle)	бада	bada

stable	аткана	atkana
pigsty	чочкокана	ʧoʧkokana
cowshed	уйкана	ujkana
rabbit hutch	коенкана	koenkana
hen house	тоокана	tookana

213. Dogs. Dog breeds

dog	ит	it
sheepdog	овчарка	ovʧarka
German shepherd	немис овчаркасы	nemis ovʧarkası
poodle	пудель	pudelʲ
dachshund	такса	taksa
bulldog	бульдог	bulʲdog

boxer	боксёр	boksʲor
mastiff	мастиф	mastif
Rottweiler	ротвейлер	rotvejler
Doberman	доберман	doberman

basset	бассет	basset
bobtail	бобтейл	bobtejl
Dalmatian	далматинец	dalmatinets
cocker spaniel	кокер-спаниэль	koker-spanielʲ

| Newfoundland | ньюфаундленд | njʉfaundlend |
| Saint Bernard | сенбернар | senbernar |

husky	хаски	χaski
Chow Chow	чау-чау	ʧau-ʧau
spitz	шпиц	ʃpits
pug	мопс	mops

214. Sounds made by animals

barking (n)	үрүү	yryy
to bark (vi)	үрүү	yryy
to miaow (vi)	миёлоо	mijoloo
to purr (vi)	мырылдоо	mırıldoo

to moo (vi)	маароо	maaroo
to bellow (bull)	өкүрүү	økyryy
to growl (vi)	ырылдоо	ırıldoo

howl (n)	уулуу	uuluu
to howl (vi)	уулуу	uuluu
to whine (vi)	кыңшылоо	kıŋʃiloo

to bleat (sheep)	маароо	maaroo
to oink, to grunt (pig)	коркулдоо	korkuldoo
to squeal (vi)	чаңыруу	ʧaŋıruu

to croak (vi)	чардоо	ʧardoo
to buzz (insect)	зыңылдоо	zıŋıldoo
to chirp (crickets, grasshopper)	чырылдоо	ʧırıldoo

215. Young animals

cub	жаныбарлардын баласы	ʤanıbarlardın balası
kitten	мышыктын баласы	mıʃıktın balası
baby mouse	чычкандын баласы	ʧıʧkandın balası
puppy	күчүк	kyʧyk

leveret	бөжөк	bøʤøk
baby rabbit	бөжөк	bøʤøk
wolf cub	бөлтүрүк	bøltyryk

| fox cub | түлкү баласы | tylky balası |
| bear cub | мамалак | mamalak |

lion cub	арстан баласы	arstan balası
tiger cub	жолборс баласы	dʒolbors balası
elephant calf	пилдин баласы	pildin balası

piglet	торопой	toropoj
calf (young cow, bull)	музоо	muzoo
kid (young goat)	улак	ulak
lamb	козу	kozu
fawn (young deer)	бугунун музоосу	bugunun muzoosu
young camel	бото	boto

| snakelet (baby snake) | жылан баласы | dʒılan balası |
| froglet (baby frog) | бака баласы | baka balası |

baby bird	балапан	balapan
chick (of chicken)	балапан	balapan
duckling	өрдөктүн баласы	ørdøktyn balası

216. Birds

bird	куш	kuʃ
pigeon	көгүчкөн	køgytʃkøn
sparrow	таранчы	tarantʃı
tit (great tit)	синица	sinitsa
magpie	сагызган	sagızgan

raven	кузгун	kuzgun
crow	карга	karga
jackdaw	таан	taan
rook	чаркарга	tʃarkarga

duck	өрдөк	ørdøk
goose	каз	kaz
pheasant	кыргоол	kırgool

eagle	бүркүт	byrkyt
hawk	итэлги	itelgi
falcon	шумкар	ʃumkar
vulture	жору	dʒoru
condor (Andean ~)	кондор	kondor

swan	аккуу	akkuu
crane	турна	turna
stork	илегилек	ilegilek

parrot	тотукуш	totukuʃ
hummingbird	колибри	kolibri
peacock	тоос	toos

| ostrich | төө куш | tøø kuʃ |
| heron | көк кытан | køk kıtan |

| flamingo | фламинго | flamingo |
| pelican | биргазан | birgazan |

| nightingale | булбул | bulbul |
| swallow | чабалекей | ʧabalekej |

thrush	таркылдак	tarkıldak
song thrush	сайрагыч таркылдак	sajragıʧ tarkıldak
blackbird	кара таңдай таркылдак	kara taŋdaj tarkıldak

swift	кардыгач	kardıgaʧ
lark	торгой	torgoj
quail	бөдөнө	bødønø

woodpecker	тоңкулдак	toŋkuldak
cuckoo	күкүк	kykyk
owl	мыкый үкү	mıkıj yky
eagle owl	үкү	yky
wood grouse	керең кур	kereŋ kur
black grouse	кара кур	kara kur
partridge	кекилик	kekilik

starling	чыйырчык	ʧıjırʧık
canary	канарейка	kanarejka
hazel grouse	токой чили	tokoj ʧili
chaffinch	зяблик	zʲablik
bullfinch	снегирь	snegirʲ

seagull	ак чардак	ak ʧardak
albatross	альбатрос	alʲbatros
penguin	пингвин	pingvin

217. Birds. Singing and sounds

to sing (vi)	сайроо	sajroo
to call (animal, bird)	кыйкыруу	kıjkıruu
to crow (cock)	"күкирику" деп кыйкыруу	kykiriky' dep kıjkıruu
cock-a-doodle-doo	күкирику	kykiriky

to cluck (hen)	какылдоо	kakıldoo
to caw (crow call)	каркылдоо	karkıldoo
to quack (duck call)	бакылдоо	bakıldoo
to cheep (vi)	чыйылдоо	ʧıjıldoo
to chirp, to twitter	чырылдоо	ʧırıldoo

218. Fish. Marine animals

bream	лещ	leʃʧ
carp	карп	karp
perch	окунь	okunʲ
catfish	жаян	dʒajan
pike	чортон	ʧorton

| salmon | лосось | lososʲ |
| sturgeon | осётр | osʲotr |

herring	сельдь	selʲdʲ
Atlantic salmon	сёмга	sʲomga
mackerel	скумбрия	skumbrija
flatfish	камбала	kambala

zander, pike perch	судак	sudak
cod	треска	treska
tuna	тунец	tunets
trout	форель	forelʲ

eel	угорь	ugorʲ
electric ray	скат	skat
moray eel	мурена	murena
piranha	пиранья	piranja

shark	акула	akula
dolphin	дельфин	delʲfin
whale	кит	kit

crab	краб	krab
jellyfish	медуза	meduza
octopus	сегиз бут	segiz but

starfish	деңиз жылдызы	deŋiz dʒıldızı
sea urchin	деңиз кирписи	deŋiz kirpisi
seahorse	деңиз тайы	deŋiz tajı

oyster	устрица	ustritsa
prawn	креветка	krevetka
lobster	омар	omar
spiny lobster	лангуст	langust

219. Amphibians. Reptiles

| snake | жылан | dʒılan |
| venomous (snake) | уулуу | uuluu |

viper	кара чаар жылан	kara tʃaar dʒılan
cobra	кобра	kobra
python	питон	piton
boa	удав	udav

grass snake	сары жылан	sarı dʒılan
rattle snake	шакылдак жылан	ʃakıldak dʒılan
anaconda	анаконда	anakonda

lizard	кескелдирик	keskeldirik
iguana	игуана	iguana
monitor lizard	эчкемер	etʃkemer
salamander	саламандра	salamandra
chameleon	хамелеон	χameleon

scorpion	чаян	ʧajan
turtle	ташбака	taʃbaka
frog	бака	baka
toad	курбака	kurbaka
crocodile	крокодил	krokodil

220. Insects

insect	курт-кумурска	kurt-kumurska
butterfly	көпөлөк	køpøløk
ant	кумурска	kumurska
fly	чымын	ʧımın
mosquito	чиркей	ʧirkej
beetle	коңуз	koŋuz

wasp	аары	aarı
bee	бал аары	bal aarı
bumblebee	жапан аары	dʒapan aarı
gadfly (botfly)	көгөөн	køgøøn

| spider | жөргөмүш | dʒørgømyʃ |
| spider's web | желе | dʒele |

dragonfly	ийнелик	ijnelik
grasshopper	чегиртке	ʧegirtke
moth (night butterfly)	көпөлөк	køpøløk

cockroach	таракан	tarakan
tick	кене	kene
flea	бүргө	byrgø
midge	майда чымын	majda ʧımın

locust	чегиртке	ʧegirtke
snail	үлүл	ylyl
cricket	кара чегиртке	kara ʧegirtke
firefly	жалтырак коңуз	dʒaltırak koŋuz
ladybird	айланкөчөк	ajlankøʧøk
cockchafer	саратан коңуз	saratan koŋuz

leech	сүлүк	sylyk
caterpillar	каз таман	kaz taman
earthworm	жер курту	dʒer kurtu
larva	курт	kurt

221. Animals. Body parts

beak	тумшук	tumʃuk
wings	канаттар	kanattar
foot (of bird)	чеңгел	ʧeŋgel
feathers (plumage)	куштун жүнү	kuʃtun dʒyny
feather	канат	kanat
crest	көкүлчө	køkylʧø

gills	бакалоор	bakaloor
spawn	балык уругу	balık urugu
larva	курт	kurt
fin	сүзгүч	syzgytʃ
scales (of fish, reptile)	кабырчык	kabırtʃık

fang (canine)	азуу тиш	azuu tiʃ
paw (e.g. cat's ~)	таман	taman
muzzle (snout)	тумшук	tumʃuk
maw (mouth)	ооз	ooz
tail	куйрук	kujruk
whiskers	мурут	murut

| hoof | туяк | tujak |
| horn | мүйүз | myjyz |

carapace	калканч	kalkantʃ
shell (of mollusc)	үлүл кабыгы	ylyl kabıgı
eggshell	кабык	kabık

| animal's hair (pelage) | жүн | dʒyn |
| pelt (hide) | тери | teri |

222. Actions of animals

to fly (vi)	учуу	utʃuu
to fly in circles	айлануу	ajlanuu
to fly away	учуп кетүү	utʃup ketyy
to flap (~ the wings)	канаттарын кагуу	kanattarın kaguu

to peck (vi)	чукуу	tʃukuu
to sit on eggs	жумуртка басуу	dʒumurtka basuu
to hatch out (vi)	жумуртадан чыгуу	dʒumurtkadan tʃıguu
to build a nest	уя токуу	uja tokuu

to slither, to crawl	сойлоо	sojloo
to sting, to bite (insect)	чагуу	tʃaguu
to bite (ab. animal)	каап алуу	kaap aluu

to sniff (vt)	жыттоо	dʒıttoo
to bark (vi)	үрүү	yryy
to hiss (snake)	ышкыруу	ıʃkıruu

| to scare (vt) | коркутуу | korkutuu |
| to attack (vt) | тап берүү | tap beryy |

to gnaw (bone, etc.)	кемирүү	kemiryy
to scratch (with claws)	тытуу	tıtuu
to hide (vi)	жашынуу	dʒaʃınuu

to play (kittens, etc.)	ойноо	ojnoo
to hunt (vi, vt)	аңчылык кылуу	antʃılık kıluu
to hibernate (vi)	чээнге кирүү	tʃeenge kiryy
to go extinct	кырылуу	kırıluu

223. Animals. Habitats

| habitat | жашоо чөйрөсү | ʤaʃoo ʧøjrøsy |
| migration | миграция | migratsija |

mountain	тоо	too
reef	риф	rif
cliff	зоока	zooka

forest	токой	tokoj
jungle	джунгли	ʤungli
savanna	саванна	savanna
tundra	тундра	tundra

steppe	талаа	talaa
desert	чөл	ʧøl
oasis	оазис	oazis

sea	деңиз	deŋiz
lake	көл	køl
ocean	мухит	muχit

swamp (marshland)	саз	saz
freshwater (adj)	тузсуз суулу көл	tuzsuz suulu køl
pond	жасалма көлмө	ʤasalma kølmø
river	дарыя	darıja

den (bear's ~)	ийин	ijin
nest	уя	uja
tree hollow	көндөй	køŋdøj
burrow (animal hole)	ийин	ijin
anthill	кумурска уюгу	kumurska ujʉgu

224. Animal care

| zoo | зоопарк | zoopark |
| nature reserve | корук | koruk |

breeder (cattery, kennel, etc.)	питомник	pitomnik
open-air cage	вольер	voljer
cage	капас	kapas
kennel	иттин кепеси	ittin kepesi

dovecot	кептеркана	kepterkana
aquarium (fish tank)	аквариум	akvarium
dolphinarium	дельфинарий	delʲfinarij

to breed (animals)	багуу	baguu
brood, litter	тукум	tukum
to tame (vt)	колго үйрөтүү	kolgo yjrøtyy
to train (animals)	үйрөтүү	yjrøtyy
feed (fodder, etc.)	жем, чөп	ʤem, ʧøp
to feed (vt)	жем берүү	ʤem beryy

pet shop	зоодукөн	zoodykøn
muzzle (for dog)	тумшук кап	tumʃuk kap
collar (e.g., dog ~)	ит каргысы	it kargısı
name (of animal)	лакап ат	lakap at
pedigree (of dog)	мал теги	mal tegi

225. Animals. Miscellaneous

pack (wolves)	үйүр	yjyr
flock (birds)	топ	top
shoal, school (fish)	топ	top
herd (horses)	үйүр	yjyr

| male (n) | эркек | erkek |
| female (n) | ургаачы | urgaatʃı |

hungry (adj)	ачка	atʃka
wild (adj)	жапайы	dʒapajı
dangerous (adj)	коркунучтуу	korkunutʃtuu

226. Horses

| horse | жылкы | dʒılkı |
| breed (race) | тукум | tukum |

| foal | кулун | kulun |
| mare | бээ | bee |

mustang	мустанг	mustang
pony	пони	poni
draught horse	жүк ташуучу ат	dʒyk taʃuutʃu at

| mane | жал | dʒal |
| tail | куйрук | kujruk |

hoof	туяк	tujak
horseshoe	така	taka
to shoe (vt)	такалоо	takaloo
blacksmith	темирчи	temirtʃi

saddle	ээр	eer
stirrup	үзөнгү	yzøngy
bridle	жүгөн	dʒygøn
reins	тизгин	tizgin
whip (for riding)	камчы	kamtʃı

rider	чабандес	tʃabandes
to saddle up (vt)	ээр токуу	eer tokuu
to mount a horse	ээрге отуруу	eerge oturuu

| gallop | текиреӊ-таскак | tekireŋ-taskak |
| to gallop (vi) | таскактатуу | taskaktatuu |

trot (n)	таскак	taskak
at a trot (adv)	таскактап	taskaktap
to go at a trot	таскактатуу	taskaktatuu
racehorse	күлүк ат	kylyk at
horse racing	ат чабыш	at ʧabıʃ
stable	аткана	atkana
to feed (vt)	жем берүү	dʒem beryy
hay	чөп	ʧøp
to water (animals)	сугаруу	sugaruu
to wash (horse)	тазалоо	tazaloo
horse-drawn cart	араба	araba
to graze (vi)	оттоо	ottoo
to neigh (vi)	кишенөө	kiʃenøø
to kick (to buck)	тээп жиберүү	teep dʒiberyy

Flora

227. Trees

tree	дарак	darak
deciduous (adj)	жалбырактуу	dʒalbıraktuu
coniferous (adj)	ийне жалбырактуулар	ijne dʒalbıraktuular
evergreen (adj)	дайым жашыл	dajım dʒaʃıl
apple tree	алма бак	alma bak
pear tree	алмурут бак	almurut bak
sweet cherry tree	гилас	gilas
sour cherry tree	алча	altʃa
plum tree	кара өрүк	kara øryk
birch	ак кайың	ak kajıŋ
oak	эмен	emen
linden tree	жөкө дарак	dʒøkø darak
aspen	бай терек	baj terek
maple	клён	klʲon
spruce	кара карагай	kara karagaj
pine	карагай	karagaj
larch	лиственница	listvennitsa
fir tree	пихта	piχta
cedar	кедр	kedr
poplar	терек	terek
rowan	четин	tʃetin
willow	мажүрүм тал	madʒyrym tal
alder	ольха	olʲχa
beech	бук	buk
elm	кара жыгач	kara dʒıgatʃ
ash (tree)	ясень	jasenʲ
chestnut	каштан	kaʃtan
magnolia	магнолия	magnolija
palm tree	пальма	palʲma
cypress	кипарис	kiparis
mangrove	мангро дарагы	mangro daragı
baobab	баобаб	baobab
eucalyptus	эвкалипт	evkalipt
sequoia	секвойя	sekvoja

228. Shrubs

bush	бадал	badal
shrub	бадал	badal

| grapevine | жүзүм | dʒyzym |
| vineyard | жүзүмдүк | dʒyzymdyk |

raspberry bush	дан куурай	dan kuuraj
blackcurrant bush	кара карагат	kara karagat
redcurrant bush	кызыл карагат	kızıl karagat
gooseberry bush	крыжовник	krıdʒovnik

acacia	акация	akatsija
barberry	бөрү карагат	børy karagat
jasmine	жасмин	dʒasmin

juniper	кара арча	kara artʃa
rosebush	роза бадалы	roza badalı
dog rose	ит мурун	it murun

229. Mushrooms

mushroom	козу карын	kozu karın
edible mushroom	желе турган козу карын	dʒele turgan kozu karın
poisonous mushroom	уулуу козу карын	uuluu kozu karın
cap (of mushroom)	козу карындын телпеги	kozu karındın telpegi
stipe (of mushroom)	аякчасы	ajaktʃası

cep, penny bun	ак козу карын	ak kozu karın
orange-cap boletus	подосиновик	podosinovik
birch bolete	подберёзовик	podberʲozovik
chanterelle	лисичка	lisitʃka
russula	сыроежка	sıroedʒka

morel	сморчок	smortʃok
fly agaric	мухомор	muxomor
death cap	поганка	poganka

230. Fruits. Berries

| fruit | мөмө-жемиш | mømø-dʒemiʃ |
| fruits | мөмө-жемиш | mømø-dʒemiʃ |

apple	алма	alma
pear	алмурут	almurut
plum	кара өрүк	kara øryk

strawberry (garden ~)	кулпунай	kulpunaj
sour cherry	алча	altʃa
sweet cherry	гилас	gilas
grape	жүзүм	dʒyzym

raspberry	дан куурай	dan kuuraj
blackcurrant	кара карагат	kara karagat
redcurrant	кызыл карагат	kızıl karagat
gooseberry	крыжовник	krıdʒovnik

cranberry	клюква	klukva
orange	апельсин	apel'sin
tangerine	мандарин	mandarin
pineapple	ананас	ananas
banana	банан	banan
date	курма	kurma

lemon	лимон	limon
apricot	өрүк	øryk
peach	шабдаалы	ʃabdaalı
kiwi	киви	kivi
grapefruit	грейпфрут	grejpfrut

berry	жер жемиш	dʒer dʒemiʃ
berries	жер жемиштер	dʒer dʒemiʃter
cowberry	брусника	brusnika
wild strawberry	кызылгат	kızılgat
bilberry	кара моюл	kara mojul

231. Flowers. Plants

| flower | гүл | gyl |
| bouquet (of flowers) | десте | deste |

rose (flower)	роза	roza
tulip	жоогазын	dʒoogazın
carnation	гвоздика	gvozdika
gladiolus	гладиолус	gladiolus

cornflower	ботокөз	botokøz
harebell	коңгуроо гүл	konguroo gyl
dandelion	каакым-кукум	kaakım-kukum
camomile	ромашка	romaʃka

aloe	алоэ	aloe
cactus	кактус	kaktus
rubber plant, ficus	фикус	fikus

lily	лилия	lilija
geranium	герань	geranj
hyacinth	гиацинт	giatsint

mimosa	мимоза	mimoza
narcissus	нарцисс	nartsiss
nasturtium	настурция	nasturtsija

orchid	орхидея	orχideja
peony	пион	pion
violet	бинапша	binapʃa

pansy	алагүл	alagyl
forget-me-not	незабудка	nezabudka
daisy	маргаритка	margaritka
poppy	кызгалдак	kızgaldak

| hemp | наша | naʃa |
| mint | жалбыз | dʒalbız |

| lily of the valley | ландыш | landıʃ |
| snowdrop | байчечекей | bajtʃetʃekej |

nettle	чалкан	tʃalkan
sorrel	ат кулак	at kulak
water lily	чөмүч баш	tʃømytʃ baʃ
fern	папоротник	paporotnik
lichen	лишайник	liʃajnik

conservatory (greenhouse)	күнөскана	kynøskana
lawn	газон	gazon
flowerbed	клумба	klumba

plant	өсүмдүк	øsymdyk
grass	чөп	tʃøp
blade of grass	бир тал чөп	bir tal tʃøp

leaf	жалбырак	dʒalbırak
petal	гүлдүн желекчеси	gyldyn dʒelektʃesi
stem	сабак	sabak
tuber	жемиш тамыр	dʒemiʃ tamır

| young plant (shoot) | өсмө | øsmø |
| thorn | тикен | tiken |

to blossom (vi)	гүлдөө	gyldøø
to fade, to wither	соолуу	sooluu
smell (odour)	жыт	dʒıt
to cut (flowers)	кесүү	kesyy
to pick (a flower)	үзүү	yzyy

232. Cereals, grains

grain	дан	dan
cereal crops	дан эгиндери	dan eginderi
ear (of barley, etc.)	машак	maʃak

wheat	буудай	buudaj
rye	кара буудай	kara buudaj
oats	сулу	sulu
millet	таруу	taruu
barley	арпа	arpa
maize	жүгөрү	dʒygøry
rice	күрүч	kyrytʃ
buckwheat	гречиха	gretʃixa

pea plant	нокот	nokot
kidney bean	төө буурчак	tøø buurtʃak
soya	соя	soja
lentil	жасмык	dʒasmık
beans (pulse crops)	буурчак	buurtʃak

233. Vegetables. Greens

vegetables	жашылча	dʒaʃiltʃa
greens	көк чөп	køk tʃøp
tomato	помидор	pomidor
cucumber	бадыраӊ	badıraŋ
carrot	сабиз	sabiz
potato	картошка	kartoʃka
onion	пияз	pijaz
garlic	сарымсак	sarımsak
cabbage	капуста	kapusta
cauliflower	гүлдүү капуста	gyldyy kapusta
Brussels sprouts	брюссель капустасы	brʉsselʲ kapustası
broccoli	брокколи капустасы	brokkoli kapustası
beetroot	кызылча	kızıltʃa
aubergine	баклажан	bakladʒan
marrow	кабачок	kabatʃok
pumpkin	ашкабак	aʃkabak
turnip	шалгам	ʃalgam
parsley	петрушка	petruʃka
dill	укроп	ukrop
lettuce	салат	salat
celery	сельдерей	selʲderej
asparagus	спаржа	spardʒa
spinach	шпинат	ʃpinat
pea	нокот	nokot
beans	буурчак	buurtʃak
maize	жүгөрү	dʒygøry
kidney bean	төө буурчак	tøø buurtʃak
pepper	калемпир	kalempir
radish	шалгам	ʃalgam
artichoke	артишок	artiʃok

REGIONAL GEOGRAPHY

Countries. Nationalities

234. Western Europe

Europe	Европа	evropa
European Union	Европа Биримдиги	evropa birimdigi
European (n)	европалык	evropalık
European (adj)	европалык	evropalık

Austria	Австрия	avstrija
Austrian (masc.)	австриялык	avstrijalık
Austrian (fem.)	австриялык аял	avstrijalık ajal
Austrian (adj)	австриялык	avstrijalık

Great Britain	Улуу Британия	uluu britanija
England	Англия	anglija
British (masc.)	англичан	anglitʃan
British (fem.)	англичан аял	anglitʃan ajal
English, British (adj)	англиялык	anglijalık

Belgium	Бельгия	belʲgija
Belgian (masc.)	бельгиялык	belʲgijalık
Belgian (fem.)	бельгиялык аял	belʲgijalık ajal
Belgian (adj)	бельгиялык	belʲgijalık

Germany	Германия	germanija
German (masc.)	немис	nemis
German (fem.)	немис аял	nemis ajal
German (adj)	Германиялык	germanijalık

Netherlands	Нидерланддар	niderlanddar
Holland	Голландия	gollandija
Dutch (masc.)	голландиялык	gollandijalık
Dutch (fem.)	голландиялык аял	gollandijalık ajal
Dutch (adj)	голландиялык	gollandijalık

Greece	Греция	gretsija
Greek (masc.)	грек	grek
Greek (fem.)	грек аял	grek ajal
Greek (adj)	грециялык	gretsijalık

Denmark	Дания	danija
Dane (masc.)	даниялык	danijalık
Dane (fem.)	даниялык аял	danijalık ajal
Danish (adj)	даниялык	danijalık
Ireland	Ирландия	irlandija
Irish (masc.)	ирландиялык	irlandijalık

| Irish (fem.) | ирланд аял | irland ajal |
| Irish (adj) | ирландиялык | irlandijalık |

Iceland	Исландия	islandija
Icelander (masc.)	исландиялык	islandijalık
Icelander (fem.)	исланд аял	island ajal
Icelandic (adj)	исландиялык	islandijalık

Spain	Испания	ispanija
Spaniard (masc.)	испаниялык	ispanijalık
Spaniard (fem.)	испан аял	ispan ajal
Spanish (adj)	испаниялык	ispanijalık

Italy	Италия	italija
Italian (masc.)	итальялык	italjalık
Italian (fem.)	итальялык аял	italjalık ajal
Italian (adj)	итальялык	italjalık

Cyprus	Кипр	kipr
Cypriot (masc.)	киприк	kiprlik
Cypriot (fem.)	киприк аял	kiprlik ajal
Cypriot (adj)	киприк	kiprlik

Malta	Мальта	malʲta
Maltese (masc.)	мальталык	malʲtalık
Maltese (fem.)	мальталык аял	malʲtalık ajal
Maltese (adj)	мальталык	malʲtalık

Norway	Норвегия	norvegija
Norwegian (masc.)	норвегиялык	norvegijalık
Norwegian (fem.)	норвегиялык аял	norvegijalık ajal
Norwegian (adj)	норвегиялык	norvegijalık

Portugal	Португалия	portugalija
Portuguese (masc.)	португал	portugal
Portuguese (fem.)	португал аял	portugal ajal
Portuguese (adj)	португалиялык	portugalijalık

Finland	Финляндия	finlʲandija
Finn (masc.)	финн	finn
Finn (fem.)	финн аял	finn ajal
Finnish (adj)	финляндиялык	finlʲandijalık

France	Франция	frantsija
French (masc.)	француз	frantsuz
French (fem.)	француз аял	frantsuz ajal
French (adj)	француз	frantsuz

Sweden	Швеция	ʃvetsija
Swede (masc.)	швед	ʃved
Swede (fem.)	швед аял	ʃved ajal
Swedish (adj)	швед	ʃved

Switzerland	Швейцария	ʃvejtsarija
Swiss (masc.)	швейцариялык	ʃvejtsarijalık
Swiss (fem.)	швейцар аял	ʃvejtsar ajal

Swiss (adj)	швейцариялык	ʃvejtsarijalık
Scotland	Шотландия	ʃotlandija
Scottish (masc.)	шотландиялык	ʃotlandijalık
Scottish (fem.)	шотланд аял	ʃotland ajal
Scottish (adj)	шотландиялык	ʃotlandijalık

Vatican	Ватикан	vatikan
Liechtenstein	Лихтенштейн	liχtenʃtejn
Luxembourg	Люксембург	lʉksemburg
Monaco	Монако	monako

235. Central and Eastern Europe

Albania	Албания	albanija
Albanian (masc.)	албан	alban
Albanian (fem.)	албаниялык аял	albanijalık ajal
Albanian (adj)	албаниялык	albanijalık

Bulgaria	Болгария	bolgarija
Bulgarian (masc.)	болгар	bolgar
Bulgarian (fem.)	болгар аял	bolgar ajal
Bulgarian (adj)	болгар	bolgar

Hungary	Венгрия	vengrija
Hungarian (masc.)	венгр	vengr
Hungarian (fem.)	венгр аял	vengr ajal
Hungarian (adj)	венгр	vengr

Latvia	Латвия	latvija
Latvian (masc.)	латыш	latıʃ
Latvian (fem.)	латыш аял	latıʃ ajal
Latvian (adj)	латвиялык	latvijalık

Lithuania	Литва	litva
Lithuanian (masc.)	литвалык	litvalık
Lithuanian (fem.)	литвалык аял	litvalık ajal
Lithuanian (adj)	литвалык	litvalık

Poland	Польша	polʲʃa
Pole (masc.)	поляк	polʲak
Pole (fem.)	поляк аял	polʲak ajal
Polish (adj)	польшалык	polʲʃalık

Romania	Румыния	rumınija
Romanian (masc.)	румын	rumın
Romanian (fem.)	румын аял	rumın ajal
Romanian (adj)	румын	rumın

Serbia	Сербия	serbija
Serbian (masc.)	серб	serb
Serbian (fem.)	серб аял	serb ajal
Serbian (adj)	сербиялык	serbijalık
Slovakia	Словакия	slovakija
Slovak (masc.)	словак	slovak

| Slovak (fem.) | словак аял | slovak ajal |
| Slovak (adj) | словакиялык | slovakijalık |

Croatia	Хорватия	χorvatija
Croatian (masc.)	хорват	χorvat
Croatian (fem.)	хорват аял	χorvat ajal
Croatian (adj)	хорватиялык	χorvatijalık

Czech Republic	Чехия	ʧeχija
Czech (masc.)	чех	ʧeχ
Czech (fem.)	чех аял	ʧeχ ajal
Czech (adj)	чех	ʧeχ

Estonia	Эстония	estonija
Estonian (masc.)	эстон	eston
Estonian (fem.)	эстон аял	eston ajal
Estonian (adj)	эстониялык	estonijalık

Bosnia and Herzegovina	Босния жана	bosnija ʤana
Macedonia (Republic of ~)	Македония	makedonija
Slovenia	Словения	slovenija
Montenegro	Черногория	ʧernogorija

236. Former USSR countries

Azerbaijan	Азербайжан	azerbajʤan
Azerbaijani (masc.)	азербайжан	azerbajʤan
Azerbaijani (fem.)	азербайжан аял	azerbajʤan ajal
Azerbaijani, Azeri (adj)	азербайжан	azerbajʤan

Armenia	Армения	armenija
Armenian (masc.)	армян	armʲan
Armenian (fem.)	армян аял	armʲan ajal
Armenian (adj)	армениялык	armenijalık

Belarus	Беларусь	belarusʲ
Belarusian (masc.)	белорус	belorus
Belarusian (fem.)	белорус аял	belorus ajal
Belarusian (adj)	белорус	belorus

Georgia	Грузия	gruzija
Georgian (masc.)	грузин	gruzin
Georgian (fem.)	грузин аял	gruzin ajal
Georgian (adj)	грузин	gruzin

Kazakhstan	Казакстан	kazakstan
Kazakh (masc.)	казак	kazak
Kazakh (fem.)	казак аял	kazak ajal
Kazakh (adj)	казак	kazak

Kirghizia	Кыргызстан	kırgızstan
Kirghiz (masc.)	кыргыз	kırgız
Kirghiz (fem.)	кыргыз аял	kırgız ajal
Kirghiz (adj)	кыргыз	kırgız

Moldova, Moldavia	Молдова	moldova
Moldavian (masc.)	молдаван	moldavan
Moldavian (fem.)	молдаван аял	moldavan ajal
Moldavian (adj)	молдовалык	moldovalık

Russia	Россия	rossija
Russian (masc.)	орус	orus
Russian (fem.)	орус аял	orus ajal
Russian (adj)	орус	orus

Tajikistan	Тажикистан	tadʒikistan
Tajik (masc.)	тажик	tadʒik
Tajik (fem.)	тажик аял	tadʒik ajal
Tajik (adj)	тажик	tadʒik

Turkmenistan	Туркмения	turkmenija
Turkmen (masc.)	түркмөн	tyrkmøn
Turkmen (fem.)	түркмөн аял	tyrkmøn ajal
Turkmenian (adj)	түркмөн	tyrkmøn

Uzbekistan	Өзбекистан	øzbekistan
Uzbek (masc.)	өзбек	øzbek
Uzbek (fem.)	өзбек аял	øzbek ajal
Uzbek (adj)	өзбек	øzbek

Ukraine	Украина	ukraina
Ukrainian (masc.)	украин	ukrain
Ukrainian (fem.)	украин аял	ukrain ajal
Ukrainian (adj)	украиналык	ukrainalık

237. Asia

Asia	Азия	azija
Asian (adj)	азиаттык	aziattık

Vietnam	Вьетнам	vjetnam
Vietnamese (masc.)	вьетнамдык	vjetnamdık
Vietnamese (fem.)	вьетнам аял	vjetnam ajal
Vietnamese (adj)	вьетнамдык	vjetnamdık

India	Индия	indija
Indian (masc.)	индиялык	indijalık
Indian (fem.)	индиялык аял	indijalık ajal
Indian (adj)	индиялык	indijalık

Israel	Израиль	izrailʲ
Israeli (masc.)	израильдик	izrailʲdik
Israeli (fem.)	израильдик аял	izrailʲdik ajal
Israeli (adj)	израильдик	izrailʲdik

Jew (n)	еврей	evrej
Jewess (n)	еврей аял	evrej ajal
Jewish (adj)	еврей	evrej
China	Кытай	kıtaj

Chinese (masc.)	кытай	kıtaj
Chinese (fem.)	кытай аял	kıtaj ajal
Chinese (adj)	кытай	kıtaj

Korean (masc.)	кореялык	korejalık
Korean (fem.)	кореялык аял	korejalık ajal
Korean (adj)	кореялык	korejalık

Lebanon	Ливан	livan
Lebanese (masc.)	ливан	livan
Lebanese (fem.)	ливан аял	livan ajal
Lebanese (adj)	ливандык	livandık

Mongolia	Монголия	mongolija
Mongolian (masc.)	монгол	mongol
Mongolian (fem.)	монгол аял	mongol ajal
Mongolian (adj)	монгол	mongol

Malaysia	Малазия	malazija
Malaysian (masc.)	малазиялык	malazijalık
Malaysian (fem.)	малазиялык аял	malazijalık ajal
Malaysian (adj)	малазиялык	malazijalık

Pakistan	Пакистан	pakistan
Pakistani (masc.)	пакистандык	pakistandık
Pakistani (fem.)	пакистан аял	pakistan ajal
Pakistani (adj)	пакистан	pakistan

Saudi Arabia	Сауд Аравиясы	saud aravijası
Arab (masc.)	араб	arab
Arab (fem.)	араб аял	arab ajal
Arab, Arabic (adj)	араб	arab

Thailand	Таиланд	tailand
Thai (masc.)	таиландык	tailandık
Thai (fem.)	таиландык аял	tailandık ajal
Thai (adj)	таиланд	tailand

Taiwan	Тайвань	tajvanʲ
Taiwanese (masc.)	тайвандык	tajvandık
Taiwanese (fem.)	тайвандык аял	tajvandık ajal
Taiwanese (adj)	тайван	tajvan

Turkey	Түркия	tyrkija
Turk (masc.)	түрк	tyrk
Turk (fem.)	түрк аял	tyrk ajal
Turkish (adj)	түрк	tyrk

Japan	Япония	japonija
Japanese (masc.)	япондук	japonduk
Japanese (fem.)	япондук аял	japonduk ajal
Japanese (adj)	япондук	japonduk

Afghanistan	Оогонстан	ooganstan
Bangladesh	Бангладеш	bangladeʃ
Indonesia	Индонезия	indonezija

Jordan	Иордания	iordanija
Iraq	Ирак	irak
Iran	Иран	iran
Cambodia	Камбожа	kambodʒa
Kuwait	Кувейт	kuvejt

Laos	Лаос	laos
Myanmar	Мьянма	mjanma
Nepal	Непал	nepal
United Arab Emirates	Бириккен Араб	birikken arab
	Эмираттары	emirattarı

Syria	Сирия	sirija
Palestine	Палестина	palestina
South Korea	Түштүк Корея	tyʃtyk koreja
North Korea	Түндүк Корея	tundyk koreja

238. North America

United States of America	Америка Кошмо Штаттары	amerika koʃmo ʃtattarı
American (masc.)	америкалык	amerikalık
American (fem.)	америкалык аял	amerikalık ajal
American (adj)	америкалык	amerikalık

Canada	Канада	kanada
Canadian (masc.)	канадалык	kanadalık
Canadian (fem.)	канадалык аял	kanadalık ajal
Canadian (adj)	канадалык	kanadalık

Mexico	Мексика	meksika
Mexican (masc.)	мексикалык	meksikalık
Mexican (fem.)	мексикалык аял	meksikalık ajal
Mexican (adj)	мексикалык	meksikalık

239. Central and South America

Argentina	Аргентина	argentina
Argentinian (masc.)	аргентиналык	argentinalık
Argentinian (fem.)	аргентиналык аял	argentinalık ajal
Argentinian (adj)	аргентиналык	argentinalık

Brazil	Бразилия	brazilija
Brazilian (masc.)	бразилиялык	brazilijalık
Brazilian (fem.)	бразилиялык аял	brazilijalık ajal
Brazilian (adj)	бразилиялык	brazilijalık

Colombia	Колумбия	kolumbija
Colombian (masc.)	колумбиялык	kolumbijalık
Colombian (fem.)	колумбиялык аял	kolumbijalık ajal
Colombian (adj)	колумбиялык	kolumbijalık
Cuba	Куба	kuba

Cuban (masc.)	кубалык	kubalık
Cuban (fem.)	кубалык аял	kubalık ajal
Cuban (adj)	кубалык	kubalık

Chile	Чили	tʃili
Chilean (masc.)	чилилик	tʃililik
Chilean (fem.)	чилилик аял	tʃililik ajal
Chilean (adj)	чилилик	tʃililik

Bolivia	Боливия	bolivija
Venezuela	Венесуэла	venesuela
Paraguay	Парагвай	paragvaj
Peru	Перу	peru
Suriname	Суринам	surinam
Uruguay	Уругвай	urugvaj
Ecuador	Эквадор	ekvador

The Bahamas	Багам аралдары	bagam araldarı
Haiti	Гаити	gaiti
Dominican Republic	Доминикан Республикасы	dominikan respublikası
Panama	Панама	panama
Jamaica	Ямайка	jamajka

240. Africa

Egypt	Египет	egipet
Egyptian (masc.)	египтик мырза	egiptik mırza
Egyptian (fem.)	египтик аял	egiptik ajal
Egyptian (adj)	египеттик	egipettik

Morocco	Марокко	marokko
Moroccan (masc.)	марокколук	marokkoluk
Moroccan (fem.)	марокколук аял	marokkoluk ajal
Moroccan (adj)	марокколук	marokkoluk

Tunisia	Тунис	tunis
Tunisian (masc.)	тунистик	tunistik
Tunisian (fem.)	тунистик аял	tunistik ajal
Tunisian (adj)	тунистик	tunistik

Ghana	Гана	gana
Zanzibar	Занзибар	zanzibar
Kenya	Кения	kenija
Libya	Ливия	livija
Madagascar	Мадагаскар	madagaskar

Namibia	Намибия	namibija
Senegal	Сенегал	senegal
Tanzania	Танзания	tanzanija
South Africa	ТАР	tar

African (masc.)	африкалык	afrikalık
African (fem.)	африкалык аял	afrikalık ajal
African (adj)	африкалык	afrikalık

241. Australia. Oceania

Australia	Австралия	avstralija
Australian (masc.)	австралиялык	avstralijalık
Australian (fem.)	австралиялык аял	avstralijalık ajal
Australian (adj)	австралиялык	avstralijalık
New Zealand	Жаңы Зеландия	dʒaŋı zelandija
New Zealander (masc.)	жаңы зеландиялык	dʒaŋı zelandijalık
New Zealander (fem.)	жаңы зеландиялык аял	dʒaŋı zelandijalık ajal
New Zealand (as adj)	жаңы зеландиялык	dʒaŋı zelandijalık
Tasmania	Тасмания	tasmanija
French Polynesia	Француз Полинезиясы	frantsuz polinezijası

242. Cities

Amsterdam	Амстердам	amsterdam
Ankara	Анкара	ankara
Athens	Афина	afina
Baghdad	Багдад	bagdad
Bangkok	Бангкок	bangkok
Barcelona	Барселона	barselona
Beijing	Пекин	pekin
Beirut	Бейрут	bejrut
Berlin	Берлин	berlin
Mumbai (Bombay)	Бомбей	bombej
Bonn	Бонн	bonn
Bordeaux	Бордо	bordo
Bratislava	Братислава	bratislava
Brussels	Брюссель	brusselʲ
Bucharest	Бухарест	buxarest
Budapest	Будапешт	budapeʃt
Cairo	Каир	kair
Kolkata (Calcutta)	Калькутта	kalʲkutta
Chicago	Чикаго	tʃikago
Copenhagen	Копенгаген	kopengagen
Dar-es-Salaam	Дар-эс-Салам	dar-es-salam
Delhi	Дели	deli
Dubai	Дубай	dubaj
Dublin	Дублин	dublin
Düsseldorf	Дюссельдорф	dusselʲdorf
Florence	Флоренция	florentsija
Frankfurt	Франкфурт	frankfurt
Geneva	Женева	dʒeneva
The Hague	Гаага	gaaga
Hamburg	Гамбург	gamburg

Hanoi	Ханой	χanoj
Havana	Гавана	gavana
Helsinki	Хельсинки	χelʲsinki
Hiroshima	Хиросима	χirosima
Hong Kong	Гонконг	gonkong

Istanbul	Стамбул	stambul
Jerusalem	Иерусалим	ierusalim
Kyiv	Киев	kiev
Kuala Lumpur	Куала-Лумпур	kuala-lumpur
Lisbon	Лиссабон	lissabon
London	Лондон	london
Los Angeles	Лос-Анджелес	los-andʒeles
Lyons	Лион	lion

Madrid	Мадрид	madrid
Marseille	Марсель	marselʲ
Mexico City	Мехико	meχiko
Miami	Майями	majami
Montreal	Монреаль	monrealʲ
Moscow	Москва	moskva
Munich	Мюнхен	munχen

Nairobi	Найроби	najrobi
Naples	Неаполь	neapolʲ
New York	Нью-Йорк	njʉ-jork
Nice	Ницца	nitstsa
Oslo	Осло	oslo
Ottawa	Оттава	ottava

Paris	Париж	paridʒ
Prague	Прага	praga
Rio de Janeiro	Рио-де-Жанейро	rio-de-dʒanejro
Rome	Рим	rim

Saint Petersburg	Санкт-Петербург	sankt-peterburg
Seoul	Сеул	seul
Shanghai	Шанхай	ʃanχaj
Singapore	Сингапур	singapur
Stockholm	Стокгольм	stokgolʲm
Sydney	Сидней	sidnej

Taipei	Тайпей	tajpej
Tokyo	Токио	tokio
Toronto	Торонто	toronto
Venice	Венеция	venetsija
Vienna	Вена	vena
Warsaw	Варшава	varʃava
Washington	Вашингтон	waʃington

243. Politics. Government. Part 1

| politics | саясат | sajasat |
| political (adj) | саясий | sajasij |

politician	саясатчы	sajasattʃı
state (country)	мамлекет	mamleket
citizen	жаран	dʒaran
citizenship	жарандык	dʒarandık

| national emblem | улуттук герб | uluttuk gerb |
| national anthem | мамлекеттик гимн | mamlekettik gimn |

government	өкмөт	økmøt
head of state	мамлекет башчысы	mamleket baʃtʃısı
parliament	парламент	parlament
party	партия	partija

| capitalism | капитализм | kapitalizm |
| capitalist (adj) | капиталистик | kapitalistik |

| socialism | социализм | sotsializm |
| socialist (adj) | социалистик | sotsialistik |

communism	коммунизм	kommunizm
communist (adj)	коммунистик	kommunistik
communist (n)	коммунист	kommunist

democracy	демократия	demokratija
democrat	демократ	demokrat
democratic (adj)	демократиялык	demokratijalık
Democratic party	демократиялык партия	demokratijalık partija

| liberal (n) | либерал | liberal |
| Liberal (adj) | либералдык | liberaldık |

| conservative (n) | консерватор | konservator |
| conservative (adj) | консервативдик | konservativdik |

republic (n)	республика	respublika
republican (n)	республикачы	respublikatʃı
Republican party	республикалык	respublikalık

elections	шайлоо	ʃajloo
to elect (vt)	шайлоо	ʃajloo
elector, voter	шайлоочу	ʃajlootʃu
election campaign	шайлоо кампаниясы	ʃajloo kampanijası

voting (n)	добуш	dobuʃ
to vote (vi)	добуш берүү	dobuʃ beryy
suffrage, right to vote	добуш берүү укугу	dobuʃ beryy ukugu

candidate	талапкер	talapker
to be a candidate	талапкерлигин көрсөтүү	talapkerligin kørsøtyy
campaign	кампания	kampanija

| opposition (as adj) | оппозициялык | oppozitsijalık |
| opposition (n) | оппозиция | oppozitsija |

| visit | визит | vizit |
| official visit | расмий визит | rasmij vizit |

international (adj)	эл аралык	el aralık
negotiations	сүйлөшүүлөр	syjløʃyylør
to negotiate (vi)	сүйлөшүүлөр жүргүзүү	syjløʃyylør ʤyrgyzyy

244. Politics. Government. Part 2

society	коом	koom
constitution	конституция	konstitutsija
power (political control)	бийлик	bijlik
corruption	коррупция	korruptsija

law (justice)	мыйзам	mıjzam
legal (legitimate)	мыйзамдуу	mıjzamduu

justice (fairness)	адилеттик	adilettik
just (fair)	адилеттүү	adilettyy

committee	комитет	komitet
bill (draft law)	мыйзам долбоору	mıjzam dolbooru
budget	бюджет	bʉdʒet
policy	саясат	sajasat
reform	реформа	reforma
radical (adj)	радикалдуу	radikalduu

power (strength, force)	күч	kytʃ
powerful (adj)	кудуреттүү	kudurettyy
supporter	жактоочу	ʤaktooʧu
influence	таасир	taasir

regime (e.g. military ~)	түзүм	tyzym
conflict	чыр-чатак	ʧır-ʧatak
conspiracy (plot)	заговор	zagovor
provocation	айгак аракети	ajgak araketi

to overthrow (regime, etc.)	кулатуу	kulatuu
overthrow (of government)	кулатуу	kulatuu
revolution	ыңкылап	ıŋkılap

coup d'état	төңкөрүш	tøŋkøryʃ
military coup	аскердик төңкөрүш	askerdik tøŋkøryʃ

crisis	каатчылык	kaatʧılık
economic recession	экономикалык төмөндөө	ekonomikalık tømøndøø
demonstrator (protester)	демонстрант	demonstrant
demonstration	демонстрация	demonstratsija
martial law	согуш абалында	soguʃ abalında
military base	аскер базасы	asker bazası

stability	туруктуулук	turuktuuluk
stable (adj)	туруктуу	turuktuu

exploitation	эзүү	ezyy
to exploit (workers)	эзүү	ezyy
racism	расизм	rasizm

racist	расист	rasist
fascism	фашизм	faʃizm
fascist	фашист	faʃist

245. Countries. Miscellaneous

foreigner	чет өлкөлүк	ʧet ølkølyk
foreign (adj)	чет өлкөлүк	ʧet ølkølyk
abroad (in a foreign country)	чет өлкөдө	ʧet ølkødø

emigrant	эмигрант	emigrant
emigration	эмиграция	emigratsija
to emigrate (vi)	башка өлкөгө көчүү	baʃka ølkøgø køʧyy

the West	Батыш	batıʃ
the East	Чыгыш	ʧıgıʃ
the Far East	Алыскы Чыгыш	alıskı ʧıgıʃ
civilization	цивилизация	tsıvilizatsija
humanity (mankind)	адамзат	adamzat
the world (earth)	аалам	aalam
peace	тынчтык	tınʧtık
worldwide (adj)	дүйнөлүк	dyjnølyk

homeland	мекен	meken
people (population)	эл	el
population	калк	kalk
people (a lot of ~)	адамдар	adamdar
nation (people)	улут	ulut
generation	муун	muun
territory (area)	аймак	ajmak
region	регион	region
state (part of a country)	штат	ʃtat

tradition	салт	salt
custom (tradition)	үрп-адат	yrp-adat
ecology	экология	ekologija

Indian (Native American)	индеец	indeets
Gypsy (masc.)	цыган	tsıgan
Gypsy (fem.)	цыган аял	tsıgan ajal
Gypsy (adj)	цыгандык	tsıgandık

empire	империя	imperija
colony	колония	kolonija
slavery	кулчулук	kulʧuluk
invasion	басып келүү	basıp kelyy
famine	ачарчылык	aʧarʧılık

246. Major religious groups. Confessions

| religion | дин | din |
| religious (adj) | диний | dinij |

faith, belief	диний ишеним	dinij iʃenim
to believe (in God)	ишенүү	iʃenyy
believer	динчил	dintʃil

| atheism | атеизм | ateizm |
| atheist | атеист | ateist |

Christianity	Христианчылык	xristiantʃılık
Christian (n)	христиан	xristian
Christian (adj)	христиандык	xristiandık

Catholicism	Католицизм	katolitsizm
Catholic (n)	католик	katolik
Catholic (adj)	католиктер	katolikter

Protestantism	Протестантизм	protestantizm
Protestant Church	Протестанттык чиркөө	protestanttık tʃirkøø
Protestant (n)	протестанттар	protestanttar

Orthodoxy	Православие	pravoslavie
Orthodox Church	Православдык чиркөө	pravoslavdık tʃirkøø
Orthodox (n)	православдык	pravoslavdık

Presbyterianism	Пресвитерианчылык	presviteriantʃılık
Presbyterian Church	Пресвитериандык чиркөө	presviteriandık tʃirkøø
Presbyterian (n)	пресвитериандык	presviteriandık

| Lutheranism | Лютерандык чиркөө | lʉterandık tʃirkøø |
| Lutheran (n) | лютерандык | lʉterandık |

| Baptist Church | Баптизм | baptizm |
| Baptist (n) | баптист | baptist |

| Anglican Church | Англикан чиркөөсү | anglikan tʃirkøøsy |
| Anglican (n) | англикан | anglikan |

| Mormonism | Мормондук | mormonduk |
| Mormon (n) | мормон | mormon |

| Judaism | Иудаизм | iudaizm |
| Jew (n) | иудей | iudej |

| Buddhism | Буддизм | buddizm |
| Buddhist (n) | буддист | buddist |

| Hinduism | Индуизм | induizm |
| Hindu (n) | индуист | induist |

Islam	Ислам	islam
Muslim (n)	мусулман	musulman
Muslim (adj)	мусулмандык	musulmandık

Shiah Islam	Шиизм	ʃiizm
Shiite (n)	шиит	ʃiit
Sunni Islam	Суннизм	sunnizm
Sunnite (n)	суннит	sunnit

247. Religions. Priests

priest	поп	pop
the Pope	Рим Папасы	rim papası
monk, friar	кечил	ketʃil
nun	кечил аял	ketʃil ajal
pastor	пастор	pastor
abbot	аббат	abbat
vicar (parish priest)	викарий	vikarij
bishop	епископ	episkop
cardinal	кардинал	kardinal
preacher	диний үгүттөөчү	dinij ygyttøøtʃy
preaching	үгүт	ygyt
parishioners	чиркөө коомунун мүчөлөрү	tʃirkøø koomunun mytʃøløry
believer	динчил	dintʃil
atheist	атеист	ateist

248. Faith. Christianity. Islam

Adam	Адам ата	adam ata
Eve	Обо эне	obo ene
God	Кудай	kudaj
the Lord	Алла талаа	alla talaa
the Almighty	Кудуреттүү	kudurettyy
sin	күнөө	kynøø
to sin (vi)	күнөө кылуу	kynøø kıluu
sinner (masc.)	күнөөкөр	kynøøkør
sinner (fem.)	күнөөкөр аял	kynøøkør ajal
hell	тозок	tozok
paradise	бейиш	bejiʃ
Jesus	Иса	isa
Jesus Christ	Иса Пайгамбар	isa pajgambar
the Holy Spirit	Ыйык Рух	ıjık ruχ
the Saviour	Куткаруучу	kutkaruutʃu
the Virgin Mary	Бүбү Мариям	byby marijam
the Devil	Шайтан	ʃajtan
devil's (adj)	шайтан	ʃajtan
Satan	Шайтан	ʃajtan
satanic (adj)	шайтандык	ʃajtandık
angel	периште	periʃte
guardian angel	сактагыч периште	saktagıtʃ periʃte

angelic (adj)	периште	periʃte
apostle	апостол	apostol
archangel	архангель	arχangelʲ
the Antichrist	антихрист	antiχrist
Church	Чиркөө	ʧirkøø
Bible	библия	biblija
biblical (adj)	библиялык	biblijalık
Old Testament	Эзелки осуят	ezelki osujat
New Testament	Жаңы осуят	dʒaŋı osujat
Gospel	Евангелие	evangelie
Holy Scripture	Ыйык	ijık
Heaven	Жаннат	dʒannat
Commandment	парз	parz
prophet	пайгамбар	pajgambar
prophecy	пайгамбар сөзү	pajgambar søzy
Allah	Аллах	allaχ
Mohammed	Мухаммед	muχammed
the Koran	Куран	kuran
mosque	мечит	meʧit
mullah	мулла	mulla
prayer	дуба	duba
to pray (vi, vt)	дуба кылуу	duba kıluu
pilgrimage	зыярат	zıjarat
pilgrim	зыяратчы	zıjaratʧı
Mecca	Мекке	mekke
church	чиркөө	ʧirkøø
temple	ибадаткана	ibadatkana
cathedral	чоң чиркөө	ʧoŋ ʧirkøø
Gothic (adj)	готикалуу	gotikaluu
synagogue	синагога	sinagoga
mosque	мечит	meʧit
chapel	кичинекей чиркөө	kiʧinekej ʧirkøø
abbey	аббаттык	abbattık
monastery	монастырь	monastırʲ
bell (church ~s)	коңгуроо	konguroo
bell tower	коңгуроо мунарасы	konguroo munarası
to ring (ab. bells)	коңгуроо кагуу	konguroo kaguu
cross	крест	krest
cupola (roof)	купол	kupol
icon	икона	ikona
soul	жан	dʒan
fate (destiny)	тагдыр	tagdır
evil (n)	жамандык	dʒamandık
good (n)	жакшылык	dʒakʃılık
vampire	кан соргуч	kan sorguʧ

witch (evil ~)	жез тумшук	dʒez tumʃuk
demon	шайтан	ʃajtan
spirit	арбак	arbak

| redemption (giving us ~) | күнөөнү жуу | kynøøny dʒuu |
| to redeem (vt) | күнөөнү жуу | kynøøny dʒuu |

church service, mass	ибадат	ibadat
to say mass	ибадат кылуу	ibadat kıluu
confession	сыр төгүү	sır tøgyy
to confess (vi)	сыр төгүү	sır tøgyy

saint (n)	ыйык	ıjık
sacred (holy)	ыйык	ıjık
holy water	ыйык суу	ıjık suu

ritual (n)	диний ырым-жырым	dinij ırım-dʒırım
ritual (adj)	диний ырым-жырым	dinij ırım-dʒırım
sacrifice	курмандык	kurmandık

superstition	ырым-жырым	ırım-dʒırım
superstitious (adj)	ырымчыл	ırımtʃıl
afterlife	тиги дүйнө	tigi dyjnø
eternal life	түбөлүк жашоо	tybølyk dʒaʃoo

MISCELLANEOUS

249. Various useful words

background (green ~)	фон	fon
balance (of situation)	теңдем	teŋdem
barrier (obstacle)	тоскоолдук	toskoolduk
base (basis)	түп	typ
beginning	башталыш	baʃtalıʃ
category	категория	kategorija
cause (reason)	себеп	sebep
choice	тандоо	tandoo
coincidence	дал келгендик	dal kelgendik
comfortable (~ chair)	ыңгайлуу	ıngajluu
comparison	салыштырма	salıʃtırma
compensation	ордун толтуруу	ordun tolturuu
degree (extent, amount)	даража	daradʒa
development	өнүгүү	ønygyy
difference	айырма	ajırma
effect (e.g. of drugs)	таасир	taasir
effort (exertion)	күч аракет	kytʃ araket
element	элемент	element
end (finish)	бүтүү	bytyy
example (illustration)	мисал	misal
fact	далил	dalil
frequent (adj)	бат-бат	bat-bat
growth (development)	өсүү	øsyy
help	жардам	dʒardam
ideal	идеал	ideal
kind (sort, type)	түр	tyr
labyrinth	лабиринт	labirint
mistake, error	ката	kata
moment	учур	utʃur
object (thing)	объект	obʰjekt
obstacle	тоскоолдук	toskoolduk
original (original copy)	түпнуска	typnuska
part (~ of sth)	бөлүгү	bølygy
particle, small part	бөлүкчө	bølyktʃø
pause (break)	тыныгуу	tınıguu
position	позиция	pozitsija
principle	усул	usul
problem	көйгөй	køjgøj
process	жараян	dʒarajan

progress	өнүгүү	ønygyy
property (quality)	касиет	kasiet
reaction	реакция	reaktsija
risk	тобокел	tobokel

secret	сыр	sır
series	катар	katar
shape (outer form)	тариз	tariz
situation	кырдаал	kırdaal
solution	чечүү	tʃetʃyy

standard (adj)	стандарттуу	standarttuu
standard (level of quality)	стандарт	standart
stop (pause)	токтотуу	toktotuu
style	стиль	stilʲ

system	тутум	tutum
table (chart)	жадыбал	dʒadıbal
tempo, rate	темп	temp
term (word, expression)	атоо	atoo
thing (object, item)	буюм	bujum

truth (e.g. moment of ~)	чындык	tʃındık
turn (please wait your ~)	кезек	kezek
type (sort, kind)	түр	tyr
urgent (adj)	шашылыш	ʃaʃılıʃ
urgently	шашылыш	ʃaʃılıʃ

utility (usefulness)	пайда	pajda
variant (alternative)	вариант	variant
way (means, method)	ыкма	ıkma
zone	алкак	alkak

250. Modifiers. Adjectives. Part 1

additional (adj)	кошумча	koʃumtʃa
ancient (~ civilization)	байыркы	bajırkı
artificial (adj)	жасалма	dʒasalma
back, rear (adj)	арткы	artkı
bad (adj)	жаман	dʒaman

beautiful (~ palace)	укмуштай	ukmuʃtaj
beautiful (person)	сулуу	suluu
big (in size)	чоң	tʃoŋ
bitter (taste)	ачуу	atʃuu
blind (sightless)	сокур	sokur

calm, quiet (adj)	тынч	tıntʃ
careless (negligent)	шалаакы	ʃalaakı
caring (~ father)	камкор	kamkor
central (adj)	борбордук	borborduk

| cheap (low-priced) | арзан | arzan |
| cheerful (adj) | куунак | kuunak |

children's (adj)	балдар	baldar
civil (~ law)	жарандык	dʒarandık
clandestine (secret)	жашыруун	dʒaʃıruun

clean (free from dirt)	таза	taza
clear (explanation, etc.)	түшүнүктүү	tyʃynyktyy
clever (intelligent)	акылдуу	akılduu
close (near in space)	жакын	dʒakın
closed (adj)	жабык	dʒabık

cloudless (sky)	булутсуз	bulutsuz
cold (drink, weather)	муздак, суук	muzdak, suuk
compatible (adj)	сыйышкыч	sıjıʃkıtʃ
contented (satisfied)	курсант	kursant
continuous (uninterrupted)	үзгүлтүксүз	yzgyltyksyz

cool (weather)	салкын	salkın
dangerous (adj)	коркунучтуу	korkunutʃtuu
dark (room)	караңгы	karaŋgı
dead (not alive)	өлүк	ølyk
dense (fog, smoke)	коюу	kojuu

destitute (extremely poor)	кедей	kedej
different (not the same)	ар кандай	ar kandaj
difficult (decision)	оор	oor
difficult (problem, task)	кыйын	kıjın
dim, faint (light)	күңүрт	kyŋyrt

dirty (not clean)	кир	kir
distant (in space)	алыс	alıs
dry (clothes, etc.)	кургак	kurgak
easy (not difficult)	женил	dʒenil

empty (glass, room)	бош	boʃ
even (e.g. ~ surface)	тегиз	tegiz
exact (amount)	так	tak
excellent (adj)	мыкты	mıktı
excessive (adj)	ашыкча	aʃıktʃa

expensive (adj)	кымбат	kımbat
exterior (adj)	тышкы	tıʃkı
far (the ~ East)	алыс	alıs
fast (quick)	тез	tez
fatty (food)	майлуу	majluu

fertile (land, soil)	түшүмдүү	tyʃymdyy
flat (~ panel display)	жалпак	dʒalpak
foreign (adj)	чет өлкөлүк	tʃet ølkølyk
fragile (china, glass)	морт	mort

free (at no cost)	акысыз	akısız
free (unrestricted)	эркин	erkin
fresh (~ water)	тузсуз	tuzsuz
fresh (e.g. ~ bread)	жаңы	dʒaŋı
frozen (food)	тоңдурулган	toŋdurulgan
full (completely filled)	толо	tolo

gloomy (house, forecast)	караңгы	karaŋgı
good (book, etc.)	жакшы	dʒakʃı
good, kind (kindhearted)	боорукер	booruker
grateful (adj)	ыраазы	ıraazı

happy (adj)	бактылуу	baktıluu
hard (not soft)	катуу	katuu
heavy (in weight)	оор	oor
hostile (adj)	кастык	kastık
hot (adj)	ысык	ısık

huge (adj)	зор	zor
humid (adj)	нымдуу	nımduu
hungry (adj)	ачка	atʃka
ill (sick, unwell)	оорулуу	ooruluu
immobile (adj)	кыймылсыз	kıjmılsız

important (adj)	маанилүү	maanilyy
impossible (adj)	мүмкүн эмес	mymkyn emes
incomprehensible	түшүнүксүз	tyʃynyksyz
indispensable (adj)	керектүү	kerektyy
inexperienced (adj)	тажрыйбасыз	tadʒrıjbasız

insignificant (adj)	арзыбаган	arzıbagan
interior (adj)	ички	itʃki
joint (~ decision)	бирге	birge
last (e.g. ~ week)	мурунку	murunku

last (final)	акыркы	akırkı
left (e.g. ~ side)	сол	sol
legal (legitimate)	мыйзамдуу	mıjzamduu
light (in weight)	жеңил	dʒeŋil
light (pale color)	ачык	atʃık

limited (adj)	чектелген	tʃektelgen
liquid (fluid)	суюк	sujuk
long (e.g. ~ hair)	узак	uzak
loud (voice, etc.)	катуу	katuu
low (voice)	акырын	akırın

251. Modifiers. Adjectives. Part 2

main (principal)	негизги	negizgi
matt, matte	жалтырабаган	dʒaltırabagan
meticulous (job)	тыкан	tıkan
mysterious (adj)	сырдуу	sırduu
narrow (street, etc.)	кууш	kuuʃ

native (~ country)	өз	øz
nearby (adj)	жакынкы	dʒakınkı
needed (necessary)	керектүү	kerektyy
negative (~ response)	терс	ters
neighbouring (adj)	коңшу	konʃu
nervous (adj)	тынчы кеткен	tıntʃı ketken

new (adj)	жаңы	dʒaŋı
next (e.g. ~ week)	кийинки	kijinki
nice (agreeable)	сүйкүмдүү	syjkymdyy

pleasant (voice)	жагымдуу	dʒagımduu
normal (adj)	кадимки	kadimki
not big (adj)	анчейин эмес	antʃejin emes
not difficult (adj)	анчейин оор эмес	antʃejin oor emes

obligatory (adj)	милдеттүү	mildettyy
old (house)	эски	eski
open (adj)	ачык	atʃık
opposite (adj)	карама-каршы	karama-karʃı
ordinary (usual)	жөнөкөй	dʒønøkøj

original (unusual)	бөтөнчө	bøtøntʃø
past (recent)	өтүп кеткен	øtyp ketken
permanent (adj)	туруктуу	turuktuu
personal (adj)	жекелик	dʒekelik
polite (adj)	сылык	sılık

poor (not rich)	кедей	kedej
possible (adj)	мүмкүн	mymkyn
present (current)	учурда	utʃurda
previous (adj)	мурунку	murunku
principal (main)	негизги	negizgi

private (~ jet)	жеке	dʒeke
probable (adj)	ыктымал	ıktımal
prolonged (e.g. ~ applause)	узак	uzak
public (open to all)	коомдук	koomduk

punctual (person)	так	tak
quiet (tranquil)	тынч	tıntʃ
rare (adj)	сейрек	sejrek
raw (uncooked)	чийки	tʃijki

right (not left)	оң	oŋ
right, correct (adj)	туура	tuura
ripe (fruit)	бышкан	bıʃkan
risky (adj)	тобокелдүү	tobokeldyy
sad (~ look)	кайгылуу	kajgıluu

sad (depressing)	муңдуу	muŋduu
safe (not dangerous)	коопсуз	koopsuz
salty (food)	туздуу	tuzduu
satisfied (customer)	ыраазы	ıraazı

second hand (adj)	мурдагы	murdagı
shallow (water)	тайыз	tajız
sharp (blade, etc.)	курч	kurtʃ
short (in length)	кыска	kıska

short, short-lived (adj)	кыска мөөнөттүү	kıska møønøttyy
short-sighted (adj)	алыстан көрө албоо	alıstan kørø alboo
significant (notable)	маанилүү	maanilyy

| similar (adj) | окшош | okʃoʃ |
| simple (easy) | жөнөкөй | dʒønøkøj |

skinny	арык	arık
small (in size)	кичине	kitʃine
smooth (surface)	жылма	dʒılma
soft (~ toys)	жумшак	dʒumʃak
solid (~ wall)	бекем	bekem

sour (flavour, taste)	кычкыл	kıtʃkıl
spacious (house, etc.)	кең	keŋ
special (adj)	атайын	atajın
straight (line, road)	түз	tyz
strong (person)	күчтүү	kytʃtyy

stupid (foolish)	акылсыз	akılsız
suitable (e.g. ~ for drinking)	жарактуу	dʒaraktuu
sunny (day)	күн ачык	kyn atʃık
superb, perfect (adj)	сонун	sonun
swarthy (adj)	кара тору	kara toru

sweet (sugary)	таттуу	tattuu
tanned (adj)	күнгө күйгөн	kyngø kyjgøn
tasty (delicious)	даамдуу	daamduu
tender (affectionate)	назик	nazik

the highest (adj)	жогорку	dʒogorku
the most important	эң маанилүү	eŋ maanilyy
the nearest	эң жакынкы	eŋ dʒakınkı
the same, equal (adj)	окшош	okʃoʃ

thick (e.g. ~ fog)	коюу	kojuu
thick (wall, slice)	калың	kalıŋ
thin (person)	арык	arık
tight (~ shoes)	тар	tar
tired (exhausted)	чарчаңкы	tʃartʃaŋkı

tiring (adj)	чарчатуучу	tʃartʃatuutʃu
transparent (adj)	тунук	tunuk
unclear (adj)	ачык эмес	atʃık emes
unique (exceptional)	окшоштугу жок	okʃoʃtugu dʒok
various (adj)	түрлүү	tyrlyy

warm (moderately hot)	жылуу	dʒıluu
wet (e.g. ~ clothes)	суу	suu
whole (entire, complete)	бүтүн	bytyn
wide (e.g. ~ road)	кең	keŋ
young (adj)	жаш	dʒaʃ

MAIN 500 VERBS

252. Verbs A-C

to accompany (vt)	жолдоо	dʒoldoo
to accuse (vt)	айыптоо	ajıptoo
to acknowledge (admit)	моюнга алуу	mojʉnga aluu
to act (take action)	аракет кылуу	araket kıluu
to add (supplement)	кошуу	koʃuu
to address (speak to)	кайрылуу	kajrıluu
to admire (vi)	суктануу	suktanuu
to advertise (vt)	жарнамалоо	dʒarnamaloo
to advise (vt)	кеңеш берүү	keŋeʃ beryy
to affirm (assert)	сөзүнө туруу	søzynø turuu
to agree (say yes)	макул болуу	makul boluu
to aim (to point a weapon)	мээлөө	meeløø
to allow (sb to do sth)	уруксат берүү	uruksat beryy
to amputate (vt)	кесип таштоо	kesip taʃtoo
to answer (vi, vt)	жооп берүү	dʒoop beryy
to apologize (vi)	кечирим суроо	ketʃirim suroo
to appear (come into view)	көрүнүү	kørynyy
to applaud (vi, vt)	кол чабуу	kol tʃabuu
to appoint (assign)	дайындоо	dajındoo
to approach (come closer)	жакындоо	dʒakındoo
to arrive (ab. train)	келүү	kelyy
to ask (~ sb to do sth)	суроо	suroo
to aspire to ...	умтулуу	umtuluu
to assist (help)	жардам берүү	dʒardam beryy
to attack (mil.)	кол салуу	kol saluu
to attain (objectives)	жетүү	dʒetyy
to avenge (get revenge)	өч алуу	øtʃ aluu
to avoid (danger, task)	качуу	katʃuu
to award (give medal to)	сыйлоо	sıjloo
to battle (vi)	согушуу	soguʃuu
to be (vi)	болуу	boluu
to be a cause of ...	... себеп болуу	... sebep boluu
to be afraid	коркуу	korkuu
to be angry (with ...)	ачуулануу	atʃuulanuu
to be at war	согушуу	soguʃuu
to be based (on ...)	негиз кылуу	negiz kıluu
to be bored	зеригүү	zerigyy

to be convinced	катуу ишенген	katuu iʃengen
to be enough	жетиштүү болуу	dʒetiʃtyy boluu
to be envious	көрө албоо	kørø alboo
to be indignant	нааразы болуу	naarazı boluu
to be interested in ...	... кызыгуу	... kızıguu
to be lost in thought	ойлонуу	ojlonuu
to be lying (~ on the table)	жатуу	dʒatuu
to be needed	керек болуу	kerek boluu
to be perplexed (puzzled)	башы маң болуу	baʃı maŋ boluu
to be preserved	сакталуу	saktaluu
to be required	зарыл болуу	zarıl boluu
to be surprised	таң калуу	taŋ kaluu
to be worried	сарсанаа болуу	sarsanaa boluu
to beat (to hit)	уруу	uruu
to become (e.g. ~ old)	болуу	boluu
to behave (vi)	алып жүрүү	alıp dʒyryy
to believe (think)	ишенүү	iʃenyy
to belong to ...	таандык болуу	taandık boluu
to berth (moor)	келип токтоо	kelip toktoo
to blind (other drivers)	көздү уялтуу	køzdy ujaltuu
to blow (wind)	үйлөө	yjløø
to blush (vi)	кызаруу	kızaruu
to boast (vi)	мактануу	maktanuu
to borrow (money)	карызга акча алуу	karızga aktʃa aluu
to break (branch, toy, etc.)	сындыруу	sındıruu
to breathe (vi)	дем алуу	dem aluu
to bring (sth)	алып келүү	alıp kelyy
to burn (paper, logs)	күйгүзүү	kyjgyzyy
to buy (purchase)	сатып алуу	satıp aluu
to call (~ for help)	чакыруу	tʃakıruu
to call (yell for sb)	чакыруу	tʃakıruu
to calm down (vt)	тынчтандыруу	tıntʃtandıruu
can (v aux)	жасай алуу	dʒasaj aluu
to cancel (call off)	жокко чыгаруу	dʒokko tʃıgaruu
to cast off (of a boat or ship)	жөнөө	dʒønøø
to catch (e.g. ~ a ball)	кармоо	karmoo
to change (~ one's opinion)	өзгөртүү	øzgørtyy
to change (exchange)	өзгөртүү	øzgørtyy
to charm (vt)	өзүнө тартуу	øzynø tartuu
to choose (select)	тандоо	tandoo
to chop off (with an axe)	чаап таштоо	tʃaap taʃtoo
to clean (e.g. kettle from scale)	тазалоо	tazaloo
to clean (shoes, etc.)	тазалоо	tazaloo
to clean up (tidy)	жыйнаштыруу	dʒıjnaʃtıruu
to close (vt)	жабуу	dʒabuu

to comb one's hair	тарануу	taranuu
to come down (the stairs)	ылдый түшүү	ıldıj tyʃyy
to come out (book)	жарык көрүү	dʒarık køryy
to compare (vt)	салыштыруу	salıʃtıruu
to compensate (vt)	ордун толтуруу	ordun tolturuu
to compete (vi)	атаандашуу	ataandaʃuu
to compile (~ a list)	түзүү	tyzyy
to complain (vi, vt)	арыздануу	arızdanuu
to complicate (vt)	татаалдантуу	tataaldantuu
to compose (music, etc.)	чыгаруу	tʃıgaruu
to compromise (reputation)	беделин түшүрүү	bedelin tyʃyryy
to concentrate (vi)	оюн топтоо	ojʉn toptoo
to confess (criminal)	моюнга алуу	mojʉnga aluu
to confuse (mix up)	адаштыруу	adaʃtıruu
to congratulate (vt)	куттуктоо	kuttuktoo
to consult (doctor, expert)	кеңешүү	keŋeʃyy
to continue (~ to do sth)	улантуу	ulantuu
to control (vt)	көзөмөлдөө	køzømøldøø
to convince (vt)	ишендирүү	iʃendiryy
to cooperate (vi)	кызматташуу	kızmattaʃuu
to coordinate (vt)	ыңтайга келтирүү	ıŋtajga keltiryy
to correct (an error)	түзөтүү	tyzøtyy
to cost (vt)	туруу	turuu
to count (money, etc.)	эсептөө	eseptøø
to count on ...	... ишенүү	... iʃenyy
to crack (ceiling, wall)	жарака кетүү	dʒaraka ketyy
to create (vt)	жаратуу	dʒaratuu
to crush, to squash (~ a bug)	тебелөө	tebeløø
to cry (weep)	ыйлоо	ıjloo
to cut off (with a knife)	кесип алуу	kesip aluu

253. Verbs D-G

to dare (~ to do sth)	батынып баруу	batınıp baruu
to date from ...	күн боюнча	kyn bojʉntʃa
to deceive (vi, vt)	алдоо	aldoo
to decide (~ to do sth)	чечүү	tʃetʃyy
to decorate (tree, street)	кооздоо	koozdoo
to dedicate (book, etc.)	арноо	arnoo
to defend (a country, etc.)	коргоо	korgoo
to defend oneself	коргонуу	korgonuu
to demand (request firmly)	талап кылуу	talap kıluu
to denounce (vt)	чагым кылуу	tʃagım kıluu
to deny (vt)	тануу, төгүндөө	tanuu, tøgyndøø
to depend on ...	... көзүн кароо	... køzyn karoo
to deprive (vt)	ажыратуу	adʒıratuu

to deserve (vt)	акылуу болуу	akıluu boluu
to design (machine, etc.)	түзүлүшүн берүү	tyzylyʃyn beryy
to desire (want, wish)	каалоо	kaaloo
to despise (vt)	киши катарына албоо	kiʃi katarına alboo

to destroy (documents, etc.)	жок кылуу	dʒok kıluu
to differ (from sth)	айырмалануу	ajırmalanuu
to dig (tunnel, etc.)	казуу	kazuu
to direct (point the way)	багыттоо	bagıttoo

to disappear (vi)	жоголуп кетүү	dʒogolup ketyy
to discover (new land, etc.)	таап ачуу	taap atʃuu
to discuss (vt)	талкуулоо	talkuuloo
to distribute (leaflets, etc.)	таратуу	taratuu

to disturb (vt)	тынчын алуу	tıntʃin aluu
to dive (vi)	сүңгүү	syŋgyy
to divide (math)	бөлүү	bølyy
to do (vt)	жасоо	dʒasoo

to do the laundry	кир жуу	kir dʒuu
to double (increase)	эки эселөө	eki eseløø
to doubt (have doubts)	күмөн саноо	kymøn sanoo
to draw a conclusion	тыянак чыгаруу	tijanak tʃıgaruu

to dream (daydream)	кыялдануу	kıjaldanuu
to dream (in sleep)	түш көрүү	tyʃ køryy
to drink (vi, vt)	ичүү	itʃyy
to drive a car	айдоо	ajdoo
to drive away (scare away)	кубалап салуу	kubalap saluu

to drop (let fall)	түшүрүп алуу	tyʃyryp aluu
to drown (ab. person)	чөгүү	tʃøgyy
to dry (clothes, hair)	кургатуу	kurgatuu
to eat (vi, vt)	тамактануу	tamaktanuu

to eavesdrop (vi)	аңдып тыңшоо	aŋdıp tıŋʃoo
to emit (diffuse - odor, etc.)	таратуу	taratuu
to enjoy oneself	көңүл ачуу	køŋyl atʃuu
to enter (on the list)	жазып коюю	dʒazıp kodʒɥu

to enter (room, house, etc.)	кирүү	kiryy
to entertain (amuse)	көңүл көтөрүү	køŋyl køtøryy
to equip (fit out)	жабдуу	dʒabduu
to examine (proposal)	карап чыгуу	karap tʃıguu

to exchange (sth)	алмашуу	almaʃuu
to excuse (forgive)	кечирүү	ketʃiryy
to exist (vi)	чыгуу	tʃıguu
to expect (anticipate)	күтүү	kytyy

to expect (foresee)	алдын ала билүү	aldın ala bilyy
to expel (from school, etc.)	чыгаруу	tʃıgaruu
to explain (vt)	түшүндүрүү	tyʃyndyryy
to express (vt)	сөз менен айтып берүү	søz menen ajtıp beryy
to extinguish (a fire)	өчүрүү	øtʃyryy

to fall in love (with …)	сүйүп калуу	syjyp kaluu
to fancy (vt)	жактыруу	dʒaktıruu
to feed (provide food)	тамак берүү	tamak beryy

to fight (against the enemy)	согушуу	soguʃuu
to fight (vi)	мушташуу	muʃtaʃuu
to fill (glass, bottle)	толтуруу	tolturuu
to find (~ lost items)	таап алуу	taap aluu

to finish (vt)	бүтүрүү	bytyryy
to fish (angle)	балык улоо	balık uloo
to fit (ab. dress, etc.)	ылайык келүү	ılajık kelyy
to flatter (vt)	жасакерденүү	dʒasakerdenyy

to fly (bird, plane)	учуу	utʃuu
to follow … (come after)	… ээрчүү	… eertʃyy
to forbid (vt)	тыюу салуу	tıjuu saluu
to force (compel)	мажбурлоо	madʒburloo

to forget (vi, vt)	унутуу	unutuu
to forgive (pardon)	кечирүү	ketʃiryy
to form (constitute)	түзүү	tyzyy
to get dirty (vi)	булгап алуу	bulgap aluu

to get infected (with …)	жуктуруп алуу	dʒukturup aluu
to get irritated	кыжырлануу	kıdʒırlanuu
to get married	аял алуу	ajalʲaluu
to get rid of …	… кутулуу	… kutuluu

to get tired	чарчоо	tʃartʃoo
to get up (arise from bed)	туруу	turuu
to give (vt)	берүү	beryy
to give a bath (to bath)	сууга түшүрүү	suuga tyʃyryy

to give a hug, to hug (vt)	кучакташуу	kutʃaktaʃuu
to give in (yield to)	жол берүү	dʒol beryy
to glimpse (vt)	байкоо	bajkoo
to go (by car, etc.)	жүрүү	dʒyryy

to go (on foot)	басуу	basuu
to go for a swim	сууга түшүү	suuga tyʃyy
to go out (for dinner, etc.)	чыгуу	tʃıguu
to go to bed (go to sleep)	уйкуга кетүү	ujkuga ketyy

to greet (vt)	саламдашуу	salamdaʃuu
to grow (plants)	өстүрүү	østyryy
to guarantee (vt)	кепилдик берүү	kepildik beryy
to guess (the answer)	жандырмагын табуу	dʒandırmagın tabuu

254. Verbs H-M

to hand out (distribute)	таркатуу	tarkatuu
to hang (curtains, etc.)	илүү	ilyy
to have (vt)	бар болуу	bar boluu

to have a bath	жуунуу	dʒuunuu
to have a try	аракет кылуу	araket kıluu
to have breakfast	эртең менен тамактануу	erteŋ menen tamaktanuu
to have dinner	кечки тамакты ичүү	ketʃki tamaktı itʃyy
to have lunch	түштөнүү	tyʃtønyy
to head (group, etc.)	баш болуу	baʃ boluu
to hear (vt)	угуу	uguu
to heat (vt)	ысытуу	ısıtuu
to help (vt)	жардам берүү	dʒardam beryy
to hide (vt)	жашыруу	dʒaʃıruu
to hire (e.g. ~ a boat)	жалдап алуу	dʒaldap aluu
to hire (staff)	жалдоо	dʒaldoo
to hope (vi, vt)	үмүттөнүү	ymyttønyy
to hunt (for food, sport)	аңчылык кылуу	aŋtʃılık kıluu
to hurry (vi)	шашуу	ʃaʃuu
to imagine (to picture)	элестетүү	elestetyy
to imitate (vt)	тууроо	tuuroo
to implore (vt)	өтүнүү	øtynyy
to import (vt)	импорттоо	importtoo
to increase (vi)	көбөйүү	købøjyy
to increase (vt)	чоңойтуу	tʃoŋojtuu
to infect (vt)	жуктуруу	dʒukturuu
to influence (vt)	таасир этүү	taasir etyy
to inform (e.g. ~ the police about ...)	билдирүү	bildiryy
to inform (vt)	маалымат берүү	maalımat beryy
to inherit (vt)	мураска ээ болуу	muraska ee boluu
to inquire (about ...)	билүү	bilyy
to insert (put in)	коюу	kojɵu
to insinuate (imply)	кыйытып айтуу	kıjıtıp aytuu
to insist (vi, vt)	көшөрүү	køʃøryy
to inspire (vt)	шыктандыруу	ʃıktandıruu
to instruct (teach)	үйрөтүү	yjrøtyy
to insult (offend)	кордоо	kordoo
to interest (vt)	кызыктыруу	kızıktıruu
to intervene (vi)	кийлигишүү	kijligiʃyy
to introduce (sb to sb)	тааныштыруу	taanıʃtıruu
to invent (machine, etc.)	ойлоп табуу	ojlop tabuu
to invite (vt)	чакыруу	tʃakıruu
to iron (clothes)	үтүктөө	ytyktøø
to irritate (annoy)	кыжырын келтирүү	kıdʒırın keltiryy
to isolate (vt)	бөлүп коюу	bølyp kojɵu
to join (political party, etc.)	кошулуу	koʃuluu
to joke (be kidding)	тамашалоо	tamaʃaloo
to keep (old letters, etc.)	сактоо	saktoo
to keep silent, to hush	унчукпоо	untʃukpoo
to kill (vt)	өлтүрүү	øltyryy

to knock (on the door)	такылдатуу	takıldatuu
to know (sb)	таануу	taanuu
to know (sth)	билүү	bilyy
to laugh (vi)	күлүү	kylyy
to launch (start up)	жандыруу	dʒandıruu

to leave (~ for Mexico)	кетүү	ketyy
to leave (forget sth)	калтыруу	kaltıruu
to leave (spouse)	таштап кетүү	taʃtap ketyy
to liberate (city, etc.)	бошотуу	boʃotuu
to lie (~ on the floor)	жатуу	dʒatuu

to lie (tell untruth)	калп айтуу	kalp ajtuu
to light (campfire, etc.)	от жагуу	ot dʒaguu
to light up (illuminate)	жарык кылуу	dʒarık kıluu
to limit (vt)	чектөө	tʃektøø

to listen (vi)	угуу	uguu
to live (~ in France)	жашоо	dʒaʃoo
to live (exist)	жашоо	dʒaʃoo
to load (gun)	октоо	oktoo
to load (vehicle, etc.)	жүктөө	dʒyktøø

to look (I'm just ~ing)	көрүү	køryy
to look for ... (search)	... издөө	... izdøø
to look like (resemble)	окшош болуу	okʃoʃ boluu

| to lose (umbrella, etc.) | жоготуу | dʒogotuu |
| to love (e.g. ~ dancing) | сүйүү | syjyy |

to love (sb)	сүйүү	syjyy
to lower (blind, head)	түшүрүү	tyʃyryy
to make (~ dinner)	даярдоо	dajardoo

| to make a mistake | ката кетирүү | kata ketiryy |
| to make angry | ачуусун келтирүү | atʃuusun keltiryy |

to make easier	жеңилдентүү	dʒeŋildentyy
to make multiple copies	көбөйтүү	købøjtyy
to make the acquaintance	таанышуу	taanıʃuu

| to make use (of ...) | пайдалануу | pajdalanuu |
| to manage, to run | башкаруу | baʃkaruu |

to mark (make a mark)	белгилөө	belgiløø
to mean (signify)	маанини билдирүү	maanini bildiryy
to memorize (vt)	эстеп калуу	estep kaluu

| to mention (talk about) | айтып өтүү | ajtıp øtyy |
| to miss (school, etc.) | калтыруу | kaltıruu |

to mix (combine, blend)	аралаштыруу	aralaʃtıruu
to mock (make fun of)	шылдыңдоо	ʃıldıŋdoo
to move (to shift)	ордунан жылдыруу	ordunan dʒıldıruu
to multiply (math)	көбөйтүү	købøjtyy
must (v aux)	тийиш	tijiʃ

255. Verbs N-R

to name, to call (vt)	атоо	atoo
to negotiate (vi)	сүйлөшүүлөр жүргүзүү	syjløʃyylør dʒyrgyzyy
to note (write down)	белгилее	belgiløø
to notice (see)	байкоо	bajkoo
to obey (vi, vt)	баш ийүү	baʃ ijyy
to object (vi, vt)	каршы болуу	karʃı boluu
to observe (see)	байкоо	bajkoo
to offend (vt)	көңүлгө тийүү	køŋylgø tijyy
to omit (word, phrase)	калтырып кетүү	kaltırıp ketyy
to open (vt)	ачуу	atʃuu
to order (in restaurant)	буйрутма кылуу	bujrutma kıluu
to order (mil.)	буйрук кылуу	bujruk kıluu
to organize (concert, party)	уюштуруу	ujuʃturuu
to overestimate (vt)	ашыра баалоо	aʃıra baaloo
to own (possess)	ээ болуу	ee boluu
to participate (vi)	катышуу	katıʃuu
to pass through (by car, etc.)	өтүп кетүү	øtup ketyy
to pay (vi, vt)	төлөө	tøløø
to peep, to spy on	шыкалоо	ʃıkaloo
to penetrate (vt)	жылжып кирүү	dʒıldʒıp kiryy
to permit (vt)	уруксат берүү	uruksat beryy
to pick (flowers)	үзүү	yzyy
to place (put, set)	жайгаштыруу	dʒajgaʃtıruu
to plan (~ to do sth)	пландаштыруу	plandaʃtıruu
to play (actor)	ойноо	ojnoo
to play (children)	ойноо	ojnoo
to point (~ the way)	көрсөтүү	kørsøtyy
to pour (liquid)	куюу	kujuu
to pray (vi, vt)	дуба кылуу	duba kıluu
to prefer (vt)	артык көрүү	artık køryy
to prepare (~ a plan)	даярдоо	dajardoo
to present (sb to sb)	тааныштыруу	taanıʃtıruu
to preserve (peace, life)	сактоо	saktoo
to prevail (vt)	үстөмдүк кылуу	ystømdyk kıluu
to progress (move forward)	илгерилее	ilgeriløø
to promise (vt)	убада берүү	ubada beryy
to pronounce (vt)	айтуу	ajtuu
to propose (vt)	сунуштоо	sunuʃtoo
to protect (e.g. ~ nature)	коргоо	korgoo
to protest (vi)	нааразычылык билдирүү	naarazıtʃılık bildiryy
to prove (vt)	далилдее	dalildøø
to provoke (vt)	көкүтүү	køkytyy
to pull (~ the rope)	тартуу	tartuu
to punish (vt)	жазалоо	dʒazaloo

to push (~ the door)	түртүү	tyrtyy
to put away (vt)	катып коюу	katıp kojuu
to put in order	иретке келтирүү	iretke keltiryy
to put, to place	коюу	kojuu

to quote (cite)	сөзүн келтирүү	søzyn keltiryy
to reach (arrive at)	жетүү	dʒetyy
to read (vi, vt)	окуу	okuu
to realize (a dream)	ишке ашыруу	iʃke aʃıruu
to recognize (identify sb)	тануу	taanuu

to recommend (vt)	сунуштоо	sunuʃtoo
to recover (~ from flu)	сакаюу	sakajuu
to redo (do again)	кайра жасатуу	kajra dʒasatuu
to reduce (speed, etc.)	кичирейтүү	kitʃirejtyy

to refuse (~ sb)	баш тартуу	baʃ tartuu
to regret (be sorry)	өкүнүү	økynyy
to reinforce (vt)	чындоо	tʃındoo
to remember (Do you ~ me?)	унутпоо	unutpoo

| to remember (I can't ~ her name) | эстөө | estøø |

to remind of ...	... эстетүү	... estetyy
to remove (~ a stain)	кетирүү	ketiryy
to remove (~ an obstacle)	жок кылуу	dʒok kıluu

to rent (sth from sb)	батирге алуу	batirge aluu
to repair (mend)	оңдоо	oŋdoo
to repeat (say again)	кайталоо	kajtaloo
to report (make a report)	билдирүү	bildiryy

to reproach (vt)	жемелөө	dʒemeløø
to reserve, to book	камдык буйрутмалоо	kamdık bujrutmaloo
to restrain (hold back)	кармап туруу	karmap turuu
to return (come back)	кайтып келүү	kajtıp kelyy

to risk, to take a risk	тобокелге салуу	tobokelge saluu
to rub out (erase)	өчүрүү	øtʃyryy
to run (move fast)	чуркоо	tʃurkoo
to rush (hurry sb)	шаштыруу	ʃaʃtıruu

256. Verbs S-W

to satisfy (please)	жактыруу	dʒaktıruu
to save (rescue)	куткаруу	kutkaruu
to say (~ thank you)	айтуу	ajtuu
to scold (vt)	урушуу	uruʃuu

to scratch (with claws)	тытуу	tıtuu
to select (to pick)	ылгоо	ılgoo
to sell (goods)	сатуу	satuu
to send (a letter)	жөнөтүү	dʒønøtyy
to send back (vt)	артка жөнөтүү	artka dʒønøtyy

to sense (~ danger)	сезүү	sezyy
to sentence (vt)	өкүм чыгаруу	økym tʃıgaruu
to serve (in restaurant)	тейлөө	tejløø

to settle (a conflict)	чечүү	tʃetʃyy
to shake (vt)	силкилдетүү	silkildetyy
to shave (vi)	кырынуу	kırınuu
to shine (gleam)	жаркырап туруу	dʒarkırap turuu

to shiver (with cold)	калтыроо	kaltıroo
to shoot (vi)	атуу	atuu
to shout (vi)	кыйкыруу	kıjkıruu
to show (to display)	көрсөтүү	kørsøtyy

to shudder (vi)	селт этүү	selt etyy
to sigh (vi)	дем алуу	dem aluu
to sign (document)	кол коюу	kol kojuu
to signify (mean)	билдирүү	bildiryy

to simplify (vt)	жөнөкөйлөтүү	dʒønøkøjløtyy
to sin (vi)	күнөө кылуу	kynøø kıluu
to sit (be sitting)	отуруу	oturuu
to sit down (vi)	отуруу	oturuu

to smell (emit an odor)	жыттануу	dʒıttanuu
to smell (inhale the odor)	жыттоо	dʒıttoo
to smile (vi)	жылмаюу	dʒılmadʒuu
to snap (vi, ab. rope)	үзүлүү	yzylyy

to solve (problem)	чечүү	tʃetʃyy
to sow (seed, crop)	себүү	sebyy
to spill (liquid)	төгүп алуу	tøgyp aluu
to spill out, scatter (flour, etc.)	чачылуу	tʃatʃıluu

to spit (vi)	түкүрүү	tykyryy
to stand (toothache, cold)	чыдоо	tʃıdoo
to start (begin)	баштоо	baʃtoo
to steal (money, etc.)	уурдоо	uurdoo

to stop (for pause, etc.)	токтоо	toktoo
to stop (please ~ calling me)	токтотуу	toktotuu
to stop talking	унчукпоо	untʃukpoo
to stroke (caress)	сылоо	sıloo

to study (vt)	окуу	okuu
to suffer (feel pain)	кайгыруу	kajgıruu
to support (cause, idea)	колдоо	koldoo
to suppose (assume)	божомолдоо	bodʒomoldoo

to surface (ab. submarine)	калкып чыгуу	kalkıp tʃıguu
to surprise (amaze)	таң калтыруу	taŋ kaltıruu
to suspect (vt)	күмөн саноо	kymøn sanoo
to swim (vi)	сүзүү	syzyy

| to take (get hold of) | алуу | aluu |
| to take a rest | эс алуу | es aluu |

to take away (e.g. about waiter)	алып кетүү	alıp ketyy
to take off (aeroplane)	учуп чыгуу	uʧup ʧıguu
to take off (painting, curtains, etc.)	алып таштоо	alıp taʃtoo
to take pictures	сүрөткө тартуу	syrøtkø tartuu
to talk to ...	... менен сүйлөшүү	... menen syjløʃyy
to teach (give lessons)	окутуу	okutuu
to tear off, to rip off (vt)	үзүп алуу	yzyp aluu
to tell (story, joke)	айтып берүү	ajtıp beryy
to thank (vt)	ыраазычылык билдирүү	ıraazıʧılık bildiryy
to think (believe)	ойлоо	ojloo
to think (vi, vt)	ойлонуу	ojlonuu
to threaten (vt)	коркутуу	korkutuu
to throw (stone, etc.)	ыргытуу	ırgıtuu
to tie to ...	байлоо	bajloo
to tie up (prisoner)	байлоо	bajloo
to tire (make tired)	чарчатуу	ʧarʧatuu
to touch (one's arm, etc.)	тийүү	tijyy
to tower (over ...)	көтөрүлүү	køtørylyy
to train (animals)	үйрөтүү	yjrøtyy
to train (sb)	машыктыруу	maʃıktıruu
to train (vi)	машыгуу	maʃıguu
to transform (vt)	башка түргө айлантуу	baʃka tyrgø ajlantuu
to translate (vt)	которуу	kotoruu
to treat (illness)	дарылоо	darıloo
to trust (vt)	ишенүү	iʃenyy
to try (attempt)	аракет кылуу	araket kıluu
to turn (e.g., ~ left)	бурулуу	buruluu
to turn away (vi)	жүз буруу	dʒyz buruu
to turn off (the light)	өчүрүү	øʧyryy
to turn on (computer, etc.)	жүргүзүү	dʒyrgyzyy
to turn over (stone, etc.)	оодаруу	oodaruu
to underestimate (vt)	баалабоо	baalaboo
to underline (vt)	баса белгилөө	basa belgiløø
to understand (vt)	түшүнүү	tyʃynyy
to undertake (vt)	чара көрүү	ʧara køryy
to unite (vt)	бириктирүү	biriktiryy
to untie (vt)	чечип алуу	ʧeʧip aluu
to use (phrase, word)	пайдалануу	pajdalanuu
to vaccinate (vt)	эмдөө	emdøø
to vote (vi)	добуш берүү	dobuʃ beryy
to wait (vt)	күтүү	kytyy
to wake (sb)	ойготуу	ojgotuu
to want (wish, desire)	каалоо	kaaloo
to warn (of the danger)	эскертүү	eskertyy

to wash (clean)	жуу	ʤuu
to water (plants)	сугаруу	sugaruu
to wave (the hand)	жаңсоо	ʤaŋsoo

to weigh (have weight)	... салмакта болуу	... salmakta boluu
to work (vi)	иштөө	iʃtøø
to worry (make anxious)	көңүлүн бөлүү	køŋylyn bølyy
to worry (vi)	толкундануу	tolkundanuu

to wrap (parcel, etc.)	ороо	oroo
to wrestle (sport)	күрөшүү	kyrøʃyy
to write (vt)	жазуу	ʤazuu
to write down	кагазга түшүрүү	kagazga tyʃyryy

www.ingramcontent.com/pod-product-compliance
Lightning Source LLC
Chambersburg PA
CBHW071325090426

42738CB00012B/2798